YES TO THE CITY

Yes to the City

Millennials and the Fight for Affordable Housing

Max Holleran

PRINCETON UNIVERSITY PRESS

PRINCETON AND OXFORD

Published by Princeton University Press
41 William Street, Princeton, New Jersey 08540
99 Banbury Road, Oxford OX2 6JX

press.princeton.edu

First paperback printing, 2024
Paperback ISBN 9780691259116

The Library of Congress has cataloged the cloth edition as follows:
Names: Holleran, Max, author.
Title: Yes to the city : millennials and the fight for affordable housing / Max Holleran.
Description: Princeton : Princeton University Press, [2022] |
    Includes bibliographical references and index.
Identifiers: LCCN 2021050086 (print) | LCCN 2021050087 (ebook) |
    ISBN 9780691200224 (hardcover) | ISBN 9780691234717 (ebook)
Subjects: LCSH: Housing. | Land use, Urban. | Generation Y. | City planning. | Housing policy. |
    BISAC: SOCIAL SCIENCE / Sociology / Urban | LAW / Housing & Urban Development
Classification: LCC HD7287 .H56 2022 (print) | LCC HD7287
    (ebook) | DDC 363.5—dc23/eng/20211018
LC record available at https://lccn.loc.gov/2021050086
LC ebook record available at https://lccn.loc.gov/2021050087

British Library Cataloging-in-Publication Data is available

Editorial: Meagan Levinson, Jacqueline Delaney
Production Editorial: Terri O'Prey
Jacket/Cover Design: Lauren Smith
Production: Erin Suydam
Publicity: Maria Whelan, Kathryn Stevens
Copyeditor: Molan Goldstein

Jacket/Cover art by Side Project / Creative Market

This book has been composed in Adobe Text and Gotham

CONTENTS

Acknowledgments   vii

Introduction   1

1   The Bay Area and the End of Affordability   19

2   Millennial YIMBYs and Boomer NIMBYs   56

3   Between a Rock and a Greenbelt: Housing and Environmental Activism in Boulder   74

4   Exclusionary Weirdness: Austin and the Battle for the Bungalows   100

5   YIMBYism Goes Global   124

Conclusion   157

Methodological Appendix   167

Notes   173

Index   195

ACKNOWLEDGMENTS

This book took shape on three continents, over five years, some of which was during a global pandemic. Despite that, I enjoyed tremendous support from former colleagues in New York and my new friends and workmates in Melbourne. Most of all, I am indebted to the housing activists who shared their time and thoughts with me.

At Princeton University Press, I would like to thank Jacqueline Delaney and Molan Goldstein. Most of all, I am so happy to have worked with my wonderful editor Meagan Levinson, who had confidence in this project from the start and was incredibly patient while all hell broke loose in 2020.

This book was built on what I learned as a PhD student at New York University, where I completed my first major project and dissertation on urbanization for tourism in the European Union. I'm thankful for the guidance offered by the many amazing people who were in NYU's Sociology Department at that time, particularly Neil Brenner, Craig Calhoun, Lynne Haney, Ruth Horowitz, Gianpaolo Baiocchi, Iddo Tavory, Richard Sennett, Jeff Manza, Colin Jerolmack, David Garland, Paula England, and Nahoko Kameo. Additionally, I was honored to work with George Shulman as an undergraduate student and continue to draw on all he taught me. I was lucky to be surrounded by a cohort of fellow graduate students in New York who expanded my knowledge in other areas of sociology, strengthened my work with their critiques, and provided solidarity over shared meals, drinks, and union meetings. In particular: Anna Skarpelis, Daniel Aldana Cohen, Caitlin Petre, David Wachsmuth, Hillary Angelo, Michael Gould-Wartofsky, Liz Koslov, Ned Crowley, Max Besbris, Adaner Usmani, Abigail Weitzman, Jacob Faber, Shelly Ronen, Peter Rich, Adam Murphree, Francisco Vieyra, Naima Brown, Muriam Haleh Davis, Mike McCarthy, Eyal Press, Zalman Newfield, Sam Dinger, Brian McCabe, Alix Rule, Sara Duvisac, Ercan Sadi, Poulami Roychowdury, Harel Shapira, Sonia Prelat, Jeannie Kim, Eliza Brown, Eric Van Deventer, Michelle O'Brien, Robert Wihr Taylor, Josh Frens-String, Jonah Birch, Madhavi Cherian, A. J. Bauer, Burcu Baykurt, Johnny Halushka,

Jaap Verheul, David Klassen, Mónica Caudillo, James Robertson, Filip Erdel-jac, Nada Matta, Ruth Braunstein, and Jeremy Cohan. Also, a shout-out to Sophie Gonick, Becky Amato, Tom Sugrue, Caitlin Zaloom, Gordon Doug-las, Jess Coffey, and Siera Dissmore, who always kept me great company at the Institute for Public Knowledge and Urban Democracy Lab.

Over my years as an academic, I have been privileged to work with scholars from around the world, especially as a member of the NYLON group. In particular, I am thankful to have met and shared my thoughts with Boris Vormann, Laura Marsh, Natalia Besedovsky, Joseph Ben Prestel, Hanna Hilbrandt, David Madden, Tim Edensor, Katherine Robinson, Fran Tonkiss, Gareth Millington, Mariya Ivancheva, Sarah Knuth, Ana Aceska, David Huyssen, Dunya van Trust, Elana Resnick, Miriam Greenberg, Mona Nicoara, Tim Bunnell, Virag Molnar, James Mark, Alberto Cossu, Linda Peake, Aaron Jakes, Romit Chowdhury, Sebastián Guzmán, Janna Besa-musca, Miguel Martinez, Lorenzo Zamponi, Kirsten Weld, Tom Slater, Davide Vampe, Rachel Bok, Agata Lisiak, Martin Fuller, Diana Petkova, Andreas Schäfer, Tanya Stancheva, Jiaying Sim, Carlos Piocos, Jamie Gil-len, Joanna Kusiak, Daniel Knight, Dace Dzenovska, Adam Kaasa, Katie Sobering, Jane M. Jacobs, Katherine Jensen, Kevin Ward, Javier Auyero, Nino Bariola, and Daiva Repečkaitė.

In my new home in Melbourne, I was supported by the many amazing people in the School for Social and Political Sciences at the University of Melbourne as well as the Melbourne Sustainable Society Institute, in par-ticular my dear colleagues and friends Ana Carballo, Clayton Chin, Evgeny Postnikov, Lisa MacKinney, Robyn Eckersley, Peter Christoff, Peter Rush, Cameo Dalley, Brendan Gleeson, Michele Acuto, Crystal Legacy, Monica Minnegal, Andy Dawson, Tammy Kohn, Fabio Mattioli, Bela Belojevic, Melissa Johnston, Sara Meger, Erik Baekkeskov, Kate Williams, Adrian Little, Carla Winston, Michelle Carmody, Barbara Barbosa Neves, Caro-lyn Whitzman, David Bissell, Tim Neale, Craig Smith, Sonja Molnar, and David Giles. I was also blessed to join a talented, supportive, and incred-ibly ambitious group of sociologists at Melbourne: Liz Dean, Ash Barnwell, Signe Ravn, Irma Mooi-Reci, Brendan Churchill, Lyn Craig, Rennie Lee, Karen Farquharson, Nikki Moodie, Dan Woodman, Leah Ruppanner, Keith McVilly, and Belinda Hewitt

Many people saw presentations of this work but only a few dug through the early drafts and gave me very useful edits: Amanda Gilbertson, Nina Serova, Alexis Kalagas, Greg Martin, Steven Roberts, and Geoffrey Mead.

They are editing heroes, unless of course there are mistakes (which are my own fault).

Through the writing of this book and my many overseas moves, I have been supported by amazing friends who have let me sleep on their couches, prepared jetlag-soothing coffee for me, and also discussed urban density in the cities they live in. My deepest gratitude to Lauren Roberts, Marisa Pereira Tully, Leah Feder, Prakash Puru, Chip Rountree, Asaf Shtull-Trauring, Muge Girisen, Seth Prins, Nicolau Puig, Cate Capsalis, Asaf Goldberg, Arielle Lawson, Laura Graber, Isabel and Philip Wohlstetter, Katherine Whitney, Alex Lopez, Javi Navarro Cano, Roy Kimmey, Damien Bright, Helen and Mark Mastache, Dan and Megan Rivoire, Brett Miller, David Sánchez Timón, Isobel and Chaya Mushka Rechter, Lauren Kelly, Anika Nicolaas Ponder, Bernd Riedel, Megan Lessard, Ignacio Hinojosa, Sangita Vyas, Julianne Chandler, and Pedro Rodriguez.

I've had two absolutely amazing mentors in my academic career, and they have both been pivotal for my intellectual development, my ability to navigate a daunting professional world, and my enjoyment of great meals from their kitchens. Thank you so much to Eric Klinenberg and Alison Young.

Thank you to my family, who have always supported my work even when academia seemed like a hard path to walk down: Tia Lessin, Carl Deal, Michael Holleran, and James Grunberger. Most of all, thanks to my best friend, twin brother, and tireless editor: Samuel Holleran.

YES TO THE CITY

Introduction

In the beginning of Sophocles' play *Oedipus at Colonus* the antihero has left Thebes, with his daughter Antigone as a guide. He is blind, disgraced, and exhausted from a life of regicide, incest, and governing a city beset by plague. On their journey the miserable pair rest on a rock in the village of Colonus. When the local population finds out their identity, they immediately try to expel them: their very proximity is a curse. The people of Colonus sympathize with the father and daughter but fear they will pollute the city, driving down its appeal to those from nearby Athens. The chorus warns:

> Evil, methinks, and long
> Thy pilgrimage on earth.
> Yet add not curse to curse and wrong to wrong.
> I warn thee, trespass not
> Within this hallowed spot . . . [1]

Who and what we live beside is a perennial problem. Most people in the United States (or ancient Greece for that matter) have invested the majority of their assets in their home. It is the main source of use and exchange value in our lives.[2] The citizens of Colonus do not hate Oedipus and Antigone; in fact they feel sorry for them. They just want the problem to go somewhere else and not to besmirch the reputation of their village.

The tendency for people to insist that disagreeable land uses be moved away from them, known as Not in My Backyard (NIMBY), is timeless: few have ever wanted to live next to a crematorium, waste-processing plant, or prison.[3] While many deride NIMBYs as curmudgeonly, elitist, and even racist, examples of this behavior are everywhere: from community activists banning together to prevent fracking to a suburban homeowner taking a stance against an unmown lawn.[4] The term has come to define the contemporary American city both as a critique of America's obsession with private property and, more troublingly, as a sign of racial and economic polarization.[5] Wealthier communities offload waste incinerators to poorer neighborhoods, creating higher asthma rates. Methadone clinics, homeless shelters, and public housing are pushed from the city center. Places with single-family homes resist apartment buildings in order to minimize traffic or, more perniciously, to avoid living among those with less means.

As American cities became less dense in the 1960s and 1970s, new communities not only blocked undesirable land uses through planning codes and zoning but they also hoarded resources.[6] Tax dollars that were once shared throughout a metropolitan region are now kept within specific suburbs to exclusively fund their schools, roads, and community centers.[7] Much of the uniquely American nature of NIMBYism also comes from resistance to racial integration of US cities in the 1970s,[8] when white flight was the prevalent migration pattern and spatial exclusion through real estate prices replaced the outright segregation of redlining and restricted covenants.

Today, NIMBYism has become a dirty word not just for its parochialism but for its anti-urbanism. NIMBYs often resist mass transit, higher-density residential neighborhoods, and anything else that disturbs the ideal of wide streets with single-family homes. Even in rapidly growing places such as Brooklyn, Austin, Denver, and Seattle, many residents hate the idea of adding more people, building structures higher than two stories, or funding public transit. The mismatch between growth and self-interest is exacerbated by the fact that most American cities have a small downtown that immediately gives way to blocks of bungalows, townhouses, and ranch homes rather than more efficient apartment buildings. Those who live in these neighborhoods are blessed with quick access to central shopping and entertainment districts, coupled with the spaciousness of suburban floor plans. This middle zone of cities is now treasured for its character—much of it is former "streetcar suburbs" connected by tram in the early twentieth century for elites who built craftsman bungalows, stone gothic-revival mini-mansions, and elegant cocoa-colored brownstones. Places like Park Slope in Brooklyn; Berkeley, California; Shaker Heights in Cleveland; or Squirrel Hill in Pittsburgh: these neighborhoods, whether historic or not, are no longer suburbs as such but rather bucolic hamlets of wealth within the hearts of cities. Most of them would like to stay that way, with residents resisting even minor plans for new housing that would bring more people and, potentially, greater socioeconomic diversity.[9]

For the most part, residents would rather not let newcomers into their neighborhoods for fear of parking shortages, overcrowded schools, messy construction projects, and, more vaguely, the destruction of "community character." But they have been coming anyway. New residents pour into cities where jobs are abundant and the quality of life is good. This has put a strain on urban housing markets, creating a boom in both construction of new buildings and the gentrification of old ones. Yet, many cities limit density to single-family homes, often due to the pressure of longtime residents who act out of NIMBY sentiments. With average rent prices at $3,500 in San Francisco and nearly that in many other cities, housing justice movements have taken on a new urgency, with some urbanists even declaring a "global housing crisis."[10] In every American city of one million people or more, nearly half of renters pay over 30 percent of their salary for housing. The number of renters has also gone up nationally by nine million in the past decade: the largest increase ever.[11] Even those who consider themselves securely in the middle class have found that they are struggling to pay rent and that homeownership is a distant dream. Interruptions in monthly wages due to the coronavirus pandemic made the situation of renters even more precarious, with millions on the brink of eviction.[12] In July 2021, one in seven American renters were still not up to date on their payments: frequently kept in their homes only because of eviction moratoriums.[13]

This book explores one particular movement: Yes in My Backyard (YIMBY), led by activists who seek to make cities more dense and to "build their way" to housing affordability. These groups have taken off in dozens of cities with large and active membership in places like Boulder, Austin, San Francisco, Boston, and Seattle as well as international offshoots in London, Vancouver, and Brisbane. Many of the groups not only campaign for new zoning rules, higher density, and better public transit but also field their own candidates for local and state office, and they have won important legislative battles in California and Colorado. While YIMBYism has become a crucial issue in Democratic Party politics in major cities such as San Francisco, Denver, and Portland, YIMBYs see themselves as nonideological coalitions that want to address urban housing shortages immediately, mostly by allowing more and larger buildings to go up with as little red tape as possible.

YIMBYs, who also refer to themselves as density activists, embrace cities in a more abstract way, by saying "yes" to bustling spaces that look and feel truly urban, often in contrast to the more sedate and spread-out American cities of the past. Many homeowners discuss apartment buildings as foreign modes of living, alluding particularly to Hong Kong as the ultimate carica-ture of vast skyscraper canyons creating an overcrowded cacophonous maze; or they voice fears that towers will suddenly collapse in the same tragic but uncommon manner as the Surfside condominium in Miami in 2021.[14] In contrast, YIMBYs often look toward Asian and European urbanism approv-ingly, maintaining that new development can create spaces brimming with life. YIMBYs employ many commonly shared approaches—adjusting zoning rules, finding solutions that use affordability mandates but also prioritize market-rate housing, representing renters rather than owners—but they are characterized by no value so much as their belief in the dignity and livability of the apartment building. If their movement were focused solely on design, it would be called "verticalism."

Increased density can take cars off the road and spur the construction of more public spaces, YIMBYs maintain, while insisting that the scale of new buildings can be moderated. They argue that multifunctional central neighborhoods that mix shopping, work, and entertainment into residen-tial real estate are fruitful for creating social and business relationships that bring people together fortuitously; particularly at a time when Americans are drifting apart and hunkering down in homogenous political and cultural spheres. As the urban sociologist Louis Wirth noted in 1938: "density thus reinforces the effect of numbers in diversifying men and their activities and in increasing the complexity of the social structure."[15] YIMBYs embrace this sentiment, arguing that the social complexity that comes with density— despite a long history of anti-urbanism in the United States that associates living closer together with poverty, crime, and ill health—builds creativity, social synergy, and cosmopolitanism.

The YIMBY movement was founded in San Francisco in 2013 by dis-gruntled millennials alarmed by rising rent prices. Sonja Trauss, one of the first members and a national leader of the movement, was a math teacher who began showing up to zoning and council meetings in which new hous-ing was under review. She found that even modest apartment buildings of two or three stories under planning review were vehemently criticized by neighbors for such problems as casting shadows and being "out of character." She saw many plans quashed or held up indefinitely. For her and likeminded young people who could only afford to live in apartments, this assault on new growth was irksome. Many of those speaking out passionately against development were older left-wing environmentalists with a hippie aesthetic and purportedly radical politics. They hoped to preserve a city of poets, misfits, and rebels. Yet, Trauss and her cohort do not see *that* city when they look around Oakland, Berkeley, or San Francisco. Instead, they see a three-caste social system in which each group studiously avoids the others: older homeowners who live in rent-stabilized apartments or, more likely, homes that had been affordable but now are worth millions; younger tech workers who can afford $4,000 in monthly rent or maybe even place a down payment on a home; and the support class of service workers who struggle mightily: everyone from cleaners and fast-food workers to nurses, teachers, and public sector employees. Increasingly, even middle-class urbanites are flung to the edges of the city. In this outer suburban ring, growth is still happening on cheap land (mostly in sprawling subdivisions) but it is badly connected to city jobs, forcing those at the bottom of the income divide to become super-commuters—sitting in traffic for two-hour stretches or boarding buses and trains before dawn to get to their workplace.

San Francisco's homes are six times more expensive than the national average.[16] From 2010 to 2019, the city's population grew by 80,000 while only 29,000 homes were built.[17] While "density bonuses" (allowing more apartments on a site in exchange for developer support of local amenities) are sometimes available in the Bay Area, the major problem is zoning: most neighborhoods only allow single-family homes and, when apartments are permitted, there is a lengthy design, community, and environmental review process. This single-family "fundamentalism" is what YIMBY activists fight against: both at the level of planning reform and at community meetings where they attempt to win over residents saying "no" to growth. After attending planning meetings, activist Sonja Trauss quickly set up the tongue-in-cheek–named BARF (Bay Area Renters Federation) in order to propose a simple economic solution to making housing prices more affordable: by increasing supply. Those who were truly concerned with the city's transformation into an unaffordable enclave of tech billionaires and their millionaire employees should rally around this idea if they hoped to maintain even a modicum of economic diversity, Trauss and the nascent YIMBY membership of BARF argued.

The first meetings for Trauss and her associates were held in bars and cafés: young people gathered around brainstorming ideas about how to shift the ideological debate from "real estate development ruins the city" to "controlled growth moderates prices and allows for new residents to contribute to existing communities." The idea was to show up to meetings that were dominated by homeowners saying "no, no, no" to every proposal and have them finally say "yes" to something. The members of BARF—young, educated, and middle class—would also become a filter for projects that would increase density, socioeconomic diversity, and transport-oriented development. They would be a kind of secondary planning commission, cheerleading growth but also pushing for design and affordability mandates in every new project. They embraced the architectural philosophy of New Urbanism, first advocated for fifty years ago—to make cities denser and livelier with more people walking and living close together. YIMBYs frame these ideas in ways that younger people can understand: through speeches to local councils about housing precarity; simple slogans about density and growth bandied around over happy hour drinks; and, perhaps most importantly, endless internet memes about the selfishness and small-mindedness of NIMBY homeowners.

The YIMBY message quickly caught on: with urban newcomers in the Bay Area, with politicians who had been foiled in their attempts to build affordable housing in the past, with developers exasperated by red tape (who courted the groups for specific projects), and—more problematically—with tech bosses looking to house their workforce (who became major donors). In just five years, the movement that began during a public comment session in San Francisco had international branches, well-attended conferences, and California state senators who identified almost exclusively with the cause. More importantly, it had redirected the public conversation around growth from "go somewhere else" to "growth is inevitable, so how can we make it better, fairer, and more sustainable."

The YIMBY movement has created a novel but problematic coalition of activists who want to make American cities denser: they borrow much from anti-gentrification housing movements, but they view their constituents as middle-class market-rate renters; and they advocate for all new development, not just affordable housing for low-income people, a concept they call "build more of everything." YIMBY groups are also strongly supported by developers and real estate agents who see their platform as a valuable grassroots defense of the construction industry that changes the public perception of developers from rapacious to civic-minded. At the same time, density is also supported by many environmentalists who maintain that living closer together is more sustainable,[18] subscribing to the philosophy that extensive land use must be curtailed to prevent erosion and to fortify cities against sea rise, urban water shortages, and wildfires.[19]

This book analyzes the substantial criticism of YIMBYism from anti-gentrification progressives who argue that YIMBY groups are merely social justice shells concealing property interests. It also shows how density activists have successfully reframed urban growth as a progressive goal for creating more equitable and sustainable cities. They often use generational rather than class terms, portraying themselves as lobbyists for rent-paying millennials who want to live a more urban life than their parents' generation. In using this framing, they activate an age divide regarding opinions of suburbia (safe and stable versus deadening and environmentally harmful) while also acknowledging the income gap created by the 2008 financial crisis: many millennials, who are well into their thirties, are nowhere near able to buy a home. YIMBYs seek a middle ground between housing justice activists and "build, baby, build" condominium developers, and they paint the true enemy as established homeowners who, they argue, have fortuitously bought into ascendant property markets only to drive out newcomers. Their answer is the wholesale densification of American cities by adding more housing stock to wealthy and desirable areas that have thus far blocked construction of new homes and, particularly, of apartment buildings.

Densification and Urban Sociology: Strangers, Danger, and the Thrill of Bustling Spaces

In 1884, when New York's Lower East Side was one of the most densely populated places in the world, the *New York Times* published a story titled "Slumming in This Town" describing how a fashionable London trend had reached the New World and how ladies and gentlemen could entertain themselves by sightseeing on the Bowery.[20] Unlike the concern shown by Progressive Era reformers, who visited the same neighborhood with a sense of opprobrium and pity, these slumming uptown gentry were fascinated by streets teeming with life. They were tired of flânerie in the staid precincts of lower Fifth Avenue and sought out a more vibrant street scene, which they found in the mix of tenements and pushcart hawkers selling *schmattas*, potatoes, herring, and everything in between. Though density was associated with urban deviance, it was interesting to look at.

Urban sociologists have long been fascinated by categorizing the city as an evolving form whose physical attributes serve distinct demographic groups. Where one lives can make socioeconomic betterment possible—or unlikely. Proponents of the Chicago school of urban sociology, most active in the 1920s, used the urban boom they saw around them to describe processes of racial and ethnic segmentation, economic stratification, and community cohesion. Urban sociologists of the time were particularly interested in how immigrants moved to dense precincts and, after a period of struggle, were able to advance to better jobs and housing conditions on the periphery of the city. Sociologists like Robert Park, Ernest Burgess, Louis Wirth, and Jane Addams described the process of succession in which impoverished migrants eventually left the teeming heart of the city—overcrowded with tenements and multifamily or intergenerational living—for transitional zones and, if they were lucky, to the new suburbs built along rail lines. These scholars sought not just to demarcate a typology of urban zones but to elevate sociology as a discipline. They described urban development as a pseudo-biological process: "[U]rban growth [may be thought of] as a resultant of organization and disorganization analogous to the anabolic and catabolic processes of metabolism in the body," Park and Burgess proposed in their seminal 1925 text *The City*.[21]

Throughout the early twentieth century, density was bemoaned as a necessary agglomeration of people and resources that allowed for metropolises to function but was also a primary factor in widespread ill health, crime, and social "deviance."[22] Being packed into neighborhoods cheek by jowl did not create new kinds of allegiances and affinities at first. Rather, as Louis Wirth put it: "The close living together and working together of individuals who have no sentimental and emotional ties foster a spirit of competition, aggrandizement, and mutual exploitation."[23] In short, people thrust together, striving to get by, often decided to look away from each other in order to preserve a modicum of privacy. They concentrated on their own advancement rather than finding solidarity with those different from them. Yet, this thinking also undersells the success of dense immigrant-filled prewar neighborhoods. Wards made up almost entirely of migrants in Chicago, New York, and Boston may have been slums, but they offered exceptional mobility through education and work opportunities (although it should be noted this only applied to immigrants of European extraction). A sense of urban ennui went hand in hand with "mutual exploitation" as Wirth suggested, but there were also campaigns for more responsible landlords, worker safety, and higher wages.[24] Eventually, density and the mixing of urban cultures produced interethnic and mixed-race marriages, civic cooperation in the government and nonprofits, labor mobilization, and even the fusion restaurants of today's Lower East Side, where tourists no longer go to gawk at poverty but to eat kosher pickles, gelato, and *xiao long bao* (sometimes all in the same afternoon).

As postwar urban sociologists and city planners began to drift away from the Chicago school's model of community studies using concentrated ethnographic portraits of a single neighborhood, they focused more on outward growth and polycentrism as an expression of the future. American cities are, after all, a physical manifestation of capitalism dependent on growth, as Joseph Schumpeter maintained: without expansion or inward renewal, the system atrophies. Already by the 1920s, Park and Burgess had noticed that "[e]ven more significant than the increasing density of urban population is its correlative tendency to overflow, and so to extend over wider areas, and to incorporate these areas into a larger communal life."[25] New theories of urbanization that emphasized regions, connectivity, and limitless growth would come to define the American urban experience and, in doing so, would cast high-density life as something antiquated, dangerous, and unseemly.

In the popular imagination of post–World War II America, concentrated street life was associated with the past: sometimes it was romanticized for movies about bootstrapping immigrants, but mostly it was maligned as a primitive state of being. Not only were urban spaces degraded as dangerous and dirty, but many observers saw their sense of community intimacy and public street life on stoops, rooftops, and stairwells as a forced closeness that disguised inner discomfort. By mid-century, with the rapid growth of suburbs, most Americans would agree with the theorist Georg Simmel, who wrote in 1903 that in cities, "the bodily proximity and narrowness of space makes the mental distance only the more visible. It is obviously only the obverse of this freedom if, under certain circumstances, one nowhere feels as lonely and lost as in the metropolitan crowd."[26]

Yet, suburbia was not the solution. As suburbia became a fact of American life in the 1960s, many who were raised there began to locate a particular brand of dejection in the dispersed built environment. It may have had luster, but it seemed to lack substance: there was nothing to walk to, the uniformity of the housing stock bespoke a wider cultural problem of conformism, and despite the tree-lined streets, green areas were often paved over, creating less fresh air than advertised. The architecture critic Jane Jacobs was the first to express high-density nostalgia in her 1961 classic *The Death and Life of Great American Cities*, in which she lamented the gradual loss of the "sidewalk ballet" of neighborhoods such as her home, New York City's Greenwich Village.[27] Tied up in this appraisal of suburbia's defects was an attempt to rehabilitate walkable central neighborhoods that were seen in the 1960s as antiquated at best and as dilapidated at worst (indeed, the book was very much a reaction to proposals to raze a large segment of Greenwich Village in the name of slum clearance).

Along with the portrait of choreographed daily comings and goings of West Villagers that Jacobs romanticized, there was a larger hope to re-create socioeconomically diverse neighborhoods with small businesses and localized governance (even to the point of left-wing libertarianism, arguably).[28] This dream was based on older cities with compact streets mixing commercial and residential zoning. Examining the winding heterogeneous laneways of Europe—in contrast to the straight lines of ascendant North American modernism—Jacobs saw diversity in density. From population to building style to economic function, she sought to create a city that transformed each step one took through it, rather than places dominated by monofunctional land use for miles on end. In time, this formulation would be taken up not only for its social goals of neighborliness and coexistence but also for the broader objectives of immigrant integration, small business incubation, and alternative transportation for sustainability goals.

Jane Jacobs and the density that she cherished went, in a matter of twenty years, from an outsider critique of the hubris of urban planning to a foundational tenet of planning schools.[29] The philosophy of New Urbanism, made popular in the 1980s and 1990s, was a refocusing of urban design on building dynamic public spaces that maximized interactions between residents.[30] This meant smaller shops that were accessible by foot (or at least better integrated with the streets around them rather than surrounded by a sea of parking), more green spaces, and a far-reaching overhaul of zoning to mix commercial and residential functions whenever possible. New Urbanism was enthusiastically heralded by urban planners as a more sustainable way to build cities that returned to pre-automotive times with bustling street life, while community leaders praised the movement for its sociable and democratic qualities: bringing people back out to the urban agoras.[31] The problem was that New Urbanism remained largely confined within the walls of architecture schools: a kind of on-paper architecture[32] that was ignored by real estate developers who were busy quickly erecting identical single-family homes on greenfield exurban sites far from stores and mass transit. Indeed, as the United States continued to sprawl in the 1990s with no sign of densification—or of mass transit investment or mixed-use development—some critics began to see the New Urbanist philosophy as a mere design shell to be slapped onto strip malls and suburban neighborhoods: an easy way to claim innovation by adding a bench and calling it a plaza, or putting a few colorfully painted townhouses into a subdivision and calling it "urban."[33]

Despite the fact that lip service to New Urbanism has been de rigueur for a quarter century within city government, the planning and architecture professions, and major national development firms, little has been done to move in this direction. City zoning laws are a big factor in these decisions that play a larger role than consumer preferences alone. As of 2019, Arlington, Texas, was zoned 89 percent for detached single-family homes; more compact Chicago was not much denser at 79 percent, showing that this housing form is not just de facto in American cities but legally mandated.[34] Density and apartments have become much more popular in gentrifying urban areas but this has not forced a systematic shift in the way that new buildings are designed. Instead, it has put more pressure on existing prewar neighborhoods with attractive street life and access to public transport. For those who appreciate the appeal of urban life, the past twenty-five years have been a profound disappointment: many people have embraced walkability, smaller homes, and vibrant streets but government has done almost nothing to incentivize this form of growth. Premium neighborhoods like Capitol Hill in Seattle or Dupont Circle in Washington, DC, grow more and more expensive. The affordable option continues to be far flung and monotonous suburbs, consternating those who would like to live the New Urbanist dream but are thwarted by the reality of housing costs.

Out of this history of stymied densification came the YIMBY movement: people steeped in knowledge about New Urbanism with a copy of the *Death and Life of Great American Cities* on their bedside table. These highly educated activists offer a marketing push to translate planning jargon, including New Urbanism, to a larger public. They focus on changing zoning codes to allow densification in places that have already experienced considerable gentrification. They seek to re-create the natural density of inner-city neighborhoods that was often diminished by 1960s slum clearance programs that bulldozed low-income houses and apartments to make way for high-rises. YIMBY activists are in a peculiar position: they assure wealthier homeowners that new construction will not create the unbearable, insalubrious density of the past, and they also assuage the fears of low-income residents that new housing will not further intensify gentrification and displacement.

The Gospel of Supply

The YIMBY movement has been criticized by many progressive housing advocates for its perceived free-market fundamentalism. It is, in the words of a longtime Seattle organizer: "just another way for centrist politicians to say that the public option is not on the table." For those involved in social movements that defend or seek to build more public housing, YIMBYism is a poor substitute. More problematically, it besmirches the reputation of state-run accommodation, adding to a long history of divestment and demonization of the sector.[35] YIMBY activists usually describe themselves as embracing a multiplicity of approaches. They maintain that even though their voice is often the loudest on plans to build market-rate housing, they push for affordability within those projects. YIMBYs also profess support for tax increases to build more public housing, or for more novel measures such as co-ops or community land trusts. Their overriding argument is two-fold: public housing will never be built in sufficient quantities to solve the housing crisis in places like San Francisco, and increasing supply broadly will provide an expanded marketplace, bringing down prices for everyone.

This tide-that-lifts-all-boats argument of housing supply is not the focus of this book, but as a central argument of the YIMBY movement it is worth looking at in more detail to better show how density activists have reframed the housing affordability debate. Some more fringe elements of the movement are truly wedded to the idea that regulatory mechanisms—that often rely on considerable public participation—are the problem: if free markets reigned supreme then supply would immediately address demand. They go further to suggest that the affordability crisis is just the tip of the iceberg when it comes to urban planning; everyone would be better served with more freedom and greater respect for private property, they maintain.[36] This group is an extreme minority of those whom I interviewed and of the conversations happening online among YIMBY activists. Rather, most YIMBYs recognize that urban housing markets are not made up of fragmented and isolated subgroups (subsidized, public, luxury, etc.) but contained within one overarching system. Thus, any infusion of new apartments broadens choices, driving down prices, keeping wealthier people out of socioeconomically transitioning areas, and lowering the cost of older units to greater levels of affordability in middle-class neighborhoods.

The housing economics that YIMBYism rests upon is a contested field that has, in the past decade, become even more heated with the growth of "supply skepticism."[37] This theory argues that new housing has the potential to actually increase suppressed demand, particularly in neighborhoods at risk of gentrification where displacement is already a problem. It also disputes the idea that there is a trickle-down effect when it comes to affordability, asserting that new units are likely to be at the luxury end of the market to maximize developer profits, having little to no impact on those struggling to pay rent.[38] Scholars holding this view are quick to dispute the efficacy of "filtering": the concept that articulates how markets supply low-income housing through the aging-out of older homes from middle-class segments of the market (and why luxury builds eventually produce more affordability lower down the real estate food chain).[39] These housing experts bolster the growing concern over development not just from homeowners but also from renters seeking to avoid increases in their monthly payments.[40] However, there is still considerable evidence that the laws of supply and demand are not broken, just frustratingly slow.

Much of the existing data shows that adding to any part of the housing market, including the higher-priced segments, eventually lowers costs.[41] Most studies in this field have shown that expanding supply slowly decreases costs for all sectors of the market. One New York City study showed that every 10 percent increase in market-rate housing in a given neighborhood would result in a 1 percent reduction in rental prices:[42] a supply effect but not one that gives much optimism to public policy officials tasked with solving the affordability crisis. However, this does not take into account the fact that many new projects, including in New York, have inclusionary zoning mandates that require affordable units within all new projects. Other cities with more available land can also have positive effects from "gentle" upzoning through new building codes that allow multiple units on a single lot: this can range from townhouses to accessory dwelling units above garages or in backyards.[43] These more suburban fixes can have the benefit of increasing housing stock while moderating the pace of development and the attendant effects of neighborhood gentrification.

All signs show that, currently, state-funded options alone cannot solve the United States' tremendous affordability crisis because of the incapacity for local and national governments to attain financing, organize construction, and, most importantly, secure public support. There is a huge gap between the desire of housing activists to launch radically expanded public housing programs and the will within state and federal government to find the money to do so. Ideologically, the United States, unlike Singapore or Sweden, is not bullish on public housing, given the history of slow completion on a relatively small scale with lackluster upkeep.[44] This presents a severe challenge to the amount of housing that is kept permanently affordable and has caused anti-gentrification activists to demand new sustainably built public housing as the major solution to the affordability crisis. A number of novel approaches have emerged since the 2008 crisis that would replace the "projects" of the 1960s with community land trusts, nonprofit housing, or a federal social housing authority tasked with purchasing bad assets and de-privatizing them.[45] Yet, YIMBY activists prefer to concentrate on supply only, without indicating what kind of housing will be prioritized. The majority are deeply skeptical that states like California will find the political capital to push through a purely "public option" for housing.

At the same time that YIMBYs advocate for a simple supply solution and point at statistics showing a slowdown in housing construction in desirable cities, they also ignore larger trends of housing market financialization that have occurred in the past two decades.[46] Growth is no longer simply a matter of providing new homes to people in need of rental housing but can serve platform-based tourist services (like Airbnb), "ghost tenants" who purchase units as a safe-deposit box for cash from abroad but reside elsewhere, or simply large financial firms that increasingly speculate in new apartments via real estate investment trusts (REITs).[47] This makes the question of *supply for whom* more important. Despite these changes, YIMBYs have trained their sights on a single achievable goal: repeal of single-family zoning across the country to increase the ability to build. The consistency and simplicity of this point is one of their major innovations and what has distinguished them from previous housing affordability activists.

The mainstream economics confirmation of YIMBY activists' main argument (supply) is not necessarily a slam dunk for their cause, especially not in cities like San Francisco where they are most active. The argument that for-profit developers need a relaxation of single-family home restrictions to build (primarily) apartments is not an attractive one. Indeed, the immiseration of the unhoused and the gargantuan struggles of working-class people to make rent in places like the Bay Area seems to have opened possibilities for much more radical solutions to the affordable housing crisis. These options, sometimes lumped into sustainability proposals under the banner of the Green New Deal, have attracted millions of people to support a new role for the government in building and maintaining housing, akin to Franklin Roosevelt's efforts during the Great Depression. Especially with the economic and public health devastation wreaked by the coronavirus pandemic, many in the housing activism space contend that now is the time for bold solutions, unlike YIMBYs who believe opening the spigot of supply would remove the biggest obstacle and go a long way in solving the crisis. This book traces the tension between YIMBYs and more radical housing movements that maintain that the time for measured steps and market-based solutions to housing affordability is well and truly over.[48]

No Room for Neighborliness in the Struggle for Housing Affordability

In 2018 the YIMBY movement held its third national conference, called YIMBY Town, in Boston. It was hosted by a community college in the majority Black and Latino neighborhood of Roxbury and was well attended.

YIMBYs from around the United States mingled to talk urban planning and densification. Yet, by 2018, the frayed relationship between YIMBYs and other housing activist groups was well known. Some Boston activists had even publicly denounced the organizers' choice to host their conference in a neighborhood in the process of gentrification. For them, the gospel of "build more of everything" was completely off-key for people struggling to stay in their homes. Low-income people in the Roxbury neighborhood did not want to see more housing because they associated growth with getting priced out.

During the last speech of the conference, the main event was moved from a theater space to a gymnasium farther into the building's interior because organizers expected some "disruptions." As the speech was underway, a loud noise came from down the hallway as nearly a hundred protesters wearing bright yellow shirts with drums, kazoos, vuvuzelas, and giant signs decrying displacement stormed toward the gym. Organizers attempted to stop their march on the keynote speech without success. The protestors flooded into the gym and immediately walked to the front of the room as the audience fell into a hushed silence (aside from the click of mobile phone cameras to document the intruders). Members of progressive Boston housing groups—Right to the City, Dorchester Not for Sale, City Life/Vida Urbana, and others—stood at the front of the room with their banners facing the crowd in a pose meant to elicit shame and chanted, "We've got the power." The conference crashers had a brass band and a bullhorn, but the YIMBYs quickly gave them the microphone in a first act of capitulation. People in the audience politely clapped.

The standoff at the national conference was punctuated by a mini teach-in about gentrification from activists who were largely people of color (the YIMBY meeting was also diverse, which mitigated the white-interloper feeling that the movement is often accused of). One woman admonished the crowd: "You don't walk into a neighborhood without asking the people who live there." Later, one of the activists told the *Boston Globe* the gist of their concerns:

> We keep being told the solution of "build, build, build" will trickle down to affordable housing in the most-impacted communities. But we don't have any proof of it. . . . We have complete proof of the opposite, which is that our folks get displaced and cannot afford the rents. It's hard to trust and support a movement that is not working for our communities.[49]

The major grievance was that building more was exactly what local activists had been trying to stop for years in order to *maintain* affordability. Furthermore, the people who advocated for the opposite were largely outsiders with a middle-class solution that seemed suspiciously geared toward their middle-class interests. As the conference crashers left, the audience erupted in loud applause. Later, the organizers released a statement in solidarity with the groups that disrupted them. Seemingly they decided the unplanned interruption was the best possible closing.

This showdown is at the heart of this book: those seeking market-rate densification of cities wish to simply join existing housing advocates as a different but complementary "flavor" of activism. YIMBYs believe this is possible; anti-gentrification groups do not. The former see themselves as expanding the struggle; the latter think the new focus is missing the crucial goal: helping those in the most need. The conflict between the two groups also shows a wider gulf within urban management and US politics more broadly: the centrist position is no longer a popular one. YIMBYs pride themselves on solving problems through compromise and incrementalism. That is a hard sell in American cities, which, at the moment, are riven with economic inequality, racial tension, and infrastructural neglect. This book shows how density activists frame urban issues and how they aim to rekindle neighborliness and the ethos of living together, and it interrogates their successes and failures in rousing a new political coalition of renters.

Structure of the Book

San Francisco—with its meteoric rent prices and booming tech economy—is ground zero for YIMBYism. The problem of housing affordability has jumped scale from a working-class issue to a middle-class one. The first chapter of the book examines how San Francisco has resisted building housing at the same rate as similar-sized cities. In 2014, YIMBY organizers began to demand immediate growth and densification and then exported this idea to other cities using conferences, slickly designed websites, podcasts, and toolkits for dealing with zoning boards. The chapter shows how the movement began as a standoff with an older generation of culturally Left former-hippie homeowners in San Francisco and Berkeley who opposed growth, splitting progressives on neighborhood issues. Last, it analyzes how YIMBYs lauded the work of anti-gentrification activists in the Mission District and Oakland but also sought to keep their own efforts separate and confined to middle-class participants, attracting the ire of tenants' organizations that felt that middle-class (disproportionately white) housing groups should act in solidarity with working-class people of color rather than in their own interest.

As cities have both expanded and re-densified in the early twenty-first century, the ethos of NIMBYism has become harder to maintain. Often, people with NIMBY incentives are part of the baby-boom generation who grew up in suburbia (and see it as the quintessential model for cities because it structured their childhoods) and are now homeowners with valuable assets that could be adversely impacted by higher density. Conversely, density activists are mostly millennials (under age forty) who struggle to afford high rents and are locked out of the housing market. The second chapter examines interview data with YIMBY activists (most of whom are millennials) as well as a small sample of homeowners (all of whom are over age fifty), in order to contrast competing generational visions of how dense American cities should be.

Those who fight to keep away development often do so to protect values seen as inherently progressive, such as preservation of historic architecture, conservation of parks and open space, and protection of communities from displacement and gentrification. Yet, YIMBYs dislike the nexus of altruism and self-interest. They maintain that those with a Not in My Backyard mentality are frequently affluent progressives who bemoan gentrification but also have zero tolerance for growth, fueling housing shortages and a high rent burden for working-class families. The second chapter concludes by asking if YIMBYism is indeed a sea change in how a new generation is thinking about cities and, if successful, whether the movement's plans would drastically change the look and feel of sprawling American cities to be more vertical and urban.[50]

Boulder, Colorado, is sometimes known as the "People's Republic of Boulder" or the town "wedged between the Rocky Mountains and reality" for its massive network of hiking trails protected by a 1967 law creating an urban greenbelt to limit growth. Even with the constraint of the greenbelt, Boulder has not significantly densified despite a growing tech economy bringing new workers and the constant pressure of a student population of over 30,000. Since 2013, YIMBY groups have successfully lobbied against several ballot initiatives to limit growth, pushing back against anti-development residents who feel that more downtown apartments will ruin Boulder's unique character. Chapter 3 analyzes how YIMBY groups navigate environmentalist objections to development:[51] often arguing for growth using the rationale that real urban greening only occurs when dense walkable urban cores are created (a feature lacking from many American cities). It also contains a historical section on Ebenezer Howard's ideal of the "garden city." This framework was successfully implemented in Boulder to establish protected public lands,[52] but without proper urban density, the model has been ineffective in controlling sprawl.

The capital of Texas has a much-repeated mantra: "Keep Austin Weird." Emblazoned on t-shirts and hissed at planning board meetings, it is invoked to guard against some of the most rapid population growth in the United States.[53] Chapter 4 shows how YIMBYs in Austin, who originally organized around expanding rail transit, began taking on anti-growth residents and sparked a war over urban authenticity.[54] Density activists see extensive construction as a means to stave off higher prices while continuing to attract new residents and preserving the "weird" spirit. Drawing on urban arts economy literature, the chapter shows why many YIMBY activists see themselves as the original Austin creatives, whose efforts in the arts and hospitality economies put the city on the national radar but who may now be victims of their own success because of rising prices.

The YIMBY movement has caught on in a range of global cities, including three groups in Australia, nine in the United Kingdom, and three in Sweden. These groups argue that urban life is no longer a cultural choice but the only path to upward mobility. The last chapter of the book broadly considers how YIMBYism transcended its American origins and found a global audience, and why this framing of housing affordability is novel in a range of international contexts. Drawing on examples from the United Kingdom and Australia, it considers how the movement has supplied a language of growth and densification that has been picked up in other Anglophone countries, even those without a strong history of NIMBY objections to apartment construction.

The book concludes by considering the future of YIMBYism and whether the fragile coalition of housing-growth advocates assembled in the past ten years can hold together and present a unified and appealing political platform for millennial voters. It also analyzes the immense challenges to high-density urban life brought on by the coronavirus pandemic, examining whether apartment living can maintain its appeal in an era of widespread epidemiological fear.

1

The Bay Area and the End of Affordability

When did San Francisco transform from a city of open arms to one of closed doors? The Bay Area was once firmly lodged in the American psyche as the place for rebels and misfits to relocate. Lawrence Ferlinghetti, a former poet laureate of San Francisco who was attracted to the freedom of sexual, pharmacological, and social experimentation, wrote a 1958 poem about flute-playing beatniks feeding grapes to squirrels in "Golden Gate Park . . . the meadow of the world."[1]

The Bay Area was the Edenic base camp for creating a new society for the Beat generation and, later, the hippies in the 1950s and 1960s. Unlike Lyndon Johnson's Great Society programs, based on extending the welfare state, these anti-establishment writers and artists wanted to push cognitive horizons by challenging bourgeois morality, particularly as it related to the suburban middle-class family that was quickly becoming the symbol of 1950s normalcy and success. Indeed, as the Bay Area spread out—creating subdivisions of single-family homes—San Francisco doubled down on its existing reputation as a freewheeling port city where revelry and disregard for moral rectitude were both a credo and an effective business model.[2] Counterculture started as a rejection of urban boosterism and the "straight" world of capitalist marketing, but it soon became its own potent brand drawing many to the city.[3]

Often it was the people shut out of self-consciously "upstanding" Bay Area suburbs like Cupertino, where only freestanding single-family homes were allowed, who were forced to live in the city.[4] They were mostly younger and single. Some chose specifically to settle away from the family-friendly suburbs, renouncing suburban conformity for the milieu of the port city. In 1959, the *San Francisco Progress* bemoaned the new dichotomy between city and region while commending smaller communities that rejected apartments in order to exile "unbecoming" behavior: "The number of sex deviates [*sic*] in this city has soared by the thousands . . . while other communities in this area have virtually eliminated them."[5]

The quick death of San Francisco as the unconventional hippie haven, and its rebirth as the technology metropolis, has been a surprise to all those who have watched over the past fifty years. Part of this reputational shift can be chalked up to broader cultural and economic forces: the divestment in cities and increased urban-suburban segregation, the decline in manufacturing, and the waning of hippie communalism for entrepreneurial individualism. Out of the ashes rose a new metropolitan region anchored by military–higher education investment in communications technology that would quickly create Silicon Valley. As Fred Turner has pointed out, some former hippie utopians were involved in these ventures and saw computing and ARPANET technologies as a means to enact a better society through invention rather than new social relations.[6] This vision, of course, was not realized.

For a time, San Francisco was celebrated as a hotbed of innovation, where young companies got matched with "unicorn" investors and emerged a few years later with initial public offerings worth billions of dollars. The city concentrated the influence of regional Silicon Valley firms, giving them new urban offices that supplied a made-over image as well as centrality to cultural amenities for employees. By the time of the 2008 economic crisis, that narrative had been rigorously interrogated as, alongside tremendous tech wealth, poverty became endemic. Quickly gentrified neighborhoods like South of Market (SoMa) provided corporate headquarters for companies seeking to cash in on the cultural capital of urbanity and escape the "silicon suburbs." Yet, right next to the headquarters of Uber, Yahoo, and Pinterest in SoMa, one of the country's worst homelessness epidemics is laid bare. The unhoused roam the streets in huge numbers as tech workers skitter to the other side of sidewalks to avoid them. The spaces below the elevated BART (Bay Area Rapid Transit) trains have become encampments reminiscent of Latin America's informal settlements but buttressed by the most expensive real estate in downtown San Francisco, where the average rent is the highest in the country at $3,650 per month in 2019.[7] The story of the rebellious city has been supplanted with that of the cruel city where the nation's highest-paid workers step over the destitute laying prostrate on their doorsteps.

Housing has become the pivotal issue in the Bay Area, as a generation of political leaders has struggled to address housing costs and homelessness, starting as early as the original tech boom (and bust) of 1995–2000. Recrimination is rife as San Francisco's affordability crisis persists with no end in sight. In 2019, President Donald Trump, with his trademark deficit in empathy, threatened to use the Environmental Protection Agency to force California to address homelessness which, in his words, was threatening to make the city "unrecognizable."[8] London Breed, the mayor of San Francisco, was compelled to admit that human feces on the streets was a growing problem, and she formed a special task force to address the issue of human waste.[9] The irony that the hottest location for the US economy is also an epicenter of misery for those excluded from it is not that surprising: the dichotomy signals an ongoing bifurcation of American prosperity, especially in successful cities. In many instances, success is no longer just a normative moniker for places with well-paying jobs, but it designates what the journalist Alec MacGillis argues are hyper-prosperous cities that suck up resources and capital from entire regions.[10]

In response to this situation, two separate infrastructures have developed: the legacy system of rent control, public housing, and mass transit; and a new, largely private system of ridesharing apps like Uber, expensive market-rate condominiums, and company-sponsored transportation services like the Google Bus, which has become infamous for pulling up to existing public stops with shining new Wi-Fi-enabled vehicles to exclusively pick up Google's own employees. The two-strata city, and the infrastructure that serves it, shows a welfare state going through retrenchment along with a boom in privatization: on one side there are digital platforms quickly expanding their user base and shareholder value; on the other there is a rusting, neglected system of public transit and social housing. A small number of tenants desperately try to hold on to their single-room occupancy (SRO) apartments, in neighborhoods like the Tenderloin, while economically fortunate newcomers compete for the same spaces, which have been converted into posh lofts.

Often lost in the "Tale of Two Cities" argument[11] is the story of the middle class. Many commentators ignore this group because it is an endangered species in expensive American cities like San Francisco and because its plight seems less pressing in comparison with the risk of homelessness. In the Bay Area, those working in support services for the tech sector—cleaning, restaurants, retail, and even teachers, firefighters, and police—have been pushed far from the city and its prosperous suburbs. They have become a class of "super-commuters," often traveling as long as three hours to reach their workplace from formerly agricultural Central Valley towns like Stockton.[12] They possess the means to pay market-rate rent (and are ineligible for subsidized housing), but only in racially segregated parts of Oakland with concentrated poverty, postindustrial exurbs like Antioch, and farther-afield farming towns. The Bay Area middle class, once encouraged to "drive until you qualify" when it came to obtaining a mortgage in outer suburbs, has now been locked out of homeownership regionally. The average home price in San Jose is $1.2 million, with prices decreasing somewhat in the other nine counties of the Bay Area, but only reaching a low of approximately $500,000 on the border of Sacramento.[13] Often those who are employed but struggling in the Bay Area feel the most overlooked: they resent the wealth that has priced them out of the city, yet they also see both public services and the wider conversation on housing focusing on those who are entirely destitute.

Increasingly, the squeezed middle class of the Bay Area does not see the housing crisis as a natural phenomenon caused by a lack of supply due to the booming tech economy. Rather, many San Franciscans view housing prices as a problem created by an artificial limit on construction caused by opposition from existing owners. In 2018, San Francisco only gave permission to build one unit of housing per every 3.45 jobs created (the worst rate in the country).[14] Seattle, which has 200,000 fewer people than San Francisco, added twice as many housing units between 2010 and 2016[15] due to its easier permitting process, rather than a more vibrant economy, as the mitigating factor. San Francisco has allowed a large degree of local control when it comes to urban development, which has given neighbors greater influence when it comes to approving designs for new housing. While this was meant to forestall or quash egregiously large or excessively ugly new builds, it has often been used, particularly by wealthier places, to stop growth altogether.

This chapter explores the inception and growth of the YIMBY movement, which began in San Francisco in 2014 to advocate for more market-rate housing construction. Unlike previous activist groups in the affordable housing landscape, YIMBYs are supply-side believers who concentrate on "building more of everything," which distinguishes them from previous housing rights groups that focused on maintaining public housing and preventing eviction in gentrifying areas like the Mission District.[16] When charismatic pro-construction YIMBYs, such as Sonja Trauss, Laura Foote, and Brian Hanlon, began showing up to zoning meetings to speak in favor of large construction projects, they cut open a pathway for an underserved demographic in the housing debate: younger professionals who also felt squeezed by rent but not so catastrophically burdened that they are facing housing insecurity. The simplicity of the "build more" message quickly attracted thousands of volunteers in the Bay Area and a mushrooming network of splinter groups and regional start-ups in California and, in very little time, the rest of the United States. By 2021, there were over thirty YIMBY groups just in California with approximately five thousand total active members. This chapter explores the inception of this movement in San Francisco and why the city's housing crisis has become a cautionary tale among density activists. As Victoria Fierce, an East Bay YIMBY organizer, puts it: "Housing is infrastructure. . . . Allowing more housing is necessary to contain the current disaster and provide long-term relief."[17]

The creation of a middle-class social movement, with middle-class participants, advocating for middle-class policies is novel in the Bay Area. The stated original goal was to expand the total housing stock in every category, opening the door to potentially working with anti-gentrification groups to create more public housing as well as with developers to push through market-rate housing (with a certain amount, usually 15% to 20%, kept at the affordable level). YIMBYs in the Bay Area pledged to confine their activism to already wealthy neighborhoods that resist density. Yet in the Bay Area, that turned out to be manifestly untrue, and much activist energy was spent in neighborhoods like Oakland and the Mission advocating for large new projects that attracted the ire of local residents and anti-gentrification activists. As Deepa Varma, of the San Francisco Tenants Union, noted of the new focus on supply alone: "[The] 'just build' mantra put forward by opinion leaders is diverting state government from the hard truth that the market has not responded to the demand of California families for affordable homes."[18] This chapter shows how YIMBYs went from an interesting activist upstart group to the harbinger of a growing rift within the affordable housing movement and, possibly, American politics more broadly.

By relying on the market in a more or less laissez-faire approach, YIMBYs attracted the wrath of San Francisco progressives. However, many within the movement would convincingly argue that some of the loudest voices protesting their efforts to build more housing were those who enjoyed "virtue signaling" from their multimillion-dollar properties, condemning the alliance between homeowners and anti-gentrification groups as partnerships that disadvantaged those with less money and more to lose. Last, the chapter shows how YIMBY activists increasingly refocused their efforts from citizen-led grassroots speaking out at meetings to expert-led legal challenges and even running for office on a purely housing platform. In doing so, they hope to gain more control over city regulatory agencies as well as to make advocating for urbanism as a way of life a political brand for millennials.

The Roots of the Affordability Crisis

San Francisco was the emblematic western boomtown. Between 1849 and 1851, it burnt down six times, only to be frantically rebuilt in order to serve gold miners and frigates. New residents were so eager to get to the gold-fields that sailors sometimes collectively abandoned their vessels, leaving the captains little choice but to run the boat aground and adding to the new port's vast shipwrecking graveyard. Indeed, in what would become a pattern, basic infrastructure was not forthcoming. Wharf construction was completed by a fractured coalition of local government and joint stock companies employing low-paid Irish-Australian "Steam Paddies" to fill in harbor land with steam-powered shovels.[19]

By the time of the 1906 earthquake, San Francisco had become the de facto capital of the western United States, worth rebuilding at any cost. It was an economically diverse gateway to Asian goods and markets, and it took advantage of its reputation as a western Wall Street to steer shipping and banking capital into the burgeoning real estate economy. By mid-century, when the model of growth in the urban core was at the point of exhaustion, the city exploited a new growth machine:[20] it embraced state-funded suburbanization with the help of federal highway money while also accepting urban renewal funds to remake the downtown with more high-rises. Between 1960 and 1981, thirty million square feet of office space was constructed:[21] one of the highest rates in the nation.[22] Once concentrated on the tip of the peninsula like a thimble on an index finger extended from San Jose, the population of only 679,00 in the 1970s was insignificant in the roster of great American metropolises.[23] Instead, like other places dispersed by sprawl, San Francisco's total metropolitan population of approximately 5.2 million in 1980[24] was strewn across nine counties that often failed to properly coordinate growth, transportation, taxation, and environmental policy.

In 1958, the city's growth coalition of developers, local government, and retail businesses, which had previously accepted federal funds and encouraged new housing, met its first opposition. A proposal to create a Golden Gate Authority that would oversee regional transportation (similar to the Port Authority of New York and New Jersey) was vigorously challenged.

Even consummate urban boosters, like the mayor of Berkeley, came out against it, proposing instead a toothless Association of Bay Area Governments that would only pen recommendations rather than wield any true power.[25] Those against regional control presented arguments in the vein of Jane Jacobs, emphasizing that coordination at a higher level would devolve into a big money plot that would destroy their existing communities. They managed to block the measure in a first blow to more streamlined governance of development and transport as a harbinger of things to come.

As historian Alison Isenberg has shown, there was also much to fear: in pursuit of urban renewal goals, real estate boosters often sought to tear down historic harborside warehouses and erase existing streets into the footprints of shopping malls while underpaying the city for their privatization. Networks of housing activists were continually mobilized in the 1960s: they could quickly turn up to protest buildings that were too large or that threatened to increase rent; even projects to refurbish public housing were viewed as likely accelerators of displacement and were resisted. Justin Herman, San Francisco's urban development czar, was baffled by the ferocity of resistance, commenting with Robert Moses–like certitude: "Meaningful and productive involvement can be done only by private citizens who have the time and capacity to become thoroughly acquainted with complex problems— otherwise, they are prone to condemn what they do not understand."[26]

Unlike in other cities going through similar changes in the 1960s, urban renewal in San Francisco faced a coalition of artists, preservationists, designers, and self-taught urbanists who vociferously objected to large-scale projects. They distrusted the expertise of urban renewal professionals and were disgusted by the scale and aesthetics of modernist glass towers. Housing activists from groups like Yerba Buena Tenants Union, Western Addition Project Area Committee, and San Francisco Neighborhood Legal Aid Foundation demanded that the municipal government improve the quality of housing stock while remaining skeptical about the government's desire or ability to address issues that primarily affected the urban poor.[27] The shock engendered by the forty-eight-story Transamerica Pyramid (built in 1969) created an effective coalition enforcing constraints on vertical development.[28] The structure was seen as a grotesque imposition onto the city's mostly horizontal surface, with one letter writer derisively saying it "would be ideal for Las Vegas."[29] San Franciscans from many walks of life began to appreciate vernacular urban landscapes of wharfs, decaying Victorian homes, and brick warehouses, and they fought off those who demeaned this aesthetic as shabby or antiquated out of true stylistic preferences as well as a knowledge that with development, displacement would most likely follow. This often took the form of defending public housing and rent control in central neighborhoods like the Tenderloin, including mass tenant organizing within the San Francisco Housing Authority.[30]

The anti-growth sentiment continued throughout the 1960s, as Californians worried that the image of a temperate coastal paradise broadcast to the rest of the country had been a little too successful. In San Francisco particularly, the rallying cry was to stop the "Manhattanization" of the city. However, the real villain of uncontrolled sprawl was Los Angeles, its rival to the South, and well before Richard Nixon became president or Ronald Reagan became governor the two cities had begun to define themselves against each other, both politically and in terms of the built environment. Objections to growth were a mixture of forces: from suburban homeowners in places like Santa Clara County that zoned 70 percent of all land for single-family homes exclusively[31] to more environmentally inspired objections in Marin County. Some calls to halt planned highways and housing were unabashedly racist: in 1964 Californians nullified the legislature's fair housing act so that landlords could continue to discriminate by race. The ballot proposition was overturned by the California State Supreme Court, and then by the US Supreme Court, but not before anti-growth sentiment attracted national attention that led then Governor Edmund Brown to excoriate the state's voters for endorsing a law that seemed more in keeping with the politics of Mississippi or Alabama.[32] Other objections to growth capitalized on a broader sense of regional competition to maintain housing prices, retain a bucolic environment, and limit the burden on public services. California became, in short, a laboratory for NIMBYism after a century of unrestrained growth.

NIMBYistic objections are often well founded. They do not just represent the selfishness of the homeowners looking over their shoulders and resisting anything that may depress property values. Concern about one's backyard is often a deeply deliberative form of community engagement[33] that addresses the carrying capacity of land with on-the-ground knowledge that is attuned to environmental quality and social cohesion. However, it can become a mindset that denies all changes made at scale, embracing some of the more pernicious aspects of American federalism and home rule. Preserving independent, devolved decision making can come from overall skepticism about "big government," but also from latent racism or an unwillingness to share space and resources with others. In California in the 1970s, this was what was beginning to develop, and after reshaping the state's tax codes and housing policy, it would also become a major force in Goldwater and Reagan Republicanism. Fear of regional coordination and a revolt against taxes (often in racialized terms that decried progressive taxation as a form of unjust redistribution to inner-city African Americans) spurred Californians to hunker down in their suburbs and resist infrastructure meant for broad public use.

In 1978, the California slow-growth movement lodged an astonishing legislative success with the passage of Proposition 13 that fundamentally reoriented urban development and property taxes in the United States. The ballot initiative, named People's Initiative to Limit Property Taxation, was the pet project of anti-tax millionaire Howard Jarvis, who sought to cap property taxes out of not just a sense of runaway rates but a distaste for what he regarded as government tyranny.[34] The law, which is still in effect, limits property taxes to one percent of a home's value. The impetus for this, as stated in the initiative, was to protect Californians on a fixed income, especially retirees. However, as a number of policy analyses have shown,[35] it has acted as a regressive tax allowing wealthier homeowners to claw back payments that once supported municipal services. After passage of the law, cities struggled to fill their budget gaps, which created a new sensibility around land use. As the geographer Alex Schafran has shown, Proposition 13 marks the increased financialization of land use but its ideological origins have more to do with traditional liberalism and "home rule" rather than neoliberal marketization. It created a new economy of most desirable development: commercial strip malls were at the top (because they paid communities impact and linkage fees that could be channeled into cash-starved public services) while affordable housing, with almost no tax revenue, was at the bottom of the hierarchy.[36] This helped speed the inequality between suburbs: some attracted high-end shops and luxury homes as others became more and more defined as worker cities for blue-collar employees. City managers maximized payments coming from new development because of constant budget emergencies while ignoring the social and environmental consequences of towns filled with strip malls but few apartment complexes.

Although city managers were at first fearful of Proposition 13, it was a hit with citizens, and facsimile policies were put into law in other states. San Francisco in particular took the slow-growth ballot measure as a sign of a new public appetite for restricting development, even if that meant saying "no" to new businesses. In 1986, the city passed Proposition M, which limited office construction to 950,000 square feet a year. At the time, it was the most restrictive measure in the United States. Political scientist Richard

DeLeon notes that by the 1990s, NIMBYistic thinking in San Francisco had become a kind of "urban feudalism" that was often defended solely on the basis of complicating regional power. The appeal of this stance often rested on a radical legacy: throwing a wrench into large-scale plans was viewed as a means to keep elites from amassing power and a way to protect the "little guy." DeLeon argues that San Francisco—instead of taming a typical urban growth machine by moderating development—created an "antiregime" that "regulates by impedimenta." This antiregime went far beyond simple quality control and became fanatical, maintains DeLeon: "The antiregime is protective, defensive, and obstructive. In the domain of land-use planning and physical development, its written and unwritten constitution can be boiled down to a single word: no."[37] Yet, the coalition of "no" was surprisingly diverse and enduring.

The new slow-growth sensibility had a tremendous impact on housing. Its backers were a coalition of downtown commercial real estate owners hoping to maximize value, activists from low-income neighborhoods seeking to stay in their homes and avoid gentrification, environmentalists, and affluent homeowners. Many of them came together as early as the 1960s to protest against the double-decker coastal Embarcadero Freeway, mobilizing tens of thousands of protestors who ultimately prevented substantial sections of the project from being built. By the 1970s and 1980s, the coalition had grown both stronger and more radical in their anti-growth demands. They fought mega-projects and new housing, sometimes projects with significant affordable housing contained within their plans. They first elected the liberal mayor Art Agnos and then became a thorn in his side by thwarting his pet projects for housing and economic rejuvenation. For example, in 1990 a proposal to build ninety-one units of housing with twenty-nine low-income apartments for artists was vociferously opposed by neighborhood residents. When the no-growth coalition lost, they claimed the site was potentially a habitat for the rare Harvestman spider, further delaying the project and adding to construction costs.[38]

San Francisco's low-growth activism was particularly adept at stopping the overhauling of planning codes to allow larger and taller buildings in the process known as "upzoning" by urban planners, which adds density and frequently multistory buildings to flatter urban neighborhoods as cities grow (it can also change codes from residential only to mixed-use commercial-residential). Many neighborhoods successfully organized against upzoning in the 1990s, often galvanized by large-scale opposition to new developments, such as the 1990 Mission Bay mixed-use harborfront project. At the same time, the tech economy was growing by leaps and bounds, putting pressure on previously low-income neighborhoods such as South of Market Street. Even high-crime neighborhoods like the Tenderloin felt increased pressure on the rental market, leading many community members to fear for their homes. Anti-gentrification groups such as the North of Market Planning Coalition were successful in protecting single-room occupancy (SRO) buildings (in contrast to other American cities). This group also downzoned the Tenderloin in 1985 to make all new structures a maximum of eighty feet rather than the previous 130 to 320 feet.[39] This created a unique swath of prime downtown real estate that was protected from development as the city around it became ever more affluent: leading to the jarring juxtaposition, described in the beginning of this chapter, of affluent tech employees going to work just blocks from the severe poverty and addiction in the streets surrounding the Tenderloin. While low-income residents have been temporarily spared being priced out of the Tenderloin, the overall strategy of a development moratorium has been utilized in much more affluent neighborhoods, helping to choke off the housing supply.

When the first dot-com bubble burst in 2000, there was a temporary reprieve for communities in San Francisco threatened by gentrification, but it was short-lived. Housing became a crucial concern because of the city's geography and its decades of slow-growth legislation. Lighter-footprint tech firms began moving from Silicon Valley to the city itself, drawn by urban amenities. As tech companies focused more on lifestyle products, they began to believe that their office parks in the suburbs were producing "silicon nerds" rather than cosmopolitans, making the relocation to a downtown office not just a means to ensure the happiness of the workforce but an attempt to produce a certain kind of worker.[40] Many of the companies that moved to the city center either had a skeletal start-up staff of under 100, paid very well, or both, making housing affordability and the quantity of new units available less of a workforce challenge than it would be for other industries.

By the time of the 2008 economic crisis, these firms were assisted by city policy as well. Incentives to move to San Francisco's center abounded. Mayor Ed Lee sought to steer growth to the Tenderloin as an economic development project although few existing residents would find employment in tech offices. In 2011, he created the Central Market Payroll Tax Exclusion that waived payroll taxes for six years for large companies. The measure was spurred by Twitter's threat to abandon their Mid-Market neighborhood central office. By the 2010s, these companies relied on public funds while eschewing local infrastructure: they made their own high-end cafeterias, provided in-house fitness services, and created party-equipped offices that replaced local happy-hour destinations. Companies like Google supply their own buses, other tech workers rely on ridesharing apps for transportation instead of taking public transit, and many companies have a fleet of bicycles that undermine public bike-share programs. The only necessity not provided is housing—at least not yet.

Private infrastructure is, of course, a perfect fit for a certain brand of technophilic libertarianism. The welfare-state public infrastructure of the mid-twentieth century can seem passé and sometimes even an impediment to creating new "smart cities" that enable mobility, employment, and services through new spatial and online interactions.[41] These new private systems denationalize previous forms of infrastructure by taking away a sense of collective ownership. For many people, this is a good thing: few feel pride in the rusting antiquated systems of the federal government. As the architectural theorist Keller Easterling has shown, local and state governments have willingly given up some sovereignty in terms of infrastructure provisioning, both as a form of cost-cutting and as an acknowledgment of their lack of capacity in the digital age.[42] Public infrastructure has become a temporal marker, signifying an era that has come and gone, eliciting sorrow from big-state progressives and glee from small-government conservatives.[43] San Francisco tech companies, more in line with the latter ideology, seek to create a new, privatized physical infrastructure to complement the digital systems they have already erected.[44] The problem is that they cannot marshal control of the municipal government. So, for the time being, they have built an auxiliary infrastructure on top of the dying public system. While many tech companies earnestly engage with urban problems and attempt to harness big data to find solutions, they rarely see a meaningful role for the public systems of the past.

The move from Silicon Valley office parks to downtown San Francisco shows a fatal flaw in the privatization of infrastructure: tech employees do not want to live in suburban tech campuses. They want to be amidst a thriving urban core, problems and all. In terms of housing options, tech employees often seek out the charm of bay-windowed Victorian houses, where they can realize not just a sense of urban authenticity[45] but also considerable investment potential from the rent gap of socioeconomically changing neighborhoods.[46] Their employers can take advantage of tax incentives for relocation (such as those provided by Mayor Ed Lee) while also transitioning from pricey suburban Silicon Valley locations to up-and-coming—that is, gentrifying—urban sites. This increasingly forces out low-income urbanites living at the center of the city, creating an image of a "whitened" city in which people of color are disappearing. Indeed, San Francisco's African American population declined by nearly 40 percent between 1990 and 2010.[47] The city government, long beset by the problem of low growth, could finally strike back at the anti-development coalitions: politicians like Ed Lee were able to welcome new businesses without building significantly more housing or constructing new office towers because of the light footprints of most tech companies and their penchant for refurbishing older buildings (at first).

In this sense, the welcoming of tech into the core of San Francisco was an attempt to prop up failing infrastructure with jobs and tax revenue, reminding us, in the words of geographers Stephen Graham and Simon Marvin, that infrastructure plans, "instead of being static material artefacts to be relied on without much thought, . . . are, in effect, processes that have to be worked towards."[48] Politicians hoped to save transit and other municipal services after the 2008 economic crisis, and they sought the help of the growing downtown tech industry. Yet, San Francisco made few inroads toward building new housing even as job growth soared and defied the downturn of the Great Recession. Soon the problem would become emblematic of the city, and the lack of solutions would paralyze municipal agencies and bitterly divide neighborhoods.

Build More of Everything

In 2014, the YIMBY movement was born with the ignominious name BARF (Bay Area Renters Federation). The name was thought up by the transplanted Philadelphia teacher Sonja Trauss, who sought to grab people's attention and also to adequately express the housing situation in San Francisco: it was so dire that just thinking about it made people want to vomit. Trauss and other founding members of BARF believe that housing activism needs a sense of levity and a more practical orientation: activists have to stop saying "no" to development projects that are not perfect. This primarily meant standing up for proposed apartment buildings that mixed market-rate and affordable dwellings, rather than holding out for wholly subsidized projects. BARF activists supported the idea of public housing, community land trusts, and other novel means to offer not-for-profit shelter, but they did not believe these ideas were sensible or scalable in the booming San Francisco real estate market that followed the expansion of app-based tech firms into the downtown. As Steven Buss, an early volunteer with the group, put it: "In order to be a YIMBY you need to say 'I want subsidized *and* market-rate housing' because if you only want one or the other it is unworkable. The market will never provide for very low-income people and the government in America is just not capable of building the amount of housing that we need to build."

Early BARF organizers began setting up meetings for like-minded renters at happy-hour teach-ins on urban density. Buss, who started attending these meeting in 2014 and works in tech like many other participants, described them as small and very DIY:

> We met at this warehouse in SoMa. The warehouse had no heating and no cooling, and I am pretty sure we were illegally running this operation out of the warehouse. Which is just pretty "on brand" for us. It was full of people like me: who were young and pissed off about the mismanagement of the city.

Buss had recently moved to San Francisco from Los Angeles and was astounded at the price of accommodation. Six months before moving to the Bay Area he began searching for an apartment for him and his fiancée, but looking on Craigslist, he found that prices kept going up. Eventually a colleague told him that his roommate was moving out and he and his partner could rent the room (for slightly more than they had paid for an entire one-bedroom apartment in Los Angeles). A couple of months later, Buss and his fiancée split up, and he was back searching for a place to live. He remembers this time as extraordinarily frustrating:

> I started to search again and everything had increased in price. . . . I ended up sleeping on the couch in my ex-fiancée's apartment for a couple months and that's not pleasant. . . . That was the last place I wanted to be. And that's the thing that radicalized me.

For many YIMBYs the language of radicalization is relative: their solutions are in keeping with mainstream urban-planning dogma, palatable to municipal governments, and downright thrilling for developers. The reason that YIMBYs often have a conversion story at all is that they are often comfortably middle class and did not previously feel the need to defend their economic interests. Yet, the extent of unaffordability in urban housing markets changed their own sense of financial security and forced them to advocate for their interests in a more assertive style. At early BARF meetings, Buss was introduced to other YIMBYs who were equally angry about the rental market. Many were tech workers with good salaries who simply could not understand how prices had gotten so out of control in San Francisco. They quickly settled on a reason: a lack of construction and an arcane permitting process that allowed existing residents to block new construction. As Buss put it:

> Discretionary review is the process that allows any random person in the city to appeal any project. They can just pay a couple hundred dollars and say: "I don't like this" and they can hold the project up for years. Literally years. The majority of the time, it is not good-faith opposition but millionaires fighting millionaires. Occasionally you get a millionaire fighting a billionaire.

The idea that San Francisco's NIMBY thinking was a battle between elites was a common thread at YIMBY meetings. If they had to choose, YIMBYs tended to side with the wealthy developers, because at least developers' aims could be tempered into a socially useful outcome (more housing). They saved special ire for progressives who bought their mansions at a discount when the city was a cheaper place. Laura Foote, a prominent YIMBY in San Francisco, said: "everyone was sick of being told they were a newcomer because they hadn't lived in the same house for thirty years." During zoning meetings for new construction she added there were two types of NIMBYs: the growth denialists who say, "I don't live in a place where I think there will have to be any growth, so smart growth isn't an issue," and those with murky ideas about how to get things built: "there are people who, when you ask them if we should have more housing, they say 'absolutely,' but if you say 'do we need more development' they'll answer 'not at all.'" This thinking also echoed the idea that residents of wealthy neighborhoods frequently conflate community development and construction, both of which they feel should take place in lower-income places.

Early meetings were often led by two of the rising stars of the YIMBY movement, Laura Foote and Sonja Trauss, but they were collaborative affairs, sometimes starting almost as a venting session over drinks and snacks. Buss remembers one early meeting in the cold SoMa warehouse when they got out a piece of butcher paper and started jotting down ideas. Other meetings were held at bars in the hope of attracting walk-ins who would come for a brief pitch talk and stay for drinks and chat about housing or other topics. For Foote, this was all about creating low-key spaces that were welcoming for those without much of an organizing background: "Get beers afterwards. Can't overestimate that. It is critical to community building. Nurtures the quality and not quantity of your community," she told me. Joe Rivano Barros, another early YIMBY participant, confirmed this, saying that meetings could last up to three hours: "YIMBYs are very social, and if you don't make your political home a social home, people will stop coming. There are always snacks and drinks," he said. Foote and others said that these social ties—and even the kvetching about housing prices—were essential to group solidarity: common grievances got people activated. As she put it:

> Someone will come out once because they are really angry; they'll come out twice because you guilt-tripped them; but if they didn't have a good time, and if they didn't bond with people and feel like they were appreciated and what they did matters, . . . they won't come back.

This early collaborative and horizontalist approach was meant to get as many people in the room as possible. It succeeded in attracting a wide swath of the political spectrum, from those working in the real estate industry to anticapitalist organizers, although this compromise would prove to be short-lived.

The first goal of YIMBY activists in San Francisco was to create a platform to amplify the voice of renters. As of 2018, 65 percent of San Franciscans rent their apartments. Of those, almost 60 percent enjoy rent control: a tremendous number for an American city. Yet, the other 40 percent are left at the whim of the rising housing prices, and some of them, with below-market apartments, may face displacement.[49] Trauss and other YIMBYs felt that renters, who spend nearly 40 percent of their income on housing in San Francisco–Oakland–Hayward,[50] were pitied but not heard. Their voices were present in debates on gentrification but not at city planning meetings that discussed expanding the housing stock. Instead, these meetings were dominated by homeowners who consistently argued against apartment buildings for reasons such as traffic, casting shadows, and depleting "community character." BARF activists were skeptical of community character, and when it was invoked, they heard hints of self-interest and protecting the status quo rather than defending a group of actual people tied together by social bonds. As Joe Matthews, a California writer sympathetic to YIMBY views, put it:

> The dark political genius of the "protecting the character of the community" argument is that it allows those who employ it to avoid responsibility for their obstructionism. They portray themselves as "stakeholders" merely trying to keep their neighborhood from getting hurt. Even worse, at a time that celebrates activism, many of these community-character protectors pose as righteous neighborhood activists.[51]

YIMBYs saw themselves as the true activists, while depicting those who resisted change as selfish and out of touch with how cities mature. As Matthews puts it: "The defense of community character is a lousy argument in normal times, because neither character nor community is static. Housing, buildings, streets, economies, and public spaces all age, and all must be maintained, updated, and renewed."[52] One of the countless YIMBY memes on the topic shows Spongebob Squarepants considering NIMBY logic in front of a smelly trash can with text that reads: "The laundromat that no one knows about that got the city to designate a historic place," riffing off a real struggle for historic designation in the Mission spearheaded by a city supervisor.[53] Given their frustration with community character and the perceived need to defend the spatial and aesthetic status quo, YIMBYs were determined to fill planning meetings with their own coalition of, mostly, market-rate renters who had neither an endangered rent-controlled apartment nor a home with a mortgage to protect.

Many of the first people to join BARF were newcomers to San Francisco who struggled to find and stay in a reasonably priced apartment. They often felt both cash-strapped and targeted for destroying existing communities. One tech worker described the group as a safe space to "be both privileged enough to be paying $4,000 in rent a month but also worried about that price. . . . The meetings were a place where no one would tell you 'You don't belong in this city' or '[You're] just another tech bro.'"

Early YIMBYs disdained NIMBY activists for their inability to see the housing crisis as a matter of supply. They also disliked many existing neighborhood groups who demonized all newcomers. Tim Redmond, writing in the now-defunct *San Francisco Bay Guardian*, a left-leaning paper focused on city culture, responded negatively to the YIMBY movement, implying that previous migrants to San Francisco had been beatniks, hippies, and gay people motivated by cultural reasons and that newcomers were motivated only for economic reasons.[54] YIMBY activists were quick to ridicule Redmond for his stance on closing the gates to the Bay Area on "greedy" newcomers because he lived in a $1.4 million house that had quadrupled in value since he bought it. Thanks to Proposition 13, Redmond only paid a 0.4 percent annual tax[55] on his home while complaining that "When you are in a hole, stop digging. If you're in a crisis, don't make it worse. And right now, building luxury housing is a net loser for the city."[56] YIMBYs see this kind of concern about housing affordability from the San Francisco old guard as disingenuous, asserting that the latter are less concerned with gentrification and simply annoyed that they will have endure more people and larger buildings. The activists roundly mock the people who "just came for the culture" as selfish and out of touch with housing economics, highlighting their incredulous attitude as proof of their provincial suburban mindset.

"Cities need to expand at some point," a woman who worked in tech and attended YIMBY meetings in Oakland and San Francisco told me. She added:

> We were really tired of being told "you're rich so shut up" because many of us either didn't feel rich because of the prices here or . . . believed, like I do, that, hey, someone has to spend money in this city and get the economy going. So, is it really so bad to be a city that attracts people who earn a good income?

In many cases, YIMBYs felt that their education and prosperity was exactly what allowed them to be good neighbors: they could devote their time to activism that required a high degree of urban planning knowledge, and they felt that their efforts would make communities more livable for all residents.[57]

By 2016, San Francisco YIMBYs were already thousands strong and expanding into new organizations and neighborhoods. Trauss had jettisoned the name BARF for the less humorous California Renters Legal Advocacy and Education Fund (CaRLA) while also lending a hand to start YIMBY Action with Laura Foote, a group that encouraged pro-density political candidates, and California YIMBY, a group that lobbies in Sacramento for new housing policies. Along with these larger organizations, neighborhood groups sprang up around the Bay Area coordinating support for individual projects seeking zoning approval. There was Grow the Richmond, Oakland YIMBY, East Bay for Everyone, Palo Alto Forward, and Livable Berkeley, to name just a few. Trauss, considered by many in the media as the main spokesperson for YIMBYs and the movement's founder, encouraged the decentralization of efforts and the creation of offshoot organizations. This was both a means to encourage localism but also a broad tent approach that allowed for a range of groups: from YIMBY socialists to YIMBY free marketeers. By the time that Donald Trump was elected in 2016, the movement was moving forward at a running pace thanks to community interest, a pithy name, and several hundred thousand dollars in grants from tech philanthropists, including the founders of Yelp and Facebook.[58] The backing of tech money at this early stage would come to haunt YIMBY groups as they sought to mediate disputes between their socialist and libertarian members and to protect their brand image as an authentically grassroots network of "pissed off rent-payers."[59]

YIMBY members were speaking at local meetings about their right to be in San Francisco, while growing their local organizations through payment of small dues, online brand-building, and relying on volunteers in lieu of hiring professional staff. They continued to attract newcomers to the city who were appalled by the mismatch between housing and jobs. This was often explained in terms of economic opportunity: people should be able to move to the center of the technology job market, where they can reap the rewards of a thriving economy. Further still, Trauss and others often reframed it as a kind of internal provincialism that mimicked Donald Trump's xenophobia. In November of 2016, Trauss, speaking in defense of an apartment project in the Mission neighborhood in front of the San Francisco Board of Supervisors, said: "In Trump's America, we're already disturbed by nativism everywhere. . . . When you . . . say that you don't want new, different people in your neighborhood, you're exactly the same as Americans all over the country that don't want immigrants. It's the same attitude."[60] For YIMBYs, saying "no" to development or to newcomers was akin to shouting "Build the wall." Yet, for Latino and undocumented San Franciscans, this comparison was ridiculous and demeaned their own life experience of living off the legal radar.

Yes in My Backyard activists tried to show that people should be able to move toward opportunities, but their increasingly bellicose attitude was quickly making them notorious in San Francisco. This was not at all troublesome to early YIMBYs. Sonja Trauss told me that the point of showing up to so many meetings was to "hear people's bullshit excuses" for why development cannot happen and then "call them on it." Similarly, Laura Foote, explained that

> The worst advice is to be nice and be positive and make sure you are only always bringing locals from the neighborhood. . . . We are not playing that game. In order to enact real structural change you need to be loud enough, you need to be shrill enough to actually attract the people who are sitting on the couch, because that's your audience. The people who are actually at that meeting don't really matter because everyone who is there came in knowing what decision they were gonna make.

Indeed, YIMBYs were gaining a reputation in San Francisco for a confrontational style and a bawdy sense of humor that belied the earnestness of most activists. Some longstanding housing groups accused them of showboating and creating unnecessary vendettas, such as when they would research their opponents and publicize the value of their homes, but the high-visibility strategy was effective, especially on social media and online forums where moderation is seldom rewarded.

Another viewpoint that made YIMBYs anathema to much of the previous housing-activism community was the notion that developers could be the best allies for those worried about affordability. Anti-gentrification activists saw developers as caring little for the well-being of their tenants: they actively displaced people in order to maximize land value. In San Francisco, this meant uprooting people in places like Oakland and the Mission in smaller mid-century homes, knocking down those structures, and replacing them with larger apartment buildings where the majority of previous residents had no hope of landing one of the few affordably priced units agreed upon during planning negotiations (if there were any at all).

YIMBYs sought to change the tone of the debate. Vilifying developers was counterproductive, they believed: developers were needed to get projects built. YIMBYS reasoned that nonprofit institutions and the city government were incapable of erecting new housing at scale, and a more useful strategy was to vet developers' projects for affordability and to help the more capable ones get planning permission. This more macro viewpoint was frustrating to traditional activists because it said exactly what hostile city planners and economic development organizations had been telling them for years as housing prices rose, in effect: "Yes, people will have to leave the neighborhood, but these new buildings are part of the big picture." As one Oakland anti-gentrification activist commented: "YIMBYs are all about saying 'Wait for it—affordability is coming, but while you wait, can you just move thirty miles away and get out of my sight?'" Indeed, the promise of YIMBY groups to work with developers to get the best possible deal to expand the housing stock for everyone rang hollow to anti-gentrification groups: for them, YIMBYs were not negotiating with developers, they *were* developers dressed up as activists.

From Outrage to Humor: Winning Hearts and Minds One Meme at a Time

In most accountings of the San Francisco housing crisis the reigning emotion is pathos, not bathos. Activists recount evictions, homelessness, and the destruction of community in order for policy makers and the general public to comprehend the enormity of housing precarity in the Bay Area. Yet, many of the YIMBY tactics have been comedic and even irreverent. Early in her career as a YIMBY provocateur, Sonja Trauss expressed her frustration with anti-development forces in the Bay Area by saying they would even resist building on a vacant lot because they had their first sexual experience there.[61]

Other activists relish using memes about their NIMBY opponents. One such meme shows a stick figure wearing a NIMBY mask, and a passerby says, "Why do you always wear that mask?" He gets no response, so he lifts the mask off to reveal a face that says, "Fuck the poor." He then pulls down the NIMBY mask, remarking: "Let's keep that on." These memes are distributed on Instagram, Twitter, Facebook, and various blogs almost daily. They testify to the pro-development, pro-density savviness for reaching people with humor rather than with pleas for earnest conversation.[62] However, for many critics of San Francisco YIMBYism they are a testament to a lack of seriousness and, worse yet, a kind of crassness and meanness that has taken housing politics to a new level of rancor. As one online poster commented about this approach: "I actually agree with most of [the YIMBYists'] points, but they take a lot of their tactics and attitudes out of the Trump playbook."[63]

One moment that stands out is the "zucchini lady" incident. At a Berkeley city council meeting in 2017, a property owner was seeking to build two units where a single-family house was located: exactly the kind of micro upzoning that density activists favor and feel should be inoffensive to neighbors. A homeowner living adjacent to the proposed project stood up during the public comment portion of the meeting and brandished a zucchini. "I brought a zucchini, because I love to garden," the woman told the council. "And in order to garden, you need sunlight. But this zucchini exists because I don't have a big two-story house next door to me right now."[64] This moment was meme-making gold for YIMBY activists in the audience. They wasted no time in ridiculing the concerned neighbor on social media, as well as speaking afterward at the public comment session, where a millennial stated: "I don't have a zucchini—it's a really great prop—but I do have my debit card. . . . It has maybe $800 on it. This is all the money I have," and going on to say that they will never own a home with a garden.[65]

The strategy of combining humor with indignation was not a new one,[66] but it gets at a central tactic of YIMBYism: make opponents look ridiculous and uncompromising and show how intransigent they are even on the smallest issues. This approach is meant to draw to the movement younger digital natives whose political sensibilities were shaped by watching *The Daily Show* rather than *60 Minutes*. This is perhaps most evident in urbanist groups such as New Urbanist Memes for Transit-Oriented Teens (NUMTOTs), which has over 200,000 followers on Facebook. Posters offer ribald "hot takes" on urban planning issues for a constituency of young people who use public and alternative transit and have no hope of buying property for the long-term future. This shift in tone concentrates on mirth making in order to uncover hypocrisy: it primes potential supporters to not trust assessments of slow-growth advocates who say that a building will be too big. It casts neighborhood groups as "hysterical hippies" who care more about their vegetables than about people becoming homeless.

Making YIMBYism fun was aimed primarily at those who opposed growth in wealthy neighborhoods, like Berkeley, but also to compete with progressive housing groups. Many of the YIMBY activists interviewed expressed their frustration with what they saw as left-wing "purity testing." They interpreted this as a self-sabotaging desire to get perfect projects approved (such as ones that contained 100% affordable housing) rather than to move along a larger quantity of projects with fewer affordable units. One example was a 2019 Board of Supervisors decision to block a sixty-three-unit apartment building with fifteen below-market apartments in the busy, already gentrified SoMa district because it would cast an 18 percent shadow on Victoria Manalo Draves Park.[67] One YIMBY activist, when asked about the tactic of mockery via online memes, said, "Well, this is San Francisco so they basically satirize themselves." Laura Foote told me that "some of the environmentalists make me crazy; . . . one literally had a funeral for a tree the other day." She added that this kind of behavior was indicative of what pro-growth activists had to deal with: the constant invocation of homeowners' rights for petty infringements on their quality of life. Foote often quips that she is a "ground truther," or a believer that the scarcity of urban land requires greater density but also a joke remixing the same science term with the similar-sounding "flat-earther" internet conspiracy theorists. It is a nod to how any too tightly held conviction can become dangerous. For YIMBYs, ideological flexibility is useful for getting things done.

YIMBY activism mirrors new trends in online political participation that diverge sharply from the door-knocking community efforts of the past. While housing affordability campaigns had previously been neighborhood-based, YIMBYs have broader scope because they explicitly represent people who are not yet in a place or are priced out of where they would like to be. This shifts the conversation from displacement to mobility. Also, given that many of those drawn to YIMBY groups are millennials or younger, online activism comes as second nature. They brought a new tone eschewing the earnestness of some progressive causes that played on a sense of moral grievance and embracing online snark and humor. As Laura Foote told me, "[a lot] of YIMBYism is against the virtue signaling of the traditional left" in San Francisco. Understanding the benefits of density necessitates a crash course in urban planning, but according to YIMBYs, it should be delivered in a series of humorous tweets mocking the narrow-mindedness of NIMBY thinking rather than a two-hundred-page white paper.

YIMBYs often attacked neighborhood groups personally for not wanting newcomers in their neighborhoods and caring more about their comfort than about housing affordability. One such YIMBY called out the head of a Bay Area slow-growth group, stating, "I'm really happy that she doesn't have to be bothered by bicycles or fourplexes."[68] This personalization of the struggle for urban density was perhaps inevitable because the YIMBY action plan is to speak out about specific proposals when they come for review in front of Bay Area councils and zoning boards. It also means that any level of abstraction that would allow for a more measured discussion is stripped away: it is about actual people and the homes they live in. Yet, while YIMBYs like to portray themselves as unmaskers of the sanctimonious San Francisco Left, they actually join a long tradition of theatricality in urban activism that has flourished in San Francisco since the 1960s, from Yippie street theater to environmentalists wearing giant fur animal suits. The desire to provide a generational boundary in both group composition and tactics speaks more to the groups' need to portray themselves as a new beginning, rather than a radical divergence in activist methods.[69]

"F*ck Neighborhood Control"

"No, you do not get total control of this little micro-unit fiefdom place you call a neighborhood. That you have whittled down into the perfect size that lets you do whatever the fuck you want. So yeah, basically: fuck neighborhood control." A YIMBY activist told me this while we were drinking mid-afternoon Tecate beers from the can in an otherwise empty San Francisco bar. We had been working up to this crescendo from a conversation about YIMBYism as a basic challenge to the scale of government control, and she had elegantly held forth on the history of suburbanization as a means for elites to exercise the maximum amount of control over their chosen communities. Now, polishing off beer number three, she was ready to take the gloves off: "Local control is my big red-flag phrase, but I can't really say that because it makes it seem like I am anti-grassroots . . . and, well, hey this is America. Everyone, Right and Left, wants to say they love localism. . . . Well, I'll say it now: I do not." The woman, who did not want to be identified due to her sense that this opinion would not go over well with colleagues, used slightly more colorful language but reiterated what many YIMBY activists believe: localism breeds selfishness, inefficiency, and shortsightedness. Instead, they maintain people need to plan cities on the scale of the entire metropolis and not through consensus within neighborhoods. This view, which some feel is anti-democratic, is defended as both practical and a response to history: where people live is no accident, neighborhoods are not naturally arising conglomerations but are intensely stratified by race and class.[70]

The idea that San Francisco is fractured in its urban governance is not new: many policy efforts have tried and failed to enact more universal codes that cover development across the Bay Area. In 2019, the Bay Area's nine counties took a step forward by proposing the CASA Compact in which the Metropolitan Transportation Commission would create nine Metropolitan Housing Enterprises to build more housing in each county, but funding would be pooled in order to give poorer zones extra help.[71] YIMBY activists support this plan because it has provisions to build quickly near transit, as well as rent control and eviction protection. Yet they also want to go a step further by stripping away community control of the development process altogether. Letting decisions be made on the city level will, they argue, decrease the ability of people to think about their interests alone. It also universalizes procedures for building that are often ad hoc. At the same time, the "3Ps" of the CASA Compact (*preservation* and *production* of affordable housing along with *protection* from displacement for tenants) is often the major point of controversy between YIMBYs and other housing activists: to many the "build more of everything" philosophy runs counter to the last goal of protecting vulnerable low-income communities.

"We want more rules, not less rules," a young YIMBY in Oakland told me. "That is the big misconception: that we are all about getting rid of urban planning," he said (while also mentioning that he had studied planning at Berkeley). "We actually just want rules that can be followed." Sonja Trauss mentioned something similar, reflecting on why universal regional rules would make development more transparent:

> Planning and design reviews don't need more amateurs with half-baked ideas. There are enough of those already. We don't care as long as it follows code, and we don't think that everyone should have a right to hold up the process for years over the color of someone's shutters. Just because you live nearby, nobody gives a shit what color you think someone else's shutters should be.

Trauss and many other YIMBY activists believe that not only are community concerns often frivolous but they are distracting from the big picture of getting more housing built. On a more basic ideological level, the activists dislike the community benefits process in which developers propose structures and then local governments wrangle for affordable housing within the plan or demand new parks and schools. Their feeling is that this process works well for communities that have a lot of resources and place-based advantages that attract competition. However, by making each project unique, community benefits are a constant struggle. Laura Foote, concurred saying: "We need to undermine the narrative of hyper-localism. . . . Lots of people bought into the idea that we should only organize in our backyard, but the whole message of this YIMBY thing is that everything has regional implications."

Regional cooperation is seen as not just an economy of scale when it comes to making urban policy but a means to decouple people from their neighborhoods and the self-interest that comes with them. The emotional bond of place and community for San Francisco YIMBYs is not a benefit; it is what makes people start acting selfishly and irrationally. Joe Rivano Barros, who describes himself as a progressive YIMBY deeply concerned with both housing supply and gentrification, said that community groups in wealthy parts of the Bay Area had often ginned up the opposition by failing to accept any kind of middle ground when it comes to neighborhood change:

> There's a real failure of imagination to think about what dense neighborhoods will look like. There are not usually twenty-story buildings, like you might see in a financial district and you won't be able to see the sun ever again. We are just talking about a few stories. If you go to European cities this is the norm, and it makes very charming very walkable neighborhoods with a high quality of life. There's a lot of fearmongering.

As YIMBY groups grew in size and capacity, they began to target areas outside of San Francisco proper in order to show that the burden of new housing would have to be spread equally: most notably in wealthy suburbs that have consistently resisted anything but single-family homes. Sonja Trauss started a group called Sue the Suburbs, taking advantage of a little-known state law that mandated affordability, using it to threaten wealthy towns to build more housing. Her most notable battle was in Lafayette in 2015, in which YIMBYs sued the city for additional affordable housing. They petitioned on behalf of a housing project in which even the developer had agreed to downsize its plan, arguing that the original number of units was needed and the developer should be given permission to build the entire project.[72] While the suit was ultimately unsuccessful, it put YIMBYs in the spotlight and helped bring about negotiations with other Bay Area suburbs—including Sausalito, Calabasas, and Los Altos—that were seeking to avoid similar lawsuits and negative media attention. When Trauss was asked about her aggressive tactics in the suburb of San Bruno, she told the publication *Next City*: "We're not creating conflict—we're uncovering conflict. . . . This is Martin Luther King, Jr. 101—this is Politics 101. These people are trying to promote a [housing] shortage. The conflict is when you're like, 'Fuck, my commute is an hour each way and when I get home my kids are asleep.'"[73]

YIMBYS are often dubious about suburbs as a lifestyle choice, nonetheless they feel that many suburbs could be densified if they were near a train line or closer to the city. Laura Foote clarified the split: "The difference between a town and a suburb is a town has apartments, and suburbia is a residential-only sprawling hellscape." Yet part of this attack was an even broader assault on the conventions of twentieth-century zoning dictating that residential and commercial areas should be divided from each other. As Steven Buss put it: "If I had to pick [the one most effective thing to change] it would be form-based zoning. This takes into account the political realities in San Francisco. Form-based zoning would let you put whatever you want, at whatever density you want, in a building that meets particular physical characteristics. It gets rid of exclusionary zoning; there's no such thing as residential and commercial zones. It's just: this is how big the building can be in this part of town." While this opinion may sound unprovocative, it is in fact a severe departure from the current use-based zoning that dominates most of American urban planning. Only small experiments have begun to use it but, if put into effect widely, it could spell the end of purely residential areas as we know them. On the other hand, it could also create a hodgepodge of uses in which car garages are next to yoga studios abutting marijuana grow houses. However, few people expect it to result in this kind of mishmash. For the most part, it is like many YIMBY solutions: middle-of-the-road practices long advocated for by the planning establishment but repackaged with feisty language and GIFs.

Sidestepping Subsidies

The growth of the YIMBY movement in San Francisco was achieved through confrontation: first, by calling out homeowners who resisted development; then by haranguing municipalities that would only allow single-family homes to be built; and last, by deriding established housing activists for being do-nothings who prevented expansion of the housing stock. "They started to really piss people off," a housing activist from Oakland in her sixties told me.

"People were like, 'Who are these bros and why are they shouting at people who have been in this movement for twenty years?" the activist said. For her, YIMBYs were not activists at all but angry rich people trying to use dubious housing economics to gain popular support for gentrification. Indeed, she noted that YIMBYs had purposefully alienated other housing activists in San Francisco, and this view, according to the YIMBYs themselves, was not entirely false.

Sonja Trauss and Laura Foote noted that their movement was a complement to corollary public housing campaigns, but they quickly began disagreeing about the specifics with on-the-ground groups. Trauss stated it simply: "For those people who say that you can't grow your way out, I have asked them, 'What do you think we should do?' and they don't have an alternative. There's no other plan but to build." Growth also means gentrification for many unless it could be put in the very wealthiest neighborhoods. This is what YIMBYs had promised in their platform: they would seek to upzone the most desirable places where people wanted to live and that are already expensive. As well-educated upper-middle-class white people, they would pressure others with a similar socioeconomic background to "move over" and allow some apartment buildings in their prestigious neighborhoods. This would, in turn, take pressure off quickly changing areas like the Mission and Oakland, where less-wealthy communities of color were getting displaced. But two things began happening around 2016: YIMBY activists reneged on their promise to advocate for growth only in already-wealthy neighborhoods, and they de-emphasized affordability mandates in all of the projects they advocated for.

At the start of the YIMBY movement, the pitch to members was that they would help get the best deal possible from new developers: if someone wanted to build a thirty-unit apartment building in downtown San Francisco, they would assist in getting the community and Board of Supervisors to agree to it, but they would also push for the maximum number of below-market-rate apartments possible. This effort did not satisfy some who held out for 100 percent affordable and started splinter groups with names like PHIMBY (Public Housing in My Backyard). Sonja Trauss, and several other informants, said that this was basically a false choice: "We are led to believe that market-rate housing has to compete with affordable housing because we don't have enough room for both kinds of housing. In fact, we have plenty of room." Other activists stated that taxes from building market-rate dwellings in the more prosperous West Bay generated revenue for subsidized housing in the East Bay, creating a symbiotic relationship. Yet, mainstream YIMBY

groups also began to subtly change their attitude, arguing that all new housing was good because even if a building was entirely made up of apartments
priced at $4,000 per month, the people who would fill them would not be
moving to transitional neighborhoods (and pushing out poorer residents).
The sites of new projects were of utmost importance. The initial mandate
was to create more housing in wealthy previously closed neighborhoods.
This was accompanied by a tacit agreement with anti-gentrification activists that YIMBYs would both stay off their "turf" and not campaign for large
developments that could possibly change neighborhood demographics.
This quickly fell by the wayside as YIMBYs began to make the low-income,
heavily Latino Mission neighborhood—which has quickly gentrified in the
past twenty years[74]—a center of their efforts.

YIMBYS endorsed specific projects within the Mission District as early
as 2015, leading to a head-on clash with anti-gentrification activists in the
area. The optics of majority-white and young YIMBYs facing off with older
and largely Latino anti-gentrification activists at city meetings also created
an unwanted image for the movement, which had already been criticized
for accepting tech money to fund their efforts. Sonja Trauss was blasé about
building in the Mission, telling me that the group was open to partnering
with anyone in any neighborhood as long as they were committed to getting things done: "We want to build more, and that's the most important
thing. It doesn't matter if it's libertarians or developers, or anti-gentrification
housing-justice people. Intentions are less important than action." Others
online were less diplomatic. As one Reddit poster mentioned in reference to
the debate over gentrification versus construction of housing: "I'm so sick
of people blocking housing in a housing shortage and then giving a flaccid
lecture about how it's the wrong housing. They gentrify themselves by letting
perfect be the enemy of good. We need more housing. Full fucking stop."[75]

Trauss's framing of YIMBYism as post-ideological was not satisfying to
many in increasingly unaffordable neighborhoods who stood to lose their
apartments. Her bluster did not help, often creating attention but also bringing avoidable controversy. Trauss tweeted in 2016 that "gentrification is reval-
uing black land and rewarding those who held out,"[76] by which she meant a
windfall for property owners of color who had suffered. Yet, others decried
it as a condemnation of those "too soft to stay the course" that ignored the
vast majority of Black renters forced out of neighborhoods. Critics of the
YIMBY movement quickly pointed out that the tweet was not just insensitive,
but it also showed that Trauss did not understand that they were fighting to
preserve the social bonds of a community, that even if people could make a

bundle by selling their house and relocating, they should not have to, as doing so would sever essential friendships and support networks.[77]

Individual YIMBY groups also began to campaign for large projects in the Mission, Oakland, and other low-income communities. The 2000–2070 Bryant Street Project in the Mission was one of the largest of its kind in the neighborhood, and the original plan, endorsed by YIMBYs, included 16 percent affordable housing. Opponents began calling the plan "the Beast on Bryant" and lamented that it would force out a local performance center called Cellspace. One of the artists told a local newspaper that "We're on a mission, in the Mission, to save the soul of San Francisco,"[78] and many other local residents agreed with him. Yet, YIMBYs argued that the new units were a good deal and were desperately needed in the neighborhood. The developer also promised to include subsidized artists' spaces within the new development. During the course of 2015–2016, plans for the site broke into open hostility between neighborhood groups and YIMBYs that was abundantly covered in local media.[79] However, when the final project was approved—now with 139 affordable units, making up 41.5 percent of the project[80]—YIMBYs chalked it up as a grand victory. For them, the conflict had been generative and had helped pressure the developer. If opponents had won, they reasoned, nothing would have been built and Latino families would have slowly, and more quietly, continued to be displaced apartment by apartment whereas now there would be 139 new places for low-income families to live. Similar to the pattern in many other cities, this conflict also showed how the spats over development in gentrifying areas was not always between low-income longtime residents and newcomers but between first- and second-wave gentrifiers, the former lamenting the loss of their bohemian haunts and the latter criticizing them for hypocrisy.

Another large project in the Mission preempted criticism of a proposed high-rise using YIMBY-like tactics, but this time deployed by a real estate firm. In 2017, the developers of 1979 Mission Street spent over $340,000 in marketing their residential project even before any hearings were scheduled.[81] The plan had attracted the unflattering moniker "the Monster in the Mission," and the developers attempted to counter-spin the project with a website called "mission4all.org" and train station ads featuring diverse San Franciscans, working as teachers, paramedics, and union laborers, under the banner "I am Not a Monster."[82] The local Mission newspaper called it a "downright Orwellian use of language" but also noted that it was very savvy because, quoting a city official, it showed that developers were no longer willing to sit back and allow their opponents to define them.[83] Many YIMBY activists also supported the project, which consisted of 331 luxury units with the promise to buy two additional parcels for 192 affordable units (most likely constructed at the city's expense).[84] On February 8, 2019, the project proposal was heard before a packed planning commission meeting with more than twice as many opponents as supporters.[85] Neighborhood residents called the development a form of "urban apartheid" and jeered at those who talked about job opportunities and adding to the housing stock. Shortly thereafter, the plan went back to the drawing board but, under such withering criticism, it was officially dead by early 2020.[86] While the "Monster" met the litmus test for the YIMBY build-more-of-everything philosophy, it was controversial for two reasons. First, the plans were vague, and second, the developers had attempted to co-opt YIMBY language using their own PR firm. This offense not only watered down the movement's own message, but it threatened to confirm the idea that the groups were nothing more than the henchmen of developers: "astroturfing" as a social movement.

Development in the Mission also began to fray the marriage of convenience between libertarian and progressive YIMBYs that had emerged in San Francisco. For the former, it seemed as if density activists were now in the building-affordable-housing game rather than just encouraging market forces. Ben Woosley, who worked in San Francisco and identified more with the libertarian side of YIMBYism, calling himself a market urbanist, was not keen to be identified with subsidized housing: "There's a nonprofit housing organization nexus that basically receives large amounts of government funding, in the hundreds of millions at least, and they are motivated to have development happen and have government funding continue." For him, this ground was well covered by other groups. Other YIMBYs were dismayed that the movement was electing to work in socioeconomically transitioning neighborhoods. Joe Rivano Barros noted that there is a lot of temptation to build in poor places: "the only areas of the city where density is possible are areas that house low-income and nonwhite folks living there." Part of this was zoning, he reasoned, but he was also very uncomfortable with YIMBYs concentrating their efforts on the Mission. He and others said that around 2016 they formed a new faction of the YIMBY movement, called YIMBY Socialist, setting up hashtags and memes about the importance of public housing, inclusionary zoning (mandates for affordable housing across neighborhoods that structure all new construction), and below-market subsidies. As he put it:

> [It was an] attempt to create a space within YIMBY Action for left-leaning members who were not interested in building housing in gentrifying neighborhoods. We're interested in building affordable housing and we're

also interested in tenants' rights. That only lasted a few months because it seemed like the organization wasn't really favorable to that point of view.

In response to the push by YIMBY progressives, another offshoot group called YIMBY Neoliberal was set up by Steven Buss and others. While the name was "100 percent a troll," Buss said, and most of the members supported subsidies and social housing, they did not want to crush capitalism. They hoped to make sure that the movement was identified with their perspective, rather than that of the socialist wing. As Buss put it: "[It] started to blow up on Twitter as a defender of progressive democracy and a response to the DSA (Democratic Socialists of America) an ostensibly democratic group, who knows, but if you look at the DSA's platform, they want to end capitalism. . . . To my dismay, the YIMBY socialists kind of faded out, and they weren't really happy with all the policies or embracing the big tent." Indeed, venturing into fights over gentrification in the Mission District alienated many members and caused them to leave the YIMBY movement for good. Rivano Barros agreed: YIMBYs began to defect to anti-gentrification groups for their social justice emphasis and focus on the struggles of poor urbanites, while YIMBYism held on to a centrist stance even amidst energized progressive organizing around climate change and Black Lives Matter.

Laura Foote was unconcerned with the growing strife within the major San Francisco YIMBY organizations: "We probably have more socialist members than libertarian members. We probably alienated the libertarian members by being vehemently pro-affordable housing. But we have won no points with the purist socialist crowd." Both Trauss and Foote told me that if people were not "pissed off at you, you probably were not getting much done," and this maximum seemed to exist internally as well. Yet, by 2017, the major YIMBY leadership had emerged as a distinctly center-left lobby that supported public housing but put the issue on the backburner in order to focus on new development with affordability clauses. These leaders were also increasingly looking beyond council meetings and online activism. They saw their movement as having developed a permanent constituency. Seeking elected office seemed like the next logical step.

Housing in the State House: Rebooting the Technocrat

Most social movements do not seek to immediately translate their on-the-ground wins into electoral politics.[87] However, YIMBY activists in San Francisco were far less concerned with appearing to be grassroots. They had already accepted hundreds of thousands of dollars from tech entrepreneurs and worked with developers, so their sense of positive and negative optics was far different from that of most Bay Area activists. Additionally, they had always prized activism done by highly educated "insiders" rather than rank-and-file "boots on the ground." After several missteps in 2016 regarding gentrification, they sought to reorient their network toward public policy, capitalizing on the expertise of their members. In many ways, they wanted to build an activist think tank that would help to draft policy and explain the benefits of their proposals to the wider public.

Brian Hanlon, an early YIMBY, was one of the people tasked with this responsibility, and the group he led, YIMBY California, was the flagship operation. It put pressure on state lawmakers in California to approve accessory dwelling units, it argued for transport-oriented development, and it sought to enact the "sue the suburbs" strategy on a regional scale by targeting the many municipalities that did not build apartments due to single-family zoning. Most of all, the new YIMBY electoral strategy was meant to enact a regional plan, finally bringing together the patchwork of land regulation around the Bay Area.

The chance to embed the build-more-of-everything idea into a political platform came in 2016 during a state senate election that narrowed to two Democratic members of San Francisco's Board of Supervisors: Scott Weiner and Jane Kim. Kim, the candidate viewed as more progressive, argued against gentrification. Weiner took a line straight from Sonja Trauss saying that the city must build more housing in order to stop escalating prices. Weiner won. He quickly became the YIMBY political mascot because of his single-minded focus on housing in the state legislature, establishing himself as the go-to person to introduce housing bills. He often received cooperation from other pro-density legislators such as Nancy Skinner and David Chiu (both from the Bay Area), and many YIMBY activists felt that his election was a watershed moment in forming a political alliance around the issues of public transport, renters' rights, and affordable housing. As the early YIMBY Joe Rivano Barros said:

> YIMBY took off like a rocket ship; usually nonprofits don't have the national profile that we do after so little time. It could take decades. But because the housing crisis was so severe here a lot of activism got noticed as novel. It gave YIMBYs the confidence to think of themselves as an important constituency that wasn't going away and could start to kind of play a role in the mayoral election.

Rivano Barros insisted that the Left would have to take advantage of the housing crisis by passing sweeping statewide laws while the issue was on people's minds due to rent burden, homelessness, and homes being destroyed by wildfires. He saw YIMBYs in the California state legislature as a first step in making housing a human right but also acknowledged the danger in associating the movement with individual politicians who might tarnish its reputation while in office.

Weiner himself was an ideal match for the YIMBY movement and very much represents the kind of politics they strive for. While he has some typical "pol" qualities—a JD from Harvard and a towering stature (he is 6′7″ tall)— he is not exceedingly charismatic, and as an officeholder he is unabashedly meticulous. He loves detail and takes pride in crafting intricate bills. In this sense, he is in line with YIMBY prerogatives by seeking centrist and often technical fixes for the housing crisis. However, despite being supported by a number of mainstream politicians, his proposals have often fallen flat. He found early success with Senate Bill 35 (2017), which streamlined approval for apartment units and mandates that cities meet Regional Housing Needs Assessments to build more affordable housing. Nevertheless, the final version of the bill was toothless, with little enforcement power and plenty of opposition from Southern Californian cities wishing to retain local control. So far, it has only been used to build a handful of new developments with below-market-rate apartments in the Bay Area.

After the disappointment of SB 35, Weiner and his YIMBY allies sought to think bigger and enact a piece of legislation that would truly force noncompliant municipalities to build more apartments. Laura Foote described Weiner as a politician who had always seen the need to grow San Francisco's housing: "Some politicians realize that we should have been building housing for a long time, so they're grateful when a group comes along and builds them the runway they can run down. That's Scott Weiner." State Senator David Chiu said this explicitly, noting that YIMBYs had given politicians the wherewithal to be pro-growth in a city where so many community meetings were dominated by those who did not want to see changes to the built environment: "I think they've provided a counterbalance. They've been changing the conversation on the local level as well as in the state," he told the *Guardian*.[88]

Weiner proposed the much more sweeping housing reform Senate Bill 827 with behind the scenes support from YIMBYs in drafting its language. The proposed law sought to rethink density in California neighborhoods: no more would communities enjoy both good transit and single-story skylines. Senate Bill 827 sought to automatically upzone areas within half a mile of a high-frequency transit stop (mostly trains) and within a quarter mile to 45–85 feet of bus stops, depending on the characteristics of the location.

This meant that many places with single-family homes near mass transit would soon have neighboring buildings that were four to eight stories tall. Predictably, there was tremendous opposition from wealthy neighborhoods, such as Beverly Hills, which built no apartments in the 1980s and 1990s and few since.[89] The bill would also allow apartments to be built without minimum parking requirements, motivating developers to force new residents to rely on public transit. The hope was that these sweeping measures would begin to chip away at the neighborhoods that had resisted multiple-unit dwellings (many cities in California are zoned 75% for single-family only, and the overall amount is 58%).[90] This legislation would transform not just urban areas close to commuter hubs, frequently scrutinized by planners, but it would have a far-reaching impact on the built environment: allowing suburban apartments in places where developers had not thought to build dense housing for decades.

The opposition to SB 827 was fierce and fast. It came from traditional opponents such as wealthy communities of homeowners in Southern California who did not want "apartment people" living in their neighborhoods but also from more surprising places. The mayor of progressive Berkeley said that it was "a declaration of war against our neighborhoods" and it was even opposed by the national Sierra Club.[91] Most of all, it publicized the growing rift between pro-density growth activists and anti-gentrification groups. An LA activist descried the bill as "'ethnic cleansing,' and compared it to Andrew Jackson's expulsion of the Cherokees."[92] Many neighborhood activists in Latino or African American neighborhoods believed that the law would not be enforced to actually build affordable housing in new developments, or that what was labeled as affordable would actually be middle income and completely inaccessible to people already living in the community. They saw it as gentrification on steroids and a Trojan horse for the real estate industry. Sonja Trauss told me that these laws always attracted protest from people who warned against "corporate Democrats" and that many politicians were scared of alienating drivers and homeowners. She insisted that YIMBYs were the true progressives and that the alliance between anti-gentrification groups and homeowners was unfortunate. Laura Foote agreed, saying that people in low-income neighborhoods would be the ones to lose out when the housing stock was not expanded.

Senate Bill 827 was killed in a committee meeting, only to be instantly revived by Scott Weiner in the form of Senate Bill 50, modified to mandate more construction in wealthy communities even if they did not have transit hubs.[93] By 2018, when the new bill was moving forward, the YIMBY movement had won more important political allies: the new mayor of San Francisco, London Breed, was an avowed YIMBY and took a more tolerant stance on construction than some of her opponents in the election. However, Breed's election had also galvanized progressive housing activists, who now saw any YIMBY endorsements as a scarlet letter of developer involvement and corporate interests. Weiner's SB 50 was particularly suspect and began to attract significant ire in anti-capitalist organizing circles. "He reframed it as housing to prevent climate change," a Latino activist from the Mission told me, "but this is really just a giveaway to real estate interests."

Protests against SB 50 continued, invigorated by opposition from communities of color as well as mainstream lawmakers: what was particularly controversial was the clause that protected vulnerable (low-income) communities. These neighborhoods had five years to plan for new density, but they sought to have an exemption in perpetuity. They began to organize and even attracted support from transport-oriented development advocacy groups—normally the most fervent allies of such of bill—who said that the gentrification risks outweighed the benefits. Meanwhile, progressive groups trashed the bill and Weiner personally, drawing attention to contributions to his re-election campaign from developers and stating that when he took office: "the professional class, particularly those in the influential real estate industry, thought they had a winner."[94] Due to the crescendo of negative voices around the bill, many politicians who originally supported the measure as a resolution to California's housing crisis began to back away, including the governor, Gavin Newsom, and the mayor of Los Angeles, Eric Garcetti. By June of 2018, activists were turning up to most of Weiner's public engagements to denounce him, including an event at UCLA where three silent protestors stood with a sign reading "WEINER OWNED BY BIG REAL ESTATE."[95] In 2019, the Los Angeles City Council unanimously opposed the bill.[96]

In January 2020, SB 50 was officially killed. Despite the breadth of the YIMBY coalition in support of constructing new housing, the unified opposition was more numerous and more vocal. Orange County conservatives with expensive homes joined forces with Latino activists from low-income communities. At issue was the uniformity of the new law and its ability to demand new housing despite context (although the enforcement mechanisms were actually fairly weak). Progressive would-be supporters worried that it would produce the same story as always: wealthy communities with superior resources would mobilize while demographically changing areas would have new projects dumped on them before residents could prepare. As a *Curbed* writer put it: "[T]o my eye, my sensitive community has already contributed more than its fair share of new housing, and then some, while weathering more change than most LA neighborhoods."[97] Those who may have been YIMBY allies in the past felt that the compromises that Weiner made in the legislative process were too great, and they began to question his loyalty to the idea of housing affordability rather than just plain growth.

Yet, the main fight of YIMBYs to end single-family zoning has been remarkably successful: recent laws were passed in Sacramento and Berkeley to end the practice. Berkeley, where zoning began over 100 years ago, was a particularly strong symbolic win for YIMBYs. While their groups remain controversial, the YIMBY mission is making its way into public policy: the state of Oregon has put a blanket ban on single-family zoning as well. State Senator Weiner also passed two long-campaigned-for bills in September of 2021: one reduced lengthy and expensive environmental reviews (often dominated by NIMBYs) for multifamily homes and the other legalized duplexes on any single-family lot. If enforced as written, this will end single-family zoning in California. However, it is worth noting that the bills, after passing through the California legislature, were only signed by Governor Gavin Newsom two days after his failed recall election: a strong signal that challenging the housing status quo still necessitates a tremendous amount of political capital.

The Curse of Infrastructure

With the defeat of SB 50, many housing activists began to ask themselves if living near public infrastructure had now become a burden: not only was it overused but it was also the focus point for new development. While some people in the Bay Area felt blessed to live near a BART stop, others worried that their proximity would make them a target. Indeed, those who are reticent about YIMBY goals and the agenda of transport-oriented-development say that similar bills, if enacted, may make it harder to build future transport hubs in wealthy communities because residents will organize against the taller buildings that go with train stops. This further endangers the already beleaguered public transit system, stigmatizing it as a potential harbinger of more (and potentially lower-income) residents. In a city already riven between the newly privatized infrastructure of the technopolis and the rusting state-run systems of the twentieth century, this strategy faces an uphill battle.

While YIMBYs helped popularize more intensive land use in the Bay Area with higher buildings, they never achieved identification with renters' rights in the ways that they hoped. Instead of successfully framing their platform as expanding renters' options to move or to stay in place without being priced out, they were increasingly seen only as the "build, baby, build" movement, cutting them off from other housing activists. In some ways, their notoriety was the product of a very successful marketing campaign around normalizing new growth and construction, but the campaign also tended to lose the more emotional stories of rent burdens and displacement that were occurring on a daily basis in San Francisco.

Bay Area YIMBYs unequivocally achieved a reorientation of the housing affordability debate around generation, rather than class, lines. They increasingly marketed their movement as a break with the past to rebuke single-family-home suburbs and embrace compact neighborhoods and walkability. Yet, just like their efforts in the Mission and other neighborhoods, the recasting of the struggle for housing affordability as a battle between baby-boomer homeowners and millennial renters highlighted a generational dispute at the expense of economic realities, namely the mass expulsion of low-income renters from the centers of cities.

2

Millennial YIMBYs and Boomer NIMBYs

As American cities face an unprecedented crisis of housing affordability, many commentators have divided housing stock generationally: between baby-boomer homeowners (born from 1945 to 1965) and millennial renters (born between 1980 and 2000). With this categorization come tropes of how the members of each generation manage their finances and plans for the future. According to one narrative, "diligent" baby boomers bought a home, started a family, and worked the same job until retirement,[1] while struggling (or potentially dilettante) millennials do shift work, date into their thirties, and live in shared apartments. Housing, in particular, has become a bellwether of the future prospects of millennials. Economic and cultural reasons for millennials' struggle to become homeowners imply the magnitude of the changes on family, conceptions of self and work, and even how cities are organized. The disparaging view of millennials' failure to "grow up" is resented within the generation, fueling a counter-narrative that emphasizes how baby boomers are responsible for economic reforms that depressed wages,[2] as well as more specific changes in urban planning policy that limited the number of new homes built in urban centers, driving up property values and decreasing affordability.

A modified version of this chapter was published as Max Holleran, "Millennial 'YIMBYs' and Boomer 'NIMBYs': Generational Views on Housing Affordability in the United States," *Sociological Review* 69, no. 4 (2021): 846–61, https://doi.org/10.1177/0038026120916121.

Millennials are less likely to age into the suburbs than the boomer generation[3] and they less frequently own their own homes as they approach middle age.[4] At the same time, urban real estate markets in desirable American cities with high-paying jobs have become increasingly unaffordable. As discussed in chapter 1, San Francisco, the city known for alternative communities of the baby-boomer generation living hand to mouth in the 1960s, is now one of the world's most expensive cities.[5] Owning a home and living with one's nuclear family are the sine qua non of middle-class adulthood in the United States. The trope of millennial Peter (or Petra) Pan—addicted to personal pleasure at the expense of stability and long-term planning—is directed toward those who cannot buy a home or who return to live with their parents. Younger adults counter this by arguing that the world created by their parents often precludes these sources of stability:[6] social and economic changes embraced during the Reagan/Thatcher era made work more contingent, stripped away the social safety net, necessitated more (and costlier) higher education for middle-class jobs, and turned buying a home into an investment vehicle rather than an asset primarily for its use value.

The greatest points of contention over housing include how many apartment buildings to build, where they should go, and how tall they should be. The demand for more housing has been greeted by homeowners with trepidation: they worry that rapid construction of apartment buildings will lower home prices and destroy the character of communities.[7] On a more fundamental level, many homeowners who grew up in the postwar suburbs still prefer the model of entirely residential neighborhoods accessed by car, despite criticism of elitism and ecological harm. Anti-growth activists, who are often members of the boomer generation, have used the considerable power of neighborhood groups and homeowners' associations, aided by the spatial and jurisdictional sprawl of American suburbs,[8] to create powerful lobbies that prevent more zoning for density, enforce height limits, curtail higher occupancy, and veto projects based on "community character." Millennials, hungry for new housing to go on the market, accuse neighborhood groups of NIMBYism. They insist that NIMBYs have it all—high equity from homeownership in desirable downtown or inner-suburb neighborhoods—and also accuse NIMBYs of refusing to let in younger buyers and renters, forcing them ever farther to the edges of cities.

YIMBY activists argue for higher density, better public transit, and a general relaxation of zoning laws that neighborhood groups fight to protect. They insist that they are not just motivated by lifestyle reasons to make a home in the inner city, pointing to compelling data that asserts urban housing markets bestow access to well-paying jobs that are increasingly unavailable in nonurban areas or declining cities.[9] Being able to live in Brooklyn, Los Angeles, or Seattle is less about being in a cultural scene for these activists, as it may have been for baby boomers, who often associated cities with distinct countercultures, and more about proximity to resources needed for financial mobility.[10] The argument is backed up by macro-level observations of how culture itself has become an important economic factor in successful cities, often sorting "winner" cities from "loser" cities.[11]

This chapter examines the contestation between pro-growth housing activists (self-styled YIMBYs) and neighborhood groups (sometimes known as NIMBYs by detractors): two factions that face off at zoning meetings, community dialogues, local elections, and even in court. It expands the previous chapter's focus on San Francisco to consider the dozens of YIMBY groups that have sprung up in American cities since 2014 when SF BARF was founded. Indeed, most of those I encountered at YIMBY meetings while writing this book were millennials or younger and, of the sixty-five activists interviewed, 80 percent were under age forty. This chapter explores how generational cohort affects the movement and pits it against homeowners who are often older. Bringing homeowners into the conversation, this chapter supplements the opinions of density activists with those of older homeowners who participate in neighborhood groups in Texas, Colorado, California, Massachusetts, and New York. Last, it shows how older homeowners often use the framing of gentrification to resist new development in their neighborhoods, sometimes partnering with anti-gentrification groups and often forming a coalition of wealthier older (and often white) homeowners in prosperous urban neighborhoods and struggling urbanites, who are primarily Black and Latino, in adjacent economically mixed neighborhoods.

All those interviewed for this book worried about the erosion of the middle class, but many simultaneously were quick to describe the political battle using age groupings—boomer/millennial—rather than a class frame.[12] Often, the constraints precluding homeownership are economically based, but arguments about housing are fought using a generational framing: something potentially more palatable in the United States where universal middle-classness is a cherished fantasy frequently drawn upon in political debates.[13] This framing has been beneficial to those lobbying for renters and apartment-dwellers without conjuring up racial and class stigma, but it is also a detriment because the debate has shifted from those entirely excluded from housing (the homeless, public housing residents, and people in danger of eviction) to more middle-class populations struggling with rent or locked out of homeownership.

Pro-growth activists often see homeowners' associations and neighborhood groups as possessing a monopoly on municipal power, frequently shutting out the opinions of renters. While much of the debate around YIMBYism has been specific and technical—dealing with zoning intricacies by activists who are also often architects—it has hit a generational note that catalyzes the perceived gap between boomer and millennial values (as well as assets) when it comes to how American cities should look and feel. The problem of affordable housing is also dependent on how each generation experienced the city growing up, what their ideal city looks like, and what normative role of family and community they assign to the home. In this sense, YIMBYism is both an economically grounded social movement of middle-class professionals, in that it responds to precarity and lack of housing supply, and an emotionally constructed movement[14] that argues for cities as a solution to a plethora of problems, from mitigating environmental harm to nurturing a more cosmopolitan outlook in an era of ascendant nativism. This chapter deconstructs these viewpoints from the perspectives of boomer and millennial activists to show how their different visions of the future American city will impact the housing affordability crisis.

The Boomer "Burb": NIMBYism, Race, and Suburbia of the 1960s

The postwar American city has been dubbed a collection of suburbs rather than the mononuclear configuration of the past.[15] Suburbanization was heavily subsidized by federal highway grants and mortgage loans to assist (white) veterans returning from the Second World War. The question of whether suburbanization was a cultural choice—based on the primacy of the nuclear family, private property, and a middle ground between city and nature—or a purely economic calculus is still hotly contested.[16] The relationship between suburbanization and urban unrest is clearer. While the first wave of sprawling development may have been a response to financial incentives given by the state, a second wave occurred after urban insurrections and violence in 1968: following the death of Martin Luther King Jr.,[17] the increasing ghettoization of urban Black neighborhoods,[18] and the militarized occupation of those neighborhoods by federal troops. The experience of urban violence and racial anxiety was a key generational childhood event[19] for baby boomers, whether in Newark, Detroit, or Los Angeles. For African Americans, the urban unrest showed the state's reneging on the promises of the civil rights movement as well as its military response to what was quickly dubbed "internal colonialism" and likened to the failing war in Vietnam.[20] Suburbia, while always containing a subtext of domestic tranquility and inflexible gender roles,[21] went from an economic choice (based on affordable housing during the home shortages of the late 1940s) to an increasingly cultural and political enclavement as a source of safety away from American cities in crisis.[22]

The first widespread usage of NIMBYism refers to postwar suburban communities where individual homeowners banded together to prevent undesirable land uses such as industry[23] and, frequently, necessary infrastructure like waste incinerators, water treatment plants, and garbage dumps, often leading to more formalized zoning regulations. NIMBYism was always a way to denote how wealthier communities are better positioned to mobilize against changes that could potentially harm their home investment or general well-being. However, it also bears a distinctly racial connotation in the American context. Before the mass suburbanization of the 1960s, urban neighborhoods had been racially demarcated through the practice of redlining, in which banks refused to provide mortgages to qualifying African Americans (and, at times, Jews and Catholics) within certain "white only" boundaries, often with tacit municipal support.[24] Wealthy communities also used "restrictive covenants" (bylaws of new subdivisions preventing ownership based on race and ethnicity) to keep out those who were considered "unsavory."[25] In doing so, these suburbs frequently set up their own minor local governments in the process, which determined a number of regulations having to do with the appearance of homes and yards. Yet, after the 1960s, homeowners relied on distance and home price to sort middle-class white homeowners in the suburbs from nonwhite renters in inner cities. At the same time, this allowed new suburban communities to use their property taxes for their exclusive benefit, ending redistributive elements of the prior system that existed when the American city was less fractured.[26] This historical legacy is exactly why American inequality is not as regional as one might think (between the coasts and the Rustbelt) but also very much a product of resource hoarding between cities such as Bridgeport, Connecticut, with an average per capita annual income of $24,000 (2019), and Westport (a ten-minute drive away in the same county), where the same figure is $114,000 per year.[27]

The quest to maintain suburban home values by keeping out certain environmentally problematic uses became known as NIMBYism, but it also applied to homeowners in first-generation American suburbs (such as Long Island, New York) who blocked construction of apartment buildings where lower-income (and often nonwhite) people might live. NIMBYism is closely related to the American legal framework of property rights that supports the single-family home as a source of stability and investment in community. This rationale is often used to defend the enormously expensive mortgage deduction that gives tax write-offs to homeowners, rather than renters, which costs the federal government over $100 billion a year[28] and is the definition of regressive taxation. The primacy of the home as a protected and sacrosanct space has also given birth to uniquely American safety measures,[29] like Florida's Stand Your Ground law, which allows homeowners to defend their property with lethal force (and was famously used to exonerate the killer of Trayvon Martin, the unarmed teenager who was shot in an Orlando gated community in 2012). In short, NIMBYism is frequently used as an epithet in urban planning circles, and it is closely tied to state policies that support suburbanism as a lifestyle as well as a philosophy of individual rights over collective community benefits.[30]

Baby boomers grew up in a world of rapidly changing housing economics with expanded ownership and construction during their childhoods,[31] making the investment far more than a place to lay their heads but also an asset to borrow against, use for retirement, or pass down to future generations. As boomers grew to adulthood, owning a place of their own became an important way to buttress against risk[32] as the social safety net was eroded, particularly given the high cost of medical treatment in the United States. A second mortgage could make the difference between sickness-induced bankruptcy or staying solvent. Buying a home became a means to entrepreneurship on the most basic level: by making long-sighted predictions about real estate markets or acquiring a second home. Homeowners interested in maintaining or increasing the value of their investment could actively monitor their neighborhoods by joining community groups that did everything from cleanup activities to programming for community building to hiring armed guards to patrol suburban streets. As one boomer described her neighborhood group in Texas: "We are like the smallest level of government, but unlike regular city politics, we all have something to lose when it comes to decision making: the value of our homes."

While the baby boomers were famously stifled by suburban life—and particularly the patriarchal assumptions of the work/living divide of an office-bound husband and a stay-at-home wife—they were also deeply influenced by the architectural form of the suburbs. While many in the boomer generation briefly took up residence in cities for college and young adulthood, they often returned to the suburbs when they had families of their own.[33] The ideal of a well-maintained front (public-facing) yard and a recreational backyard set in a bucolic location—but within commuting distance to suburban office-parks or downtown skyscrapers—was still the middle-class model of a city when the millennial generation were young children in the 1990s. In this sense, the spatial divide between commercial and residential uses is familiar and often essential to older homeowners, and there can often be a visceral response to mixed-use zoning that brings "noisy" shops, restaurants, and markets to bedroom communities in an attempt to limit car use and cluster local services.

Urban sociologists have shown that the onset of the most recent period of gentrification was often experienced most forcefully by millennials: as this generation came of age, American cities became safer and more desirable for new economic opportunities driven by information technology and the dot-com boom in the 1990s.[34] As Saskia Sassen[35] has pointed out: more outsourcing, online communication, and multinational supply chains have, in many cases, increased the centrality of large cities in the developed world as "command and control centers." This has given millennials a new sense of the economic primacy of urban spaces as well as a less easily measured, but nonetheless important, cultural pull to urban life.[36] As one informant put it: "We are the *Sex and the City* generation . . . the city was cool and glamorous again . . . [but] our parents . . . still were stuck in the *Panic in Needle Park* mentality." Yet, much of this urban boosterism of the millennial generation is not really about the city itself but about the nearby suburbs that exist in a state of development limbo: they are connected to downtowns with public transit and already have thriving commercial districts, but morphologically they are still single-family homes. This is where the generational fight about appropriate levels of density has mainly occurred.

Growth and How Urban Should the City Be?

In many ways, millennials' approach to urban life is neither special nor a product of their generational outlook: walkability was a key concern of the quintessential urbanist Jane Jacobs in her fight against highways in Manhattan in the 1960s;[37] mixed-use residential-commercial development has been expounded by every major urban planning school in the United States since the early 1980s; and the restoration of dormant manufacturing buildings into chic cafés and small businesses is a long-accepted strategy of adaptive reuse advocated by historic preservationists. However, millennials frequently maintain that it was their age group who successfully took these ideas from theory to practice, with the help of postindustrial urban economics that favored the service sector over large floor plans, intensive investment, and numerous employees.[38] It has also been during the lifespan of this generation that the anti-gentrification movement has gained the most momentum, providing a common vernacular that extends far beyond urban activism to discuss spatial justice and what egalitarian neighborhood change should look like.[39]

Many YIMBY activists are concerned with aging cities' failing infrastructure, downtowns depopulated by urban renewal, and a dearth of apartments. In this sense, they believe in the constant presence of young people to rejuvenate neighborhoods, keep a stable population, supply dynamic cultural life, and perhaps most importantly, provide a tax base. As in other facets of YIMBY activism, this viewpoint often mixes building typologies with age and class demographics—in this case the need to keep city centers "youthful," which they do not see as the same thing as gentrified.[40] As one YIMBY urban planner, a Coloradan in his thirties, said:

> It's frustrating to be in a neighborhood where you can see the skyscrapers hovering above you that are all offices and all around are just two-story houses, and the way the [place] is zoned means that apartments basically can't be built and everyone is gonna leave the offices, get in their car, and drive an hour through an endless traffic jam.

One of the key arguments that is used to support the twinning of millennial politics and urban planning priorities is that this generation has made social choices that fit more naturally into city life, specifically delaying marriage, cohabitating, renting, and eschewing car ownership.[41] These choices have also been affected by economic constraints, most dramatically the lost earnings for younger workers after the 2008 economic crisis.[42] In 2016, the American cohort of thirty-two-year-olds had 34 percent less wealth than expected, while older age groups had largely rebounded from the 2008 crisis.[43] For this reason, priorities of urban planners that increase mass transit, environmental protection, or investment in infrastructure are not framed just as a generational issue, in the sense that they are investments in the near future, but also that they follow the distinct preferences of millennials, which are sometimes at odds with the previous generation. A YIMBY activist living in Oakland, California, put the generational conflict this way:

> We feel more ownership of American cities than our parents. . . . [W]hat happened in the sixties onward was because their generation abandoned living in urban areas, or at least middle-class whites did, and we have a totally different mindset based on embracing the urban and creating racially diverse spaces, not locking ourselves up in the suburbs where everyone is white.

Often, then, the defense of cities was derived from lifestyle preferences (walkability, entertainment, and bustle) as well as from moral commitments, of which both racial diversity and reducing one's environmental footprint were major aspects.[44] While anti-gentrification social movements often explain this commitment as a correction of the baby boomers' initial involvement in civil rights and environmentalism before these struggles were unsatisfactorily concluded with institutionalization or diminished support, YIMBYs are focused on less radical public policy fixes such as zoning and transportation-oriented development. While some millennial activists in groups such as Sunrise Movement, Extinction Rebellion, and Standing Rock (climate change) as well as Black Lives Matter criticize the withdrawal from politics of baby boomers as they aged out of the civil rights movement, YIMBYs are far more interested in finding expert-driven solutions than in seeking mass membership. They approach neighborhood diversity and ecological goals with a data-driven and code-reform process that eschews many fundamentals of movement building in order to quickly pivot into the role of activist/government intermediary.[45]

With the popularization of American cities as places to thrive both socially and economically in the 1990s came increasing pressure on urban housing stock. Millennials often choose between trying to afford rents in expensive downtowns or relocating to gentrifying neighborhoods abutting urban centers. Out of this dynamic, the YIMBY movement was born in San Francisco, as shown in the previous chapter, as a way to lobby planning commissions and city councils to build more housing in desirable central neighborhoods. YIMBYs see their constituents as white middle-class millennials, while anti-gentrification groups are composed of working-class people of color and their allies. However, YIMBYs feel that by mobilizing millennials to build in wealthy neighborhoods they will prevent further gentrification, creating a win-win for the two groups. A San Francisco YIMBY said:

> Over the past twenty years all new development has been in low-income neighborhoods. It's not an accident . . . they can't mobilize the political pressure to stop it. That means that wealthy people in their sixties living in Berkeley can be left alone . . . and they still have this image of themselves as radical hippies even though their homes are worth $2 million and they won't let anyone else live there. . . . What we want is more homes in the already middle-class places so that younger people won't be faced with the choice to be a gentrifier or not coming to the city at all.

YIMBY activists are frustrated by the baby-boomer generation's refusal to allow apartment buildings in desirable areas with existing public transit, as one put it: "it's not all public policy, it's really just a particular group of older people unwilling to share their neighborhoods with others." One of their main actions is to speak out at monthly urban planning meetings in favor of any plan to build new housing. YIMBYs maintain that in many growing cities, homeowners' associations and neighborhood groups have put pressure on city councils to stop the construction of duplexes and accessory dwelling units (so-called granny flats, built above garages, that are a low-impact way to increase density). They consider these the most minimal changes needed, and the failure to enact them shows an ideological stubbornness among existing homeowners, who may express concern over the crisis of affordable housing but are unwilling to compromise their own comfort and privilege.

YIMBYs began showing up to zoning meetings in cities such as Denver, Seattle, and San Francisco, quickly realizing that zoning meetings were only attended by older people speaking out against development plans, which opened a new vulnerability in the structure of urban planning policy for pro-growth YIMBY groups.[46] "We saw this space totally dominated by a single and nonrepresentative group," a Texas YIMBY told me. "We thought, 'Hey, we live in these politicians' districts too,' and they need to see this is not how we think, and there are a hell of a lot more of us." This approach made zoning meetings the epicenter of the debate over urban growth, with density as the main topic, often dividing existing (older) owners and younger renters. Within these spaces, their confrontations were often acrimonious and dug into the meaning of progressivism in urban areas: boomer home-owners declared neighborhood composition, and the social ties that go with it, sacrosanct; while millennial YIMBYs advocated for managed change that proactively increases population and density with socioeconomic goals in mind (rather than unmanaged gentrification).

As the YIMBY movement spread to dozens of cities, it took on new meaning beyond just housing affordability: it acted as a gateway to local politics for millennials. It often came with the explicit goal of unseating established politicians who, the thinking went, could not understand the housing crisis or any of the other priorities of those under forty years old. In this sense, YIMBYism has become a form of demographic revolt among the urban (largely white) middle class, based on the technicalities of urban plan-ning codes, but embodying the many frustrations of an age cohort deeply affected by the 2008 financial crisis. It uses struggles within the field of housing affordability to argue for broader changes and greater social move-ment participation, especially by those with a high level of education in technocratic fields of administrative interest.[47] It is a highly bonded activist group composed of people with similar backgrounds, many of whom hope to offer expert advice. Although one tactic is to show up at zoning meetings and loudly protest, it is not because YIMBYs necessarily believe they are a mass movement not being heard but because they are a selective group with highly informed opinions.[48]

With fewer assets and worse job prospects than their parents had when they were approaching middle age,[49] millennial YIMBY activists have used housing as a wedge issue to motivate a deeper engagement with local politics. As one California YIMBY said:

> We know that our members read the *New York Times* and care about national politics. The issue is that they live in blue [Democratic Party] cities where they think a supposedly progressive government will take care of them. What we are trying to do is activate them . . . show them that's not true. . . . [T]hey need to get involved or no one will take care of them, and they might get driven out of the city altogether.

YIMBYs used zoning and housing as a way to discuss larger issues of generational wealth dispersal, sometimes conflating class status and generation.[50] One YIMBY activist from Texas said: "we think renters versus owners is good politics to get millennials in the door. . . . The way you get them to stay is [showing] that homeownership, or lack of, is just one way that their lives are gonna look very different from their parents." An older generation of participants in neighborhood groups frequently viewed this groundswell with bewilderment, especially because many of the debates took place within progressive politics. A homeowner in Boulder, Colorado, said: "The YIMBY viewpoint is pretty out of touch when it comes to what it takes to make a good city. . . . It's not respectful of all the things that go into making community . . . and the necessity of keeping that community a certain size so the bonds hold together." The same informant also said that YIMBYism was a weak political platform: "I get that they're pissed off about housing but where do they go from there?"

YIMBYism is a distinctly middle-class social movement often composed of professionals who feel that their expertise (frequently in city planning and architecture) has been eroded by NIMBY groups, whose arguments are primarily emotional (the unchanging nature of their communities). YIMBYs start from universalist arguments about cities and then select specific zoning cases to participate in. NIMBYism, on the other hand, is often hyper-local, with activists sometimes scaling up in order to counter arguments of their own self-interest.[51] However, YIMBYs also use emotional framings based on creating vibrant urban spaces that would be more inclusive. They could not localize these issues geographically, so they often use a generational framing in order to give the argument more resonance and connect it with the travails of millennials facing precarity. This puts forward a specific group of complainants who could replace the geographically bounded credibility of NIMBYs and assert their legitimacy as stakeholders even when they live miles from specific developments under question.

While NIMBYs were brought together through geography and home-ownership, YIMBY groups created a broad coalition of interests, from housing activists to real estate developers, often with the express understanding that these partnerships would be temporary: only to endorse a single project with a pre-negotiated percentage of affordable housing units. In this sense, YIMBY groups see themselves serving in a bridge role connecting other activists, municipal officials, and real estate developers in a capacity that sometimes mirrors the paid facilitation work that some YIMBYs participate in during their working lives as city planners. The mobility of YIMBY activists speaks both to their middle-classness (they are not bound by neighborhoods and family obligations but able to chase opportunities at great distances) and to their broader point that "newcomer" status cannot be used as a constant slur within the world of urban activism. "It used to be that you had to be 'from here' to run for office," one YIMBY in her early twenties told me, explaining that this often led to a web of nepotism and corruption and adding, "There is nothing wrong with choosing a place, moving there . . . getting involved. In fact, you would think people would be happy about that."

Generational Politics at the Neighborhood Level

"When you think about it, suburbia is really just a blip on the radar as far as history is concerned," Laura Foote, the prominent San Francisco YIMBY, told me. By some measure, the rapidity of America's suburbanization is actually a good thing: the most dramatic changes happened from 1945 until 2000, approximately, and the logic of dispersed development—while ubiquitous across the landscape—is still potentially reversible. While boomers are habituated to suburbs, many millennials say they would like to return to a world of main streets and towns organized around condensed shopping and business districts. Many boomers are also returning to urban centers in order to retire in more pedestrian-friendly spaces as their mobility declines. However, YIMBYs feel that the boomer generation has been permanently affected by their suburban childhood, closing off the potential to make substantial changes in the layout and height of cities needed to accommodate more housing. Some boomer informants confirmed this, such as a retired lawyer from Berkeley: "I like cities, but the ones with trees and parks. . . . I don't want to live in an apartment, . . . and I don't want to live with an apartment building over me." He went further to say he dislikes YIMBYs because he disapproves of their aggressive tactics and worries their efforts will displace people rather than providing more affordable housing. "I'm fine with what we have now. . . . It's a sort of small city of neighborhoods, not a bunch of big buildings. . . . I don't want to live in Tokyo." Many others emphasized that a suburban childhood had taught them that the scale of the neighborhood is two stories maximum, and places with higher density than that quickly became impersonal and foreboding with a commensurate loss of community contact and beneficial organizing.

Many YIMBYs disagree, arguing that walkability and proximity are the key criteria for building bonds between neighbors, particularly people from different backgrounds. "We've lost something more than just vast tracts of land through suburbanization," a YIMBY urban planner from Massachusetts stated. "There's also been a systematic destruction of community spaces where people come together." For her, density created more tightly woven social bonds, the loss of which increased distrust and loneliness.[52] She even went a step further, saying that the boomers' retreat to suburbia was one of the reasons that allowed them to ignore inequality and support anti-immigrant politicians such as Donald Trump: "I mean, with a more urban mindset and interactions with people different from you . . . I don't think some of this stuff would have happened." While many young people also hold conservative political beliefs, most YIMBYs see city life as an expression of a certain kind of progressive politics and a belief in cosmopolitan values such as tolerance, diversity, and dialogue. Critics maintain that it is an easy way to express the cultural veneer of progressive politics while gaining enviable quality-of-life benefits,[53] but it is also indicative of how the YIMBY movement combines the more nebulous cultural arguments of new social movements that focus on lifestyle with concrete political and economic demands rooted in precise spaces and moments of political contestation.[54] This belief is also a rebuttal to the devolved government and localism embraced by the boomer generation during the Reagan era: the YIMBY belief in regional thinking that reconjoins suburbs into a metropolitan area is a means to distribute risk across communities that fractured away from each other during successive waves of suburbanization.

YIMBY groups seek changes in zoning laws to build taller apartment buildings, but they also support more aggressive methods such as "suing the suburbs," discussed in chapter 1. "Suing the suburbs" draws on class-based animus of wealthy neighborhoods that refuse to "do their share" to help solve the Silicon Valley housing crisis. However, the strategy is far from radical and still very much within the bounds of market-driven urban growth.[55] This reflects a larger trend among YIMBY groups, who focus their attention on the ownership age-divide rather than on issues of class that have kept multiple generations of poor urbanites out of housing markets.[56] This is a combination of strategic opportunity (powerful generational framing); social movement niche (technocratic rather than radical); and political placement (center-left, rather than jostling for influence on the increasingly crowded left). One community organizer from Los Angeles, who mostly disagreed with YIMBYs but is also a millennial, commented that Los Angeles YIMBY groups hope to derive authority from broadcasting an image of practical centrism: "They want to be everything to everybody, and that is what worries me because I think it's slippery. . . . There are times when they are agreeing publicly (with anti-gentrification messages), but are they really?"

YIMBY groups are dedicated to two strategies popular in urban planning circles: (1) retrofitting suburbs to make them denser and more walkable, for example, through additional growth and more small stores; and (2) making inner-city buildings bigger and taller (as already discussed). However, within the many YIMBY groups in the United States, there are differences in opinion about the end goal of urban planning activism: many simply want to control the crisis in affordable housing, while others, who often describe themselves as libertarian-leaning, would like to disempower urban planning authorities by reducing oversight and red tape. This anti-regulatory zeal has a long history in conservative American politics but is seldom evoked in cities like Seattle, San Francisco, and Denver, known for their progressive politics. As one critic of YIMBYism, from the anti-gentrification sphere, put it: "YIMBYs are a hotbed for libertarian thinking and market-driven solutions. . . . It's a mask you can put on if you're a developer, a small-government type, or even a Republican living in 'enemy territory.'" However, there is little evidence that any but a very small minority of YIMBYs see upzoning density requirements in cities as a first step in eliminating urban planning regulation, and many support stringent environmental protections at odds with libertarian principles.

While the critique of YIMBY urban policy from the left is often directed at the involvement of real estate developers or brokers, the animating issue within the movement is the perceived capitulation of the boomer generation in addressing economic issues. In this sense, YIMBYs see their main foes as people who are otherwise political allies, particularly in national politics, but who refuse to allow more housing construction. "The people we are fighting are not country club types. They are actually the seventy-year-olds with an Obama sign in their front yard," a YIMBY sympathizer from Colorado told me. The critique of NIMBYism was that it was embraced by people who had been progressives in their youth but, once they became homeowners, were motivated to protect their assets' value.[57] For YIMBYs, the center-left of American politics has shifted in favor of people who are economic elites, and for that reason the Democratic Party and its supporters are insufficiently committed to issues such as housing, minimum wage, and job precarity because they have little experience of it. Yet, the viewpoint also dangerously repositions class, and housing precarity, as a universal generational experience,[58] rather than one suffered particularly by those with lower socioeconomic status. This is compounded by the fact that most of the YIMBY activists I interviewed are concerned about maintaining middle-classness but are also comparatively well-off professionals, indeed not a single person interviewed did not have a university education, and many graduated from prestigious schools and worked in urbanism, tech, or communications.

YIMBYs often straddled problematic political territory in this sense because they criticized mainstream Democrats while embracing an essentially market-based solution of more home construction (very much in contrast to housing justice advocates). "We really have an establishment versus insurgent issue here," a San Francisco YIMBY said:

> It's groups that normally see eye to eye—educated older hippie types and educated younger millennials, all of whom are basically white—who are fighting over the same neighborhoods and the right to be there. When the NIMBYs told us "find somewhere else," which basically means "don't move to this city," we realized that there was a major divide.

While YIMBYs were consternated that boomers could not imagine a pleasant but vertical city (with many posting on Twitter about the potential "Hong Kong-ization" of San Francisco, with a forest of high-rises towering over formerly quiet streets), the struggle is also more basic. It is about which generation wields local political power.[59] Many YIMBYs feel their organizations are a metaphor for a wider handover in political power that must occur nationally, especially around the time of the 2016 national election when most political party leaders were in their seventies. Ironically, while YIMBY groups are not afraid to use generational politics to galvanize supporters, their major policy interventions are far more conservative than calls from the newly energized socialist left—for community land trusts and more social housing.[60] One city planner who was of the boomer generation but supported the majority of densification proposals associated with YIMBYism said: "The whole framing is sort of a ruse. . . . The real issue that people care about is owners versus renters, and that's class . . . and frequently race. . . . The generational thing is sort of important but I think it's mostly a way to get younger people to care." In this sense, the generational framing can be categorized using the literature on political opportunity structure in social movements[61] for its pragmatism and goal-oriented usage, while simultaneously obscuring underlying issues to do with longer socioeconomic processes: namely, the hollowing out of the American middle class.[62]

YIMBYs acknowledged that while they found many neighborhood groups, and especially homeowners associations, to be NIMBYish—hoping they could solve urban problems by banishing them elsewhere—they learned from their organizing methods. "We wanted something for renters like they have for homeowners," one activist stated. In general, there was a respect for community organizing as a place-based phenomenon,[63] but the challenge was in uprooting the policy doxa of protecting home values above all else and displacing homeowners as a main community voice. "We tend to think of mobility as a good thing, but in this case it's not," a twenty-three-year-old YIMBY supporter told me. She maintained that millennials who had moved from city to city in search of work after the 2008 economic crisis and from neighborhood to neighborhood looking for better housing value had missed out on the opportunity to make their voices heard. Creating better structures to represent millennial interests through YIMBYism was seen as a means to give voice to an age demographic as well as to a certain group within the housing market that would become a permanent voice even if individual members moved away.

Generational Conflict and Maintaining Middle-Class Identity

The narrative of intergenerational conflict over urban space can often sound like a misdiagnosis of the housing affordability crisis. Class is perhaps the biggest determinant of whether someone faces housing insecurity: baby boomers, who are more robustly middle class, are less affected by soaring prices than millennials who are still recovering from the financial crisis of 2008.[64] The battle to maintain middle-classness[65] is one of the reasons that generational argument has reached a fever pitch, with boomers accusing the millennial generation of fecklessness[66] while millennials point to macro-structural disadvantages they have faced, which they feel baby boomers have had a hand in creating.[67] Class is certainly undervalued in the YIMBY framing of the American housing crisis, which pays undue attention to generational problems alone,[68] making the conflict seem more spatial than macroeconomic. However, at the same time, much of this narrative comes from tangible experiences of generational conflict in planning meetings and community reviews of new architecture, where YIMBY activists see older homeowners veto new projects one after another. Because so many millennial YIMBY activists have training in architecture, design, and urban planning, the local government's rebuffing of attempts to create denser neighborhoods was particularly irksome because it went against professional consensus and threatened their position both as renters and as members of a knowledge field.

Both sides of the debate around densification play on a sense of middle-class authenticity when it comes to making their claims using a generational framing. Homeowners, who are frequently baby boomers, insist that they bought into a neighborhood thinking it would be a certain way;[69] they worked hard to pay off their mortgage; and now outsiders want to change the rules and upend what their communities look and feel like. At the same time, YIMBY movement participants, who are primarily millennials, maintain that they too are good middle-class citizens who have "played by the rules" and still cannot afford rents (or homeownership) in desirable cities. Both movements fight over middle-class respectability and often unconsciously channel arguments about the virtuosity of hard work and deservedness.[70] At the same time, they also both court anti-gentrification activists in poorer neighborhoods, insisting that their approach to housing will offer better opportunities to avoid displacement. This mobilization of middle-class alliance is often looked at askance by those fighting to protect public housing or organizing in low-income communities. As an African American YIMBY organizer in Los Angeles commented: people in low-income communities of color have "had bad experiences with both groups of organizers," some saying "no" to development and some saying "yes." While he felt that more people in working-class South Los Angeles should be saying "yes" to new apartments, he could see why resisting and keeping the slowly eroding status quo (of gentrification without growth) were easier for people to wrap their heads around.

Neighborhood groups and YIMBY activists have battled each other in hyper-local spaces where age can be a more salient factor than class. The places where the movement for more density is most active are middle-class or wealthy neighborhoods, decreasing the visibility of those trying to maintain middle-class status because their suffering is relative to those in the highest economic bracket rather than, as in poorer neighborhoods, those clinging to their livelihoods, homes, and independence. At the same time, age and generation were emphasized because they were a powerful means to provide moral authority over which decisions were best for a neighborhood,[71] with neighborhood groups advocating that their members' time in a certain location was the most important factor while YIMBYs saw this source of credibility as potentially disqualifying because those with long-term attachments were unwilling to see *any* changes as positive.

When two generations have radically different experiences, a generational cleavage can result, and this is what has been occurring in American cities for several decades. It has come into play at the level of urban policy (how much public transit to fund and how much new density to endorse) as well as of public opinion (what height of buildings is livable and how much commuting is desirable). Real generational differences exist between boomers and millennials, many of which stem from fundamental visions of the city, formed in childhood, over the safety of cities and the appeal of bustling, dense metropolitan spaces. The larger question is whether a distinctly urban identity becomes something that defines the millennial generation culturally and how it will be expressed in political and economic priorities.

3

Between a Rock and a Greenbelt: Housing and Environmental Activism in Boulder

Boulder, Colorado, has long stood out as an eco-utopia at the foot of the Rocky Mountains. The community of 105,000 people is close enough to Denver to be a suburb, but its ethos is unique. The central shopping district is a red brick pedestrian mall filled with cold-pressed juice bars, buskers, tarot card readers, and more recent tenants selling high-end trekking gear. The city has one of the most extensive bike and trail systems in the country (300 miles),[1] with paved sections connecting the downtown to the University of Colorado's flagship campus perched on a hill above. Its most emblematic feature is the Flatirons: red stone masses jutting out of the Front Range of the Rocky Mountains, creating one of the most memorable city backdrops in the United States. One can walk from the university to the park at the foot of the mountains in about twenty minutes and the red sandstone slabs serve as a scrim to a lively scene of trail runners, dog walkers, climbers, and picnickers.

Boulder has matured from a college town to an affluent hub of tech start-ups and lifestyle migrants, but it has not grown much in population since the 1960s. The town's reputation has evolved considerably. Up until the 1990s, it was a cultural punchline in Colorado: Allen Ginsberg founded a Buddhist university there called the Jack Kerouac School of Disembodied Poetics (Naropa); a 2000 law designated humans as dog guardians rather than owners;[2] and for years, the main plaza in front of the central courthouse featured an encampment of transient post-hippie flower children panhandling, playing music, and selling LSD. Although Boulder is still known as a bastion of progressive politics, it is more famous as an affluent community filled with recreational opportunities and natural beauty, combining a walkable center with mountain hiking trails. However, with its reputation as an outdoor mecca, the city's housing costs are now on par with those of luxurious Colorado resort communities such as Aspen, Vail, or Telluride or much larger cities like New York and San Francisco.

Old-timers who remember the Boulder of the 1960s and 1970s—when it was a student town with few restaurants serving fare fancier than a cheeseburger—are often shocked by the cultural shift brought by new residents with large incomes: student bars replaced by swank *izakayas*, cyclists cruising by on $5,000 Italian racing bikes, and hiking trailheads packed with luxury cars. The price of the average home in Boulder was $744,300 in 2019 up from $406,000 in 2012.[3] However, this shocking climb in prices is only part of the story: the city is surrounded by satellite communities that started as farm towns but quickly ballooned in size during the 1990s when Colorado's Front Range was the fastest-growing region in the country.[4] Towns like Lafayette, Louisville, Longmont, and Broomfield became home to the teachers, nurses, firefighters, and other middle-class workers who serve Boulder but cannot afford to live there. Unlike other suburbs, the problem in Boulder is not just economic but structural and spatial. Much of the city's charm comes from its vast tracts of open space that was bought in the 1970s and 1980s to contain sprawl and limit population.

Part of what makes Boulder such a distinct destination is not just its advantageous geography—nestled at the foot of the Rocky Mountains or, as the saying goes, wedged between the mountains and reality—but the dramatic attempts made by its residents to protect the surrounding nature from development, limit population growth, and preserve community character. In 1968, the city began a process of limiting development at the foot of the Flatiron Mountains, after a ballot measure the year before. Eventually, it purchased a protective greenbelt: a municipal "land bank" of undevelopable property surrounding the city. This intervention enabled Boulder to become a leader in the field of conservation, using a $0.004 sales tax to amass land and construct recreational areas while other policies limited density, height, and co-occupancy.[5] The greenbelt was inspired by an older British tradition of municipal land conservation. However, unlike England, where greenbelts make up 13 percent of total land,[6] Boulder was going it alone at a time when fears of overpopulation were growing in the American West but skepticism around government action also prevailed. In this sense, the municipal land bank it started in 1968 was emblematic of a newer, more radical interest in environmentalism spurred by works like *Silent Spring* that called on action by the state to protect wilderness areas and human health.

The greenbelt approach has been heralded as an innovative way to create a city filled with a vibrant array of outdoor activities, but the outcome for affordable housing has not been ideal. Working- and middle-class residents have been effectively banished from the city, only permitted to enter when students need teaching, houses need building, or toilets need fixing. The advocacy group Housing Colorado makes the point that bank tellers in Boulder must spend 60 percent of their wages on housing in a marketplace that is twice as expensive as the national average.[7] More worryingly, while Boulder's greenbelt had the positive ecological effect of protecting both mountain land and a swath of prairie on Boulder's eastern edge, it has pushed development to the peripheral suburbs. This created several more towns of over 100,000 people, whose residents work in Boulder and drive across the greenbelt twice daily. Combined with height and density limits—spurred by the impulse to keep newcomers out of Boulder's Edenic center—the greenbelt keeps neighborhoods from expanding in any other direction except for leapfrogging over it.

Over the past several years, activists for increased growth have come together under the banner of YIMBYism. While most supporters of growth previously saw their grievances as economic (creating a city where all workers can live and not a place that banishes the less well-off when the sun goes down), YIMBYism has given a new spatial language to this issue that emphasizes densification.[8] Members of Boulder's main YIMBY group, Better Boulder, talk about smart growth and the need to build condensed higher-population neighborhoods before the city loses its character as a hippie haven due to the pricing out of lower-income residents, effectively borrowing the argument that anti-growth activists have used for years around cultural preservation. However, the fight has also centered on the meaning of environmentalism. While the 1968 greenbelt's major goal of land banking is supported, the capping of Boulder's population is less popular than it has ever been for fifty years. The emphasis on keeping neighborhoods of single-family homes rather than apartments is no longer seen as an aesthetic necessity or a means to keep communities at a manageable scale. It is regarded as a form of exclusion. For many younger density activists, protecting community character is tantamount to protecting a community's class composition by not allowing apartment dwellers to live amidst a city of multimillion-dollar homes.

The YIMBY fight in Boulder hinges on a key issue present in most discussions over growth: what counts as a city and what obligations come with that designation?[9] The people who oppose more housing and growth in Boulder invariably come back to one key point: their town looks more like a city every day and they do not want any of it. The narrative of "just a small college town" is often used to replace the "neighborhood is full" argument in other growth discussions. Those opposing growth point to their community's relative incapacity to bear the brunt of development regardless of whether that statement is true given current density, infrastructure, and transportation. Boulderites often argue that increases in the Colorado population need to go somewhere else that has more resources, space, or desire for newcomers. The problem is that "other places" (in this case and others) almost never actually exist and the protestations of "we are too small" are seldom accurate. Boulder is a case in point: while it may indeed be a college town, it also has important government offices, like the National Institute of Standards and Technology and the National Center for Atmospheric Research, not to mention a thriving start-up scene and nearby campuses for Ball Aerospace and IBM that have operated for nearly fifty years. YIMBYs see the inability of many Boulderites to recognize their own urbanness as a major roadblock in providing affordable housing. As one YIMBY summarized the view in an online forum: "I can't stand when people say, 'This place is great—let's keep it a secret.'" For YIMBYs seeking more density, those who misrepresent their community as a small town will not only be reflexively anti-growth but they will also be particularly displeased with apartments and high-density development that disrupts their image of a streets lined with single-family homes. As in many battles that YIMBYs are waging, one of the first steps is to convince residents to reimagine what a city can be and not to resort to anti-urbanist stereotypes of congestion, crime, and personal alienation whenever growth is mentioned.

In this chapter, I explore the connection between environmental stewardship and NIMBY thinking, showing how Boulder's 1960s foresight in building a greenbelt had the unfortunate effect of displacing growth to the periphery of the city and increasing home prices, which created a super-elite community with little racial or economic diversity. Elite status is often connected to environmentalism,[10] and in creating a city of wealthy nature lovers, Boulder has become something of a caricature of rich people searching for niche campaigns rather than bread-and-butter economic issues.[11] I begin the chapter by connecting the history of Boulder's greenbelt fight to a longer nineteenth-century campaign to create model environmental cities inspired by Ebenezer Howard's Garden City movement. Then, using oral history sources, I show how Boulder adopted this Edwardian era and somewhat utopian framework as part of a wider social movement in the 1960s that sought to raise ecological consciousness while forming new communities of affinity in the growing American West. Finally, I analyze how this model created economic pressures leading to exclusion and why disenchanted YIMBY activists are challenging anti-growth residents in an attempt to create a more economically inclusive community that embraces smart growth.

The City as Garden

The concept of the urban greenbelt goes against some of the most basic notions of how a municipality should be run, particularly in the growing cities of the early twentieth century. At that time, most mayors and city boosters wanted their towns to grow upward and outward, to absorb smaller towns through incorporation, and to use the power of their expanding populations to wrestle away governing responsibilities and authority from statehouses.[12] Selecting empty land to be used for recreation or agriculture, or simply to sit idle in a constraining ribbon around an urban area, was a hard sell given the dynamic growth of European and American cities in the late nineteenth and early twentieth century. While industrial development came to dominate British and American cities, this period was the start of nascent good government schemes that would fully bloom in the Progressive Era movement in the United States and anti-poverty programs in the United Kingdom. Indeed, it was the social reformer and co-founder of the National Trust, Octavia Hill, who coined the term "green belt" and argued that workers needed greater access to salubrious open spaces, which until that point had been hoarded in wealthy neighborhoods.[13]

Out of this tumultuous period of London's late-nineteenth-century expansion, Ebenezer Howard, a London clerk and shorthand writer, completed his masterwork *Garden Cities of Tomorrow* in 1898.[14] It led to the formation of the Garden City Association: a semi-utopian group devoted to making model cities based on an ideal population size to be permanently constrained by a "girdle" of green that would limit future growth outward. Howard, who had seen the breakneck development of Chicago as a young immigrant from England in the 1880s, was not an anti-urban transcendentalist like Thoreau and Emerson, nor did he believe that technological innovation could assuage poverty and inequality like the utopian futurist Edward Bellamy, who wrote the optimistic novel *Looking Backward* in 1888, of which Howard was a fan.

Rather he believed that the city and country needed to exist in a state of dialectical complement: using the scale of urban areas to provide for economic productivity and cultural life while retaining the bucolic landscape of the country close by to provide a level of calm and respite.

Garden Cities of Tomorrow offered a model for leafy suburban environments connected by rail to urban hubs. Superficially, they were similar to many new developments that sprang up outside of London in the 1890s. However, the book argued for a new kind of urbanization based on cooperative land trusts that would lay out communities with single-family homes that would be rented, not bought. Each community would have common facilities and would be surrounded by a greenbelt to restrict its size and provide an area for recreation. In Howard's vision, garden cities were not meant to retrofit existing villages, turning them into larger communities, but to create towns *ex nihilo* using stringent proportions for lot acreage, street curvature, and, most importantly, an ideal population size of about 32,000 people.[15] While the first cities actually built by the Garden City Association in the United Kingdom, Letchworth (1907) and Welwyn (1920), were sometimes too similar to conventional commuter rail suburbs for critics to recognize their innovativeness, Howard's larger vision was for a series of connected towns buttressed by greenbelts that would span dozens of miles. This would eliminate the need for larger central cities and, in a nod to early modernist ideas later pioneered by people like Le Corbusier, get rid of the conventional central city altogether.

As the influence of greenbelting grew around the world—with experiments in the United States, Canada, Germany, and the Netherlands—the original radicalism of Ebenezer Howard's idea was minimized. Howard had advocated for a model of community based on proto-socialists such as Robert Owen and Charles Fourier, who saw the perfection of the urban-rural relationship as a step in the amelioration of injustices caused by industrial capitalism. He was also inspired by less-progressive model communities built by companies like Cadbury, which had a chocolate production village called Bournville near Birmingham. Howard firmly believed that ownership associations could use increasing property values to make community improvements. Most of these modifications would be aesthetic, but Howard also argued that with enough construction debts paid off, greenbelt cities could embark on more ambitious social projects, such as pensions and disability schemes. In this sense, greenbelt cities were not just an urban model but a social model that anticipated the responsibilities of the postwar British welfare state while resting authority locally rather than nationally.

Greenbelt communities would help to combat the problem of land speculation present in new communities. Likewise, renting rather than buying would
ideally make places like Letchworth and Welwyn socioeconomically diverse.
The deconcentration of populations across larger metropolitan areas would give
more people the opportunity to live in wooded landscapes with wholesome
outdoor activities that would enrich childhood development and strengthen
intergenerational community bonds. Howard's cities were meant to be not
separate plots of land carved out for the exclusive use of nuclear families but
vibrant communities where people would organize theater productions,
sporting clubs, and mutual support networks. Indeed, the greenbelt cities
would be communities of affinity, attracting those with a desire to cooperate,
share their leisure time, and collectively cultivate the gardens around them.
While the idea was more suburb than kibbutz, it was still an urban model that
was expected to have sizable positive results for social cohesion.

Despite Howard's inspiration from socialist thinking on community
building and shared land, his projects were not well regarded by Fabians
or more militant socialists, notwithstanding common roots in nineteenth-
century utopianism, because of their bourgeois ethos. His critics from the
political right also lampooned the villages as hopelessly impractical and filled
with eccentrics in sandals.[16] As the British greenbelt movement became associated with the Arts and Crafts house style, many saw Howard's intervention
as mostly aesthetic rather than a true reworking of community. Increasingly,
the movement was institutionalized under the auspices of Raymond Unwin,
who metamorphosed the Garden City Association into a company that created suburbs with some design inventiveness but little to distinguish them
from the other communities ringing London during the same period.

In the United States, where a first garden city was built in Radburn, New
Jersey, in 1929, the experiment quickly became synonymous with Franklin Roosevelt's New Deal after several more communities were put up in
Maryland (Greenbelt), Wisconsin (Greendale), and Ohio (Greenhills) in
the 1930s.[17] These spaces confirmed the role of the state in city planning,
which was being redefined in the Great Depression, but their design lost
the uniqueness of the greenbelt as a growth boundary, focusing on the form
simply as a housing solution and another intervention, among many, in lay-
ing out and managing space.[18] It would take another generation for greenbelts to be reappraised as an important tool of both growth restriction and
ecological stewardship.

During the implementation of early models of greenbelt cities in the
United States and United Kingdom, the idea seemed like a clever reworking

of the traditional village commons grafted onto the real estate model of early suburban land speculation. Developers could choose to set aside some land for community uses. Providing scenic rambles was socially responsible but it would also increase property values. In the case of the New Deal towns built by Undersecretary of Agriculture Rexford Tugwell, greenbelts were salubrious additions to new public housing ventures that emphasized their superiority over polluted urban slums.[19] By the end of World War II, the average suburb looked very different from Howard's garden cities: no longer were they planned communities at the end of commuter rail lines with several modest blocks of houses. Now, with the explosion of growth for veterans and their families brought about by the mass production of suburbia—on the model of Levittown in Long Island, New York—neighborhoods were hastily erected for tens of thousands of residents with mazes of new highways to connect them to urban jobs.

By the 1950s, while suburban growth was supplying a new generation with their own spacious homes that were owned, not rented, many urbanists found that the balance between city and nature was being corrupted by suburban sprawl. Suburbs claimed to allow access to the "country" while bringing paved roads, strip malls, and thousands of vehicles into the very same tranquil spaces.[20] The new ecology of endless suburban expansion repopularized greenbelting as a means to limit municipal growth and to give urban planners a greater say over where city services were extended in order to save money. It was also an effort to curtail the formation of megalopolises like Los Angeles, where suburban neighborhoods were stitched together for dozens of miles with no center and no municipal coordination.[21] The cordon sanitaire function was reemphasized both in the United Kingdom and United States, where public attitudes toward suburbia were shifting. Rather than just putting up a ring road to contain the city, greenbelts offered a legal intervention specifically prohibiting development.[22] They were also a last hope for environmentalists who, while unable to dampen the enthusiasm for suburban life, could at least set aside a smidgen of land that was a bit of green amidst the expanding sea of "grey" thrusting outward from America's cities.

Going Green in '68

In 1968, the population of Boulder had tripled in just twenty years, growing to 60,000 people. It had been "orderly and tended toward compactness but now had a tendency toward sprawl and leapfrogging," as one contemporaneous observer put it.[23] As the population increased, the community was threatened not just by traffic jams, growing school enrolment, and the construction of new tracks of suburban housing but by a more existential menace: the loss of the scenic mountain backdrop that had come to define the city. Local advocates for controlled growth were canny practitioners of environmental politics: they knew that while the scenic backdrop was the major emotive issue that would rally the citizens behind new legislation to buy property and hold it in a public trust, they could also accomplish a number of other urban planning and ecological goals through this effort, such as flood control, park development, and bike transit.

Starting in the 1950s, a group of college professors, concerned citizens, and activists with links to the League of Women Voters had been studying the issue of environmental conservation in Boulder with special attention to the writings of Ebenezer Howard. By 1958, when they founded the advocacy group PLAN-Boulder, they had an ambitious protocol for the city to avoid the suburban sprawl creeping across the Rocky Mountain Region: to buy up Boulder's mountain backdrop and then to connect it to a ring of city-owned grasslands, former farms, and small mesas that would form a "green" moat around the city to protect it in perpetuity. This plan, while allowing for limited recreation and agricultural opportunities within the greenbelt, was predominantly an example of preservationist environmentalism rather than conservationism:[24] it attempted to save nature in a pristine form in perpetuity rather than managing that land as a public-private resource.

As a 1971 report on the greenbelt opens: "Faced with the problem of sprawl, destruction of scenic areas and loss of identity, how does a city go about preserving those natural features which initially made it unique from all other cities?"[25] This meant Boulderites envisioning what they did not want to become—which, in most imaginative renditions of an unpleasant future, was California. The "Californication of Colorado"[26] meant the expansion of housing into Boulder's western hills, canyons, and even the famous red stone outcrops of the Flatiron Mountains, viewed by many as an outright assault on the city's identity. Indeed, much of the antipathy toward California is a marker of interregional disputes over what it meant to be "western": for Coloradans it was decidedly anti-urban. Even westerners living in cities such as Boulder saw themselves as unwilling urbanites who happened to live with thousands of others, but in a different, closer-to-nature way than their East or West Coast counterparts. This ideology would come to haunt places like Phoenix,[27] Salt Lake City, and Albuquerque, where hatred of cities and belief in quick access to wilderness actually helped spur suburban development as a reluctantly agreed upon alternative to verticality, density, and anything else that smacked of urbanism.[28]

The group PLAN-Boulder was founded in the 1950s to take on just such a threat when a developer proposed building a major hotel on the Enchanted Mesa near the city's Chautauqua Hall[29] in the heart of the Flatirons Mountains. The anti-growth activists not only cut their teeth on the project arguing for the social and environmental importance of publicly held open space, they also helped shape a more comprehensive effort to secure both mountainous and flat land. The first step was to defeat the Enchanted Mesa development, which they did when they lobbied the city to issue a $105,000 bond in 1959 to buy the property and protect it from any future homes, hotels, or commercial uses. However, they went a step further, pressuring the city to enact a "Blue Line" that would prohibit the delivery of municipal services above the elevation of 5,750 feet. Without water or electric, those hoping to erect hillside homes with a view across the Front Range would be temporarily stymied due to financial considerations, but PLAN-Boulder activists also knew that this would not permanently stop new homes from climbing up the slopes of their city's treasured West End.

The Blue Line was drawn primarily by activists rather than public servants. Its creation provided encouragement for those who believed that business interests and the conservatism of Colorado politicians—forever conscious of land rights—would halt efforts to limit sprawl and protect the environment. As the math professor Bob McKelvey, who was twenty-nine when he attended one of the first PLAN-Boulder meetings in 1958, put it:

> [The f]irst engineering consideration . . . [was the line at which reservoir water would have to be pumped] . . . but when we came to realize we could put the line wherever we wanted, the whole thing broke open. I personally settled the issue one day by personally going out and drawing the line as low as I could draw it . . . and I guess that is where it still is. While we were doing this, we were always careful to say what we were doing was a stopgap measure only.[30]

For many, citizen power and environmental protection were worth fighting for with gusto, even for a group of relatively staid academics and well-heeled residents. They were motivated more by British environmental groups saving the local rambles than by the emerging ecological utopians connected to hippie culture and hence communicated their concerns using expert language and tactical legal knowledge rather than street protests. A greenbelt, in other words, would not fence in a commune of radical environmentalism but was instead a sound investment to maintain the current landscape and property values. This reflected a major tension in the environmental movement at the time: would eco groups use their advocacy as a means to argue for sweeping reforms in consumption and lifestyle or would they mostly opt to protect land that would generate revenue for tourism and home values?[31]

By the early 1960s, the piecemeal approach to anti-sprawl measures had been replaced by a concerted effort to win public support for buying up a green buffer. PLAN-Boulder's founders and members of its core brain trust (who would go on to hold important roles as mayor, state senator, and distinguished professors at the University of Colorado), had studied *Garden Cities of Tomorrow* as well as the work of the naturalist urban planner Frederick Law Olmsted (whose son visited Boulder and designed a park there in 1910). As McKelvey recalled of an early meeting when the group was formulating the greenbelt idea: "I remember hunching over a table that night when PLAN-Boulder was founded and talking excitedly about the English greenbelt cities . . . over a map liberally marked with greenbelts in red." However, the group's members needed to convince the local community that such a system of parks meant to limit growth would be financially feasible for the city to purchase as well as a sound economic decision for the future. While the western United States is defined by huge tracts of land owned by the federal government, these spaces are leased for agricultural and ranching use, and they are remote, unlike an urban greenbelt. Also, part of what makes them viable in terms of public opinion is that no state or local officials have to act: rather, ire can be directed toward Washington. In Boulder, the plan for a greenbelt formulated in the early 1960s was far less tenable for those distrustful of state intervention: it involved the City of Boulder buying land within a twenty-year period and, when necessary, taking land by eminent domain, a practice that bristled voters in still-agricultural Boulder County.

Starting in 1965, PLAN-Boulder began staging greenbelt roadshows consisting of a slideshow presented by the urban planner Jim Bowers called "Boulder Yesterday, Today, and Tomorrow." The lecture was a means to scare audiences into the realization that their eco-utopia could be wrenched away from them at any moment. More than anything, growth-control activists wanted to emphasize three things: without government action, sprawl was unstoppable; help was based on local control and advocacy, not on petitions to the federal government or large conservation organizations; and collective ownership of natural resources was the best means to protect them. This last point went against much of the ethos of urban development in the United States in which protection of "the commons" has not been prioritized.[32] But Boulder activists in the early 1960s recognized that if parcels of mountain land were sold and divided for homes, it not only would tarnish the pristine view but would mean that hiking trails and meadows where people picnicked would be segmented into backyards, new roads, and parking spaces: transforming spaces of collective leisure into fenced-off private properties for the enjoyment of single families. As Ruth Wright, a major force behind PLAN-Boulder, a lawyer, and a future state representative put it: "It became very apparent that no one was going to come in on a white horse to protect and preserve our greenbelts for us. We were going to have to do it. Federal funds might be available, but it would be on a matching basis."[33] Indeed, mobilization would have to happen at the local level by convincing residents of Boulder not just that their mountain view needed to be preserved but that they had to fortify their city—not against encroachment, like a medieval hill town—but from their own propensity to sprawl into the natural environment around them.

In 1967, PLAN-Boulder sponsored a public forum called "Greenbelts, Why and How," as the first engagement measure in the lead-up to a vote on creating an urban greenbelt that was supported by prominent citizens and business interests but had not yet been tested on the general public. Getting widespread buy-in was essential because the greenbelt was a ballot initiative that would buy land and inherently limit housing availability within the city. The mayor, Bob Knecht, opened the conference with the aphorism: "When man loses nature, he himself is lost."[34] The greenbelt ballot measure had been chiseled out by Boulder's new forward-thinking city manager, Ted Tedesco, who not only listened to the growing environmental activist movement but was excited by their ideas and momentum. Those lobbying for a greenbelt had decided on an ambitious funding scheme that would allow them a permanent pool of money to buy open space: a sales tax. Unlike bond initiatives, this would provide a source of revenue that could be used broadly rather than consulting the public on every new acquisition and having to hash out the pros and cons of each parcel as prices increased.

This more technocratic, rather than fully democratic, fix was supported by environmentalists who felt that even in a progressive city like Boulder, which was already a leader in environmental policy, the learning curve for the average citizen was steep and many people could not see environmental problems until they were so advanced that they were unsolvable. Tedesco, being a cannier political operator than many of the environmentalists of PLAN-Boulder, foresaw the threat of an exclusively greenbelt fund, and he came up with a solution that would paradoxically weld environmental and development interests. He proposed a new sales tax of 1 percent. Six-tenths of the tax collected would be used for road repair to make the booming population more mobile, while four-tenths of a cent per dollar would fund the greenbelt, which would, it was hoped, limit future growth. Businesspeople and conservationists embraced the compromise. In November 1967, the ballot measure passed with 61 percent of the vote, a resounding success for the greenbelters and only the first victory in a series of ballot initiatives. Yet, it also became an original sin in the future planning of the city: the greenbelt was embraced when construction began in 1968, but so was a program of excellent roads that allowed people to zoom past the bounds of the city into the expanding suburbs. This ironically meant containing urban growth while setting the stage for a vast new system of sprawling suburbs in Boulder County.

Winning the resources to build a greenbelt around Boulder meant that the city could set itself apart from other similar-sized municipalities in Colorado as an environmentalist experiment. However, it would also create a private club that one needed to buy into in order to enjoy the collective resources. The city acknowledged that "private lands, customarily taken for granted as part of the scenic foothills background of the west, might soon be bristling with houses." Yet, it also saw, as early as 1971, that there were "skyrocketed land values adjacent to the Greenbelt."[35] Policymakers had few tools to limit spiking property values, nor did many want to. Higher prices meant more local tax revenue with fewer residents. The main mechanism for increasing supply would have been mandating more density and building apartments instead of single-family homes, a solution that was decidedly off the table and replaced by having fewer residents with more expensive homes paying higher property taxes.

The quick acquisition of open space to create the bulk of the greenbelt was made more urgent by rising prices. As Bob McKelvey, chair of the PLAN-Boulder offshoot Citizens for Greenbelts, told the local newspaper in 1969:

> The next phase of the greenbelt program faces a serious delay. . . . [A]s Boulder's population continues to grow, commercial real estate activity is beginning to accelerate. . . . [W]e are undoubtedly the last generation in Boulder Valley able to set aside land for parks, open space, and greenbelts. Soon open land will be all used up.[36]

Indeed, rather than emphasizing the collectivist philosophy behind public ownership, many advocates chose to minimize this line of thinking (given the ideological tumult of the Cold War) and to instead frame the project as a municipal investment based on good government. As posters for the ballot initiative with smiling children playing in nature put it: "Greenbelts are for children . . . and their children."

Holding the Line: Building the Greenbelt and Managing Growth

The process of acquiring land for Boulder's greenbelt throughout the 1970s was often cumbersome despite adequate financial resources. In 1968, after passage of the greenbelt tax, Boulder hired its first land officer, Joe Wing, and created an advisory board for deciding what land to buy and at what price.[37] The citizens had resoundingly voted to protect their view, and preserving the iconic mountain backdrop (featured on the crest of the city and the advertising material of countless local businesses) was the first order of business. After that, there were thorny questions of which environmental priorities should prevail: protecting against flooding from Boulder Creek, which runs through the city center; blocking suburban growth; or creating recreational spaces? There was also the issue of how aggressive the city wanted to be with its agenda. Councilman Carl Worthington noted that the cost of New York's Central Park was $3 million in the nineteenth century, but it was now worth more than $300 million.[38] His colleague, Charles Haertling (a noted architect), was more reticent, commenting that he did not want the city to "get involved in a squeeze-play" with property owners.[39] Of particular concern was the appearance of government overreach, through the use of eminent domain, or of favoritism, through payment of inflated values for the less spectacular parcels of land away from the mountains.

The biggest challenge was to convince citizens to go the whole way and to buy up prairie parcels on the eastern edge of the city. This land formed the full belt, but it was not picturesque aside from some smaller mesas. It was flat low-intensity agricultural land with a few irrigation ditches meandering through. But this aspect also made the area cheap and a good bargain for the city. As the 1968 feasibility study argued:

> Undeveloped and open grasslands are found on the high terraces bordering the upper reaches of the floodplain. Their gently sloping surfaces offer good building sites, with little competition from agriculture. However, scarcity of water and relative inaccessibility have limited cultural development until now and have encouraged grazing activities. However, urban development will someday come to these terraces . . . prompting an immediate need to determine whether any terraces are to be included within the greenbelt area. The floodplain of South Boulder Creek, a natural physiographic boundary for the southern and eastern portions of Boulder, can provide a buffer against subdivision and subsequent urban sprawl, and should be acquired as quickly as possible.[40]

Many of the original backers of the greenbelt plan felt that the slowness of the acquisition process also benefited real estate developers who could easily surmise where purchases would be made and acquire property at the edges: they could put up a subdivision with values dramatically boosted by the adjacent parklands.

Every year that Boulder did not spend its full greenbelt fund was another twelve months of rising real estate prices in a city both growing in popularity and facing an increasingly finite supply of housing. By 1974, Ruth Wright, the godmother of PLAN-Boulder, would accuse the city council of letting "developers . . . play one city department against another in getting what they wanted."[41] Yet, overall the greenbelt was winning support: in 1971 another ballot measure passed handily a $2 million dollar bond to purchase more land; three federal Housing and Urban Development grants provided nearly $1 million dollars in matching funds; and by 1978, the city was buying large expensive parcels, such as a $2.8 million stretch of 772 acres that strategically sealed off the suburban border on the highway to Denver, twenty-seven miles to the south.

With a greenbelt encircling the city, Boulderites were forced to consider their future in a number of ways. The Ebenezer Howard greenbelt model would, in its ideal incarnation, be a regional policy that would set aside land between small cities, creating an urban-rural network. Yet, that model never worked in practice, and Boulder was no exception. One outcome of the emerald moat taking shape could actually be an increase in population and a dramatic spike in density created by new apartment buildings. Some urbanists, who mainly supported the greenbelt as an urban planning measure that gave authority back to city technocrats[42] affirmed this idea, but most of the city was firmly committed to as little growth as possible.

While the greenbelt was the child of the *Silent Spring* movement, it was also influenced by Paul Ehrlich's 1968 book, *The Population Bomb*. This neo-Malthusian prediction about global turmoil due to a mismatch between people and resources was off in its timeline, but the book was extremely influential for conservative policymakers, such as the Club of Rome, as well as environmentalists.[43] In Boulder, this issue grafted onto concerns over interstate migration and suburban sprawl. In 1971, a chapter of the group Zero Population Growth was formed in Boulder, and its members, advocates of slow (or no) growth, quickly attempted to pass legislation limiting development permits for housing.

By 1976, a resolution called the Danish Plan passed the city council with strong support from advocates of greenbelting and capped growth at

1.5–2.0 percent annually. This meant that the city would be limited in attracting large employers (a proposition that many in the increasingly wealthy city were not frightened by) and that it would try and keep the total population under 100,000 until the next century (which it successfully did). At the same time, Boulder also passed a height limit on new buildings: it was first proposed at 140 feet, which would have allowed some six- to eight-story buildings, but after public outcry from environmentalists and anti-growth advocates, it was lowered to 55 feet, the height of mature trees. With no significant reform of planning laws to build neighborhoods with structures that were not single-family homes, aside from a few exceptions of low-rise apartments and minimal public housing, the height limit locked in the current landscape of neighborhoods of bungalows and more modern three- to four-bedroom homes.[44] This guaranteed an ascending real estate market, but few would foresee just how high it would get, given the added attraction of steadily amassed parklands for wealthy new residents.

By the 1990s, twenty-five years after the greenbelt was voted in, Boulder owned an impressive 23,500 acres of open space, acquired at a cost of $99.4 million. As a writer for the local newspaper put it: Boulderites vote to buy more land "whenever they get the chance."[45] Despite the fact that the city was now largely a land manager, rather than a land buyer, the endless fortification of the greenbelt had become a more vexed issue as a new generation came to power, and as early as 1987, the local paper editorialized on the downside to limiting growth:

> For 20 years, the City of Boulder has been scarfing up open pastures and forested hillsides around its borders, creating a ring of untouchable greenbelt that effectively stops urban sprawl, preserves the natural landscape and provides thousands of acres of wildlife habitat, productive farmland and picturesque hiking trails . . . But how much is enough? There is no defined limited [sic] to the size to which Boulder's greenbelt can grow, and because of its overwhelming popularity, few policy-makers will even ask the question.[46]

Yet, the more existential question centered on who could enjoy the eco-paradise that was created from years of effort on behalf of environmentalists and low-growth groups. While the population had plateaued, housing prices had not. "Californication" may have been staved off in terms of a spike of new migrants from the coasts, but the cost of local real estate was becoming more in line with that of Boston or Santa Monica by the 1990s. Even some of the college professors who had been early voices in buying up land

to protect against development were becoming endangered in the booming housing market. Bob McKelvey, the math professor at the University
of Colorado who helped to start PLAN-Boulder, left the city for Montana
less than twenty years after his efforts began because "we found ourselves
living in what was becoming an upper-middle-class ghetto, if you can call it
that," and Missoula, to which he relocated, still had mills and working-class
people. McKelvey also reflected more broadly on the history of the greenbelt
movement and its relationship to class:

> Another social issue in Boulder [is that it] is largely an upper-middle-
> class community. . . . This didn't penetrate my consciousness at first. . . .
> I didn't understand that [open space] was an interest group. I thought
> we represented the community more broadly, but we did not focus on
> the problems of low-income people.

As McKelvey makes clear, greenbelting—like so much of the environmental movement's transformation from the 1960s to the 1980s[47]—was a creep
toward more conservative preservationist values rather than a radical search
for a new utopian society. It was carried out by well-educated people with
a set of distinct cultural preferences, like long walking trails in the woods
rather than parks with soccer pitches or dirt-bike tracks. While McKelvey
made clear that their efforts did in fact create a new urban commons, it
was not particularly beneficial to those without a lot of mobility. He also
concedes that these changes were lobbied for by the affluent. By the 1990s,
it would become abundantly clear that greenbelting boosted the concen-
tration of wealthy citizens in Boulder and made the fight over new housing
a far more contentious battle than the creation of the greenbelt ever was.

Jewels in the Emerald Belt: The End of
Affordability in Eco-Paradise

By the mid-1990s, the anti-growth coalition that had come to define Boulder's
development for thirty years had begun to fray. Property prices had not just
risen to the level of nearby Denver, the state's capital and the major business
hub for the Rocky Mountain West, but they were now high by the standards
of nationally famous destination cities. From 1980 to 1995, home prices rose
by over 100 percent with no sign of slowing down.[48] In fact, Boulder *was* a
destination, especially for wealthy outdoor enthusiasts, giving it a reputation
as a place where young affluent skiers, rock climbers, and mountain bik-
ers came to prematurely retire. The mixture of hippiedom and yuppiedom

led some old-timers to label the new arrivals from California and the East Coast as "trustifarians": a mixture of rich and rasta. However, this slight does not capture the real dynamic of housing politics in the mid-1990s. As Colorado's Front Range became the fastest-growing region in the country (it grew by 30.6% in the 1990s, and Boulder grew by only 13.6%[49]), the major mismatch in Boulder was between jobs and housing. New companies with lighter footprints were eager to set up shop in Boulder even if the city discouraged them. However, their employees would have to live in one of Boulder's satellite towns.

William Lamont, the planning director of Boulder from 1967 until 1974, recognized this disconnect between jobs and housing strategies very early on. He felt that Boulder had done a great thing creating the greenbelt, and the atmosphere of its creation made city planning an easy task that the community supported:

> When I worked in Boulder, Boulder was Camelot for planners. [In m]ost communities, planners are fighting every step of the way. In Boulder, after a few years, it was like, "Why can't you do more?" The citizens of Boulder wanted more planning.

However, Lamont also saw that Boulder was going to be an instant exemplar of the new economy, with the flagship state university, research institutes, and an extremely well-educated population. He favored a regional strategy modeled on the North Carolina "research triangle" or still nascent Silicon Valley, but he found other municipalities in Colorado too conservative when it came to funding the idea. Boulder alone was the crown jewel for innovative companies because of its combination of workforce, educational infrastructure, and beautiful location. That only became truer into the 1990s. Lamont, and many other supporters of slow growth, insisted that city officials only got one part of the equation right: they limited housing. Yet, they were incapable or unwilling to stop the creation of new jobs that grew the population despite a housing crunch that started in the 1990s and continues to this day. As Lamont observed:

> I believe that was a huge mistake, because if you've got the jobs you have to provide the housing. The reverse of that happened: we want the jobs, we want the tax revenues, but people should live someplace else. I think that Boulder in the mid-seventies sort of lost its way, primarily because of that approach in which they focused on the housing rather than on employment.

Indeed, no city is prepared to turn away good jobs, but in Boulder the policy became particularly hypocritical when combined with some of the most stringent anti-growth laws in the country. Commuting, an option that conforms to the greenbelt's growth limits but violates its environmental goals, became the only option.

Fighting for Growth

By the early 2000s, Boulder had established itself as one of America's most desirable places to live, to the consternation of many longtime residents whose viewpoints became increasingly NIMBYistic as housing prices, congestion, and commuting rose. This attitude was pronounced in Boulder but common in all of Colorado, where a new kind of regionalism was born from growth, and many Coloradans' cars sported green-and-white bumper stickers with a mountain backdrop emblazoned with the word "native." This variety of state pride has deepened the commitment of YIMBY groups in Denver and Boulder to provide housing opportunities for Coloradans no matter what year they came to the state. One of the fundamental principles of YIMBYism is the right to relocate and to pursue a better future through living in successful American cities. This often means the severing of local bonds and community that provide "legitimacy" when it comes to making collective decisions. In practice, those who move to Boulder or Denver for economic opportunities or quality of life may not be formally excluded from politics, but their opinions may be valued less because they are seen as interlopers. Often these people care the most about affordable housing because they were unable to buy into a desirable community earlier when costs were lower.

An urban planner and YIMBY supporter from Denver said, in reference to the similarly booming real estate market in the state capital:

> A person has the right to live in the community that they want to live in. And if a person says that they want to live in Denver, they should be able to do that. If we have priced [them] out whether intentionally or unintentionally, there is a significant amount of the population that can't live in Denver and that's a problem. With this core belief that people should be able to live in Denver, we then need to find ways of increasing the supply of housing. . . . If we limit the supply of housing, an essentially NIMBY position, then that's never going to contribute to our goal of more attainable housing for more people.

The planner, who has also researched housing availability in Colorado, was dismayed by the emphasis on Colorado native status playing out in Boulder and Denver, where longtime residents had begun to petition for severe limits on housing development despite a crisis in affordable housing and snarled traffic up and down the Front Range of the Rocky Mountains because of long commutes. "You can see a lot of the 'go home' attitude," he told me over lunch in downtown Denver. "It's quite hypocritical in many cases because often these are the same people [that were being told] to go home, but back in the 1980s. This whole idea of being a native . . . you have absolutely no say in where you were born. Where you are a native of is not a result of anything that *you* did." Those familiar with urban policy have found a disquieting attitude of "insiders" versus "outsiders" in cities like Boulder that have gone to great lengths to protect themselves from overdevelopment. While the influx of people has been large, the attitude toward growth has been NIMBYistic rather than environmentally responsible, many argue. It has overemphasized labeling the values and norms of newcomers rather than providing an infrastructure that allows people to make choices that require smaller homes, closer together, with less driving.

The greenbelt has come to be seen as a planning device of great imaginative insight when it was first proposed and put into effect in the 1970s, but now many housing activists are perplexed that it has become a rationale to preserve the city in aspic, locking in the same housing stock, density, and lack of public transport because of a paralyzing fear of change. In 2012, Boulderites formed an explicitly YIMBY group called Better Boulder to advocate for more affordable housing. The group is composed of a mixture of housing advocates, people working in the real estate industry, and interested citizens. In the tradition of the laid-back college town, most of their meetings take place over craft beers at a local brewery. In many ways, they are a reactive group formed after a succession of anti-growth measures came before the Boulder City Council in the late 1990s and 2000s. Members of the YIMBY group felt that Boulder was allowing an affordability problem to fester and become a housing catastrophe because there was a reticence to build and a specific bias against apartments.

Better Boulder was immediately maligned as a powerful cabal of real estate interests setting up a "citizens" group to demonstrate public buy-in for their projects. While some of the main members of the group do indeed work in the real estate industry, many others are planners and even environmentalists. "It's about selecting good growth, for apartments and residences where people use their cars less, or hopefully not at all, over bad growth which is just more big expensive houses," one YIMBY told me. Ken Hotard, a real estate agent and co-chair of the Better Boulder steering committee, recalled one of its early meetings. The members had promised a few free beers and a conversation about housing, expecting two dozen to show up, and over 200 people attended. He noted this was probably because young people who, while well educated and prosperous, found it hard to afford living in Boulder:

> The outcome is a wealthy community with a high barrier of entry for less-affluent people. They've also created an employment hub of significance with some big-name companies with high potential for growth, and there's a big university and a vibrant start-up community. All those elements suggest the city needs to accommodate more housing and a much more robust transportation system.

Hotard made clear that the momentum in the city had gone too far in the direction of people who have been homeowners for years and who, if they were to sell, would be millionaires. While many of these Boulderites are not wealthy but merely possess a valuable asset, they often fail to appreciate how the community around them cannot remain changeless but will either have to address housing affordability or become composed exclusively of elites. For Hotard, this is not just bad for a community but bad for business, and he did not mind expressing the confluence of YIMBYism and the real estate bottom line:[50]

> That's one thing I like about realtors: people say that they just want to sell expensive houses. No, they do not. That's a very narrow market. The real market goes across the entire market and it makes a more interesting community to live in. Do you really want your barista or your barber living fifty miles away?

Indeed, this point gets at one of the stranger aspects of the YIMBY alliance: the presence of real estate interests. Hotard makes the point that the industry cannot subsist on mansions alone, and this is equally true in other cities. Additionally, YIMBY groups are often supported by developers rather than property managers, making new construction of prime importance rather than the thorny issues of rent control and inclusionary zoning (which most YIMBYs support, but landlords oppose). In most cases, YIMBY groups seek to minimize the notion that they are cooperating with landlords: if it happens, they emphasize it is people who are upzoning existing properties and they name the builders, owners, and managers (who are usually local businesspeople). The movement is less adept at discussing two important issues in the affordability movement: major real estate investment firms (like Blackstone) or the use of platforms (like Airbnb). Both are key issues in Boulder, given its lucratively ascending property market and tourist potential, which has contributed to a complete decimation of affordable housing in the city: in 2016 it had the ninth worst rent burden in the nation, with over 60 percent of renters paying 30 percent of their salary in rent and almost 40 percent paying over half their salary in rent.[51]

One of the big challenges of increasing density in a community where home values have gone up substantially is to convince local residents that it will not negatively impact their investments. People who are "house rich" but potentially cash poor in a place like Boulder at the pinnacle of the real estate market are often careful to keep close track of their neighborhood to make sure their house does not depreciate in value. Hotard, and other YIMBY organizers, finds this to be a major challenge when selling the benefits of high-density housing (which is often enacted in a piecemeal manner by dividing existing larger lots):

> If you put two houses on the same piece of land, then each house will be less than the one giant one but you get twice as many people. Lots of people who are already there don't like that because they see it as a threat to home values.

The threat can also be blown out of proportion by envisioning worst-case scenarios and concentrating on the "slippery slope" argument of neighborhood development, in which a few unwise decisions provoke tremendous consequences. Hotard believes that older Boulderites sometimes see the town as a middle ground between country and city, and that leaves them feeling vulnerable even to modest proposals: "There's a lot of rancor even for a small town[:] . . . misinformation about YIMBYs building huge towers in single-family-home neighborhoods." Hotard believes Boulder has dug in over the issue of "density," with the word representing urban planning innovation for advocates and a menace of overdevelopment and a forest of high-rises for opponents. Paul Danish, the organizer of the original population-control legislation in the 1970s, has lambasted growth as "Boulder's insane densification . . . motivated by a mindless, delusional obsession with affordable housing (whatever that is) and sustainability (whatever that means)."[52] The threat of apartments has produced a surprisingly apoplectic reaction among some residents who are avowed environmentalists, raising the issue of the importance of population control within the American West's 1960s environmentalist movement rather than ecological stewardship.

Better Boulder's organizers believe they have hit a nerve with new residents of the city who are housing insecure (often despite having generous salaries), but they also recognize the uphill battle of new zoning measures that would make high-density development possible. Even small changes, like constructing duplexes and allowing for accessory dwelling units above garages and in backyards, have encountered staunch opposition. "Not sure I can quite put my finger on exactly what people dislike about density . . . a general sense of additional people taking away what you have. But what you tend to find is that the opponents are residents of single-family subdivisions, and they really don't want their lifestyle disrupted," Ken Hotard said. For some, density means the interruption of the American suburban dream that has been a powerful organizer of family and community for seventy years.

Environmental Elitism

When I talked with Anthony Meisner about Boulder's growth, he was driving across the greenbelt after work to the suburb just outside the city where he lives with his family. We both appreciated the irony that he, someone who works in real estate analytics and is involved with Better Boulder and the YIMBY movement, cannot afford to live in Boulder and was traversing the boundary that separates elite housing from (slightly) more affordable housing. Although he avidly supports the greenbelt, he is skeptical about how environmental interests are mobilized in Boulder politics and feels that "There's a lot of people with a couple million dollars who don't have to work in Boulder, and they have nothing better to do than run for public office." He is also indignant, like many, that he is forced to drive seventeen miles each direction to get to work in Boulder when, if there were more affordable housing within the city, he could live more sustainably and bike to his job.[53]

Meisner became active in Boulder YIMBYism during a particularly fraught ballot initiative that became the definitive mobilization of pro- and anti-development forces for the past twenty years. After a number of measures that would slow growth, the city put up two referendum questions in 2015: question 300 gave neighborhoods veto power over land use they did not approve of, and question 301 mandated newly built real estate to provide services or facilities that would offset its impact. Supporters of these measures knew that they would radically cap growth but argued that they were necessary, given how much the city had already "ballooned." Livable Boulder, a major supporter of halting new development, wrote in its online campaign that 2014 was an "apparent housing binge" because the city had issued 2 percent more building permits than in 2013.[54] At the same time, YIMBYs developed a well-funded coalition to oppose the measures, protesting that 2 percent more building permits was the minimum required to combat the ongoing affordability crisis that forced middle-class professionals to commute across the greenbelt daily.

Despite representing a social movement that uses public pressure to achieve policy aims, YIMBYs are often skeptical about submitting urban planning decisions to ballot referendums. While one of their major goals is to educate the public about high-density urbanism, they also feel that the general level of knowledge is still not there: people are prone to make knee-jerk decisions. In many ways, they follow a rubric similar to that of established environmental groups: prioritizing professional knowledge that is often hard for nonspecialists to grasp. For Better Boulder, the concept that all development could be vetoed at the neighborhood level was not a positive example of community control but the most pernicious kind of NIMBYism. As one Boulderite who supported new growth told me: "The measure is designed so nothing is ever passed. They know that every neighborhood will always find a flaw with development . . . either on its face or based on some trivial objection." This has also been the case with public housing in Boulder, which is supported in concept but almost never in practice when it comes to locating it in an existing neighborhood.[55] Better Boulder also maintained that the idea behind paying for more community benefits is a fantasy meant to galvanize support from people who are indignant over real estate developers taking but not giving back to the community. "The reality is, if you are going to build here, they are already gonna get a lot out of you during the approving process . . . a lot," stated a city official who asked not to be named.

In 2015, ballot measures 300 and 301 were resoundingly defeated by 61.7 percent of voters in a tremendous win for YIMBYs in a city where voting on development mostly goes the other way. Those who embraced new growth were also quick to point out that it does not need to be against the spirit of Boulder's reputation as the environmentalist avant-garde but that it must quickly correct its standing as a laggard in affordable housing and the class and racial diversity that comes with it. As one blogger wrote about the ballot measures before they failed: "Boulder could enshrine class and race exclusion in its city charter."[56] Others were quick to point out that without proactive plans to build apartments, the city could quickly become an elite bubble with support communities of lower-wage workers surrounding it. The optics of this would be particularly troubling, as Boulder's Latino population is clustered overwhelming outside the city, despite the fact that the state is over 20 percent Latino.[57] Meisner, the real estate analyst and YIMBY activist, found this to be an irony of those who supported radically anti-growth NIMBY policies:

> There are people coming into Boulder now with fifty million in the bank, and they have none of the same values. They're techie, and they like the area, and they want to be outside, and it's gorgeous. They don't care about all the bullshit politics of the past—they just don't care.

He went on to say that the old Boulderites, who do not appreciate Boulder's increasingly nouveau-riche vibe, would be very upset when the community is defined by wealth alone due to a lack of housing diversity. Despite his work pushing for housing affordability, when I asked if there was any chance that Boulder could end up as an elite outpost like Aspen, he did not hesitate to answer: "Well, I think that's probably what will happen. . . . Instead of a community that's thriving, they are going to have even more people commuting into town, and they will just figure out how to handle that." Indeed, in 2021 a ballot initiative to allow for more flexibility on roommates narrowly failed. Despite the fact that Boulder is a university town, only three unrelated people are allowed to live together, and the voters felt that even a small expansion of this ordinance (to provide for occupancy matching the number of bedrooms in a home) was a step too far toward overcrowding.[58]

For many urbanists involved in the YIMBY movement, concerns over preserving the unique character of a place can ring hollow and can display a kind of spoiled inattention to the magnitude of the housing affordability crisis in cities like Boulder. An urban planner, who did not want his name used due to the sensitivity around these issues in Colorado, summarized this attitude:

> There are three categories of NIMBY: the uninformed, spoiled, [and] selfish. The people who are spoiled are people who live in [a city] in these bucolic tree-lined streets with single-family homes, and there are parks, but two miles away from downtown with easy access to all the bells and whistles of the big city. It's the best of both worlds: you can have your city nearby but you can have your suburban-esque neighborhood with fairly little traffic. . . . The other category is the selfish: even if they recognize the problems, they are only thinking about themselves and they don't really care. They want their car, and they want to park it on their street in front of their house.

Indeed, the battle for new housing in Boulder is one of the best informed in the United States, but disagreement often comes down to two visions of environmentalism. One embraces Ebenezer Howard's admonition to live in smaller cities that are protected from the fracas of large metropoles with a buffer. But this is a very nineteenth-century idea of how a city can exist: it can be placed on the map and created on a blank slate. Whereas the built environment today is already a swath of endless suburban development and the major task is consolidating these strips into more efficient parcels. Boulder's greenbelt was a last attempt to claw back natural spaces that were either wild or agricultural because the future was already apparent in places like Los Angeles. Because of its dedication to the bucolic ideal, there was never a reckoning with what it meant to be a city at all, eschewing the efficiency provided by density. While citizens in Boulder were devoted to creating an environmental paradise, the future they feared—of an endless stretch of unimaginative suburban homes on cul-de-sacs, connected by highways and strip malls, dotted with box stores—came to pass. It sprawls all up and down the Eastern Slope of Colorado's Rocky Mountains, with the small exception of the elite college town of Boulder with its protective greenbelt.

4

Exclusionary Weirdness: Austin and the Battle for the Bungalows

One of the central conflicts of YIMBYism is representational: to whom does the city belong, and who can speak for it? Support for new urban development is often split between old-timers and newcomers: the former are the custodians of each city's unique culture, and the latter are ignorant of the stories collected in particular places. Urban sociology has shown that not only do longtime residents draw on their own social networks[1] in order to solidify positions of power over decision making—such as seats on the city council and planning board—but they also make use of a more abstract sense of authenticity[2] through mobilizing their knowledge of place. They know what store used to be on the corner; they remember the store owner's Labrador; they might even recall the name of the dog. They have weathered urban decline and growth and, in the process, have become personal repositories of local history.

American suburbanization in the second half of the twentieth century gave more cachet to people who embodied urban authenticity: newcomers from suburban "no places"[3] appreciated urbanites with an intricate network of place-based friendships and the colorful stories that come with them. In contrast, in the early part of the twentieth century, connections to neighborhoods were maligned as too ethnically based and associated with anti-modern *gemeinschaft*: the bonds of kinship, religion, and place that kept people from forming a broader worldview.[4] Today, old-timers are celebrated as living legends who withstood harder times when cities were more run-down and dangerous but simultaneously more romantic. Their networks are appreciated for providing solidarity and sometimes even life-saving support, in the case of floods, heat waves, and other disasters.[5]

However, the priorities of old-timers and newcomers are often opposed. Long-term residents are frequently comfortable with the status quo, especially when it comes to housing. They are often homeowners or enjoy relatively low rents. In working-class neighborhoods, newcomers are regarded as a possible kick-starter of gentrification as well as a broader cultural disruption. In more-affluent neighborhoods, an increased number of residents is linked to overcrowded schools or shortages of parking. Even if newcomers are from just the next town over, they may not appreciate the specific local culture of where they have moved, or they may seek to change their new town into the place they came from. Most direly, they can arrive in sufficient numbers to wrestle power away from long-term residents.[6]

Due to this fear, old-timers have often codified their priorities into local urban planning ordinances, such as minimum lot sizes for building single-family homes, density limits, and bans on nonfamilial cohabitation.[7] These laws protect the current look and feel of the city, but critics argue that they leave planners little leeway to prepare for new residents by tasking them only with the unenviable duty of simply preserving the "embalmed city."[8] This critique is very much the YIMBY viewpoint, even when it comes to cities that are generally considered success stories within the larger, more desultory story of twentieth-century American urban development. Density activists maintain that even innovative cities that have grown and prospered have often done so begrudgingly, with more than a hint of animus toward new arrivals.

Austin, Texas, has become an American "it" city: a place on the lips of both suit-wearing venture capitalists and nineteen-year-old aspiring guitarists in leather leggings. In terms of urbanism, the most popular neighborhoods are not the ones that look like a city: they are the bungalows that have withstood the onslaught of growth that Austin has gone through in the past twenty years. Most are residential, but quite a few have commercial functions just behind the facade of a peaceful bungalow. The most famous is Rainey Street, where speakeasy-style bourbon bars fill out what were once working-class homes, with patrons spilling out into the former backyards to smoke cigarettes. The street has been a historic district since 1985, protecting two blocks of one-and-a-half-story former homes from the onslaught of towers that have been erected around it.[9] In other neighborhoods, the gracefully neglected bungalows with beer bottles on the porch and funky sculptures in the front yard have become symbols of Austin's counterculture appeal. That draw has now been transformed into a gold rush of relocated tech companies and the well-heeled employees that come with them. Austin has grown to a city with a metro area of over two million people, with nearly 400,000 added between 2010 and 2017, making it the fastest-growing US city during the period.[10]

Austin began the process of amending its outdated urban master plan starting with a report in 2012 called "Imagine Austin."[11] The goal of this report was to tweak land use development in order to allow higher density, more apartments, and better connectivity between neighborhoods of single-family homes. The city started a process known as CodeNEXT that was supported by residents who were searching for housing, rent burdened, or seeking a denser city that was more walkable. There was stark opposition as well, from groups like the Austin Neighborhoods Council, which objected to the process as a giveaway to developers that would overcrowd the city and diminish its character: one member even referred to the plan in front of the city's zoning board, saying, "This is not Calcutta."[12] While the plan would have allowed growth only in busy corridors (mostly large avenues with shops), neighborhood groups opposed it vehemently, with one no-growth activist stating, "They [the city] have utter contempt for single family neighborhoods."[13]

In August of 2018, the Austin City Council scrapped the CodeNEXT plan, leaving America's fastest-growing city with no smart growth strategy, no orchestrated plan to improve density, and continued reliance on automobile-based mobility for the foreseeable future. Councilman and affordable housing activist Greg Casar remarked on the ongoing failure: "Every day we wait, we're failing current residents and generations to come."[14] Indeed, Austin, like many cities deemed successful for their economic performance and culture life, has ignored densification and comprehensive planning, because of pressure from homeowners as well as the magnitude of the task of reversing decades of policy that encouraged sprawl and highway construction.[15]

This chapter explores the rapid growth of Austin from what many perceived as an oversized college town, known for "keeping it weird,"[16] to a bustling tech hub beloved as a cultural producer and festival destination. Through examining the fight over housing densification and public transit in Austin, it analyzes how new housing movements deal with urban authenticity.[17] Unlike cities east of the Mississippi River with nineteenth-century cores, much of Austin's beloved charm is in the form of human capital rather than historic structures. The urban sociologist Sharon Zukin has argued that authenticity in cities is often located in things, not people,[18] but in Austin it is still very much the characters—the "psychedelic cowboys" and cowgirls from a previous era—that animate the city. The "weirdos" of Austin who give texture and flair to the city's nightlife are frequently considered the real patrimony of the Lone Star capital and not any specific physical structure. Yet, they are in jeopardy of disappearing: priced out as the city grows. In few other cities is housing affordability discussed as a wrenching cultural displacement as in Austin. The oppositional nature between "old Austin" and those who have flocked there in recent years has bedeviled the housing debate: focusing on issues of aesthetic self-presentation. The question of who can represent Austin has made the story into one of counterculture versus condo-owning "normies" rather than interrogating the class differences that allow some to buy property and others to languish in a merciless rental market.

As in other cities with accelerating housing costs, Austin has become a focus of densification activism. YIMBY groups in the city ask the questions: who gets to claim cultural authority, and does this position entitle them to make development decisions that affect all residents? Is it fair for cities to "belong" exclusively to their current residents and for those people to carry greater legitimacy in decisions over issues of growth? These questions have been answered with an emphatic "no" from the YIMBY movement, who argue that cities must be open to all and their planning policies should reflect a commitment to providing new housing. At the same time, this demand may threaten not only to dilute local culture but to diminish the size of marginalized communities who are forced out by those with more money and mobility. Austin has been a particularly troubling example of not just gentrification but an overall drop in African American residents,[19] drawing up painful pre–World War II memories, when the city was racially divided through redlining. Behind Austin's story of creative-class success is one of extreme housing precarity—both of historically marginalized Black and Latino residents but also of the newcomer service workers whose barbacking, Uber driving, prep cooking, and sound-checking allow the entertainment economy to function.

From Burnout to Buyout

Austin has become a darling of new urbanist thinking, based on its economic mix. For people like the "creative cities" guru Richard Florida, this mix is indicative of the future American economy.[20] While many Texas cities survive on oil and gas and other "dirty" industries, Austin thrives on tourism, cultural production (largely music), university research, and an influx of new tech companies. The city of nearly one million (with another million in the suburbs) is buoyed by the University of Texas at Austin, one of the biggest and wealthiest public research universities in the country. Before its current status as a fast-growing "it" city, the college-town feel of Austin in the 1970s was captured in the films of Richard Linklater (most notably *Dazed and Confused* [1993]) and has been described by others as having an ethos of "slacker chic," or what has long been described as its charmingly "weird" vibe.[21]

The enduring commitment to weirdness—whether in the form of a front lawn spray-painted with polka dots or of a giant freestanding backyard structure of scavenged scrap metal dubbed the Cathedral of Junk—has made the city a notable outlier in conservative Texas. However, since the early 2000s, Austin has experienced meteoric population growth as its music scene, home to the major music festivals SXSW and Austin City Limits, became increasingly monetized.[22] More importantly, a thriving tech sector emerged from previous investments in computing, starting in the 1960s when IBM and Texas Instruments made Austin their home. The model of cultural and intellectual production in Austin is a particularly attractive growth pathway in Texas because the low environmental impact of these industries stands in stark contrast to the chemical and oil businesses that many cities struggle to rein in when they are located near residential neighborhoods. This has made Austin a statewide ethical leader when it comes to green development.[23] It is not a frontrunner, however, in freeing itself from car traffic.

To the contrary, Austin and nearby San Antonio have sprawled the most of fast-growing American cities. Austin became 5 percent less dense between 2010 and 2016 as its population exploded,[24] giving credence to YIMBY fears that just because cities have high-tech economies and progressive city leaders, they will not necessarily heed the urban planning wisdom of investing in densification or transportation. In fact, many will be stuck with the status quo of sprawl because of zoning restrictions or, more simply, a lack of imaginative solutions. Even under the best of circumstances, when cities want to densify, it often means starting a public transit system from scratch, convincing chain stores to move into smaller-footprint urban shops with little parking, and cajoling developers to build smaller apartments with fewer car spaces where no precedent exists.

The struggle to accommodate new renters has been formidable in Austin. In the urban cultural imagination, the quintessential home is a bungalow, not an apartment or even a duplex. Like many cities deemed to be on top of the creative cities index for their lively entertainment scenes and postindustrial economies,[25] Austin struggles with housing affordability and competition. The increasingly expensive housing market has sparked a wider conversation about protecting urban culture, giving rise to the most recognized slogan on the subject, "Keep Austin Weird," coined in 2000 by a local radio DJ who was lamenting both the influx of newcomers and the demise of the Austin "cowboy hippie" spirit.[26] The slogan, which is now emblazoned on beer koozies and baseball hats for sale at Austin gift shops, points to the city's unique status as an island of progressives in a sea of red voters. Yet, some also view it as an exclusionary means to uncritically protect the past at the expense of preparing for the future.

Despite the coolness factor, Austin is still one of the most sprawling medium-sized cities in the United States, even with its thriving downtown packed with bars, music halls, and government office buildings.[27] New housing towers have been erected only in a small specially zoned sector of Austin's central business district in a pattern familiar to many cities, in which one area is selected for extreme density[28] while adjoining neighborhoods of single-family homes remain unmolested by upzoning thanks to their intensive lobbying. Weirdness is still a valuable commodity in the city, but many worry that it has been mistranslated not just in its marketization but as a form of nostalgia that simply perpetuates a status quo of single-family homes, very little public transit, and few apartment buildings (constructed mostly to serve college students). Housing density activists often feel that the phrase "keep Austin weird" is misused as a cudgel to talk down proposals for new growth, however modest and well designed. As one pro-density sympathizer said: "There's an unacceptable level of irony when you get a sixty-year-old lawyer with a multimillion-dollar house shouting about how the new apartment building down the street is gonna take away [all the] weirdness. . . . I mean, how are we gonna replenish our stock of weirdos?" Or as another YIMBY supporter put it on Facebook when asked why YIMBYism was important to them: "I think neighborhood character is enhanced by having more characters in my neighborhood."

YIMBYs argue that weirdness cannot preclude growth. They observe that Austin is not and never was a jumbo-sized college town. It is the state capital. It even has the biggest state capitol building in the country, right in the middle of the city, in case anyone needed reminding. As Stephanie Trinh, a YIMBY supporter and policy advisor to Austin City Council member Greg Casar, told me: "When you say, 'Keep Austin weird,' I also think it's interesting how it's this big idea of a country town with rundown bungalows . . . not a state capital and a huge research university. . . . It's kind of hard to know what past people want to go back to." Activists for housing growth in Austin believe that some of the debates over culture are red herrings that detract from the more basic NIMBY dynamics at play.

Those in favor of densification see a need for filling in low-population areas, slimming roads, investing in public transit, and changing zoning laws. They lament Austin's car dependence and observe that while the city has become a capital of cultural activities, it still has surface-level parking lots downtown, lending a sprawling vacant feeling to some parts of the central business district that should be bustling. As one YIMBY activist told me, despite his appreciation for Austin: "The urban framework is artificial and scattered. Sometimes it seems to be just set up for nightlife." Advocates for density maintain that new housing must be built immediately, and unlike in the past, it should be located near the famous Sixth Street stretch of bars and office buildings to lessen commutes as well as to stop drunk driving (by locating housing near entertainment). Density activists commend Austin for its environmentalist pedigree. Through years of struggle, Austinites created well-loved nature trails and saved a local spring from development. However, YIMBYs insist that the city cannot rest on its laurels or ignore the fact that it is still an essentially sprawling postwar western city; it cannot simply add green space and bike lanes but must also subtract low-density suburban tract housing, underused strip malls, and motorways that cut through the city center. In this sense, YIMBYism is a wake-up call to the city's transportation planners when it comes to urban form.

Kevin McLaughlin, a member of Austin's major YIMBY affiliated group AURA (formerly standing for Austinites for Urban Rail before dispensing with its acronymic origin), summarized the pressure between newcomers and "original" Austinites for the *Austin American Statesman* newspaper in 2018: "Our national discourse right now is focused on building a wall to shut people out of the opportunities that America has. . . . We should not use our zoning laws to build an invisible wall around Austin."[29] Echoing San Francisco YIMBYs, McLaughlin underscores how AURA's brand of activism is focused on reconceptualizing the right to the city[30] and showing how successful places have a responsibility to accept newcomers. While he uses the more dramatic example of international migration and the sanctuary city movement (which Austin is a part of), he would expand protection to newcomers who have less financial means than the rest of the United States. Rather than framing housing as a problem of access based on money, YIMBYs instead tend to focus on more politically neutral age categories and newcomer/old-timer status. They draw on Austin's long history as a refuge for Texans who do not fit into the rest of the state: progressives, artists, LGBTQ people, and others. The true test of tolerance, argue YIMBYs, is whether Austinites can be as welcoming with the benefits of economic success as they were when the town was a beat-up hippie haven.

The sense that housing is tied to the future demography of a city is a frequent YIMBY talking point. In Austin, it gets at urban culture as well as economic diversity. Many anti-gentrification activists say it plainly: the people who can afford to buy houses in Austin are economically productive but culturally boring. They are doctors, bankers, and brokers, not poets, painters, and performance artists. YIMBY activists push back on the idea that all newcomers are well off, and they argue that tolerance must be expressed for an evolving urban form. They maintain that Austinites must learn to accept accessory dwelling units in backyards as well as duplexes and apartment buildings if there is any hope of transforming neighborhoods of bungalows to the denser living arrangements needed to host a projected city population of 1.5 million.[31] For YIMBYs, creating a diverse housing stock is often a design metaphor for creating diverse cities. Using architecture instead of social groups can help neutralize some prototypical NIMBY fears around economic and racial diversity in neighborhoods. At the same time, arguing these issues in the wonky design-speak of urban planners can have the negative effect of muting the human costs of limited affordable housing, since the abstract terms don't fully get at the trauma of housing insecurity, rent burden, and eviction.

In Austin, YIMBYs point out that weirdness and other forms of old-timer authenticity are often NIMBYistic categories that protect those who are already in a space. They argue that cultural authenticity, even when associated with the down-at-the-heels dive bar, couch-in-the-front-yard life of "old" Austin, is not actually synonymous with lack of capital. At minimum, owners have the value of their house, in contrast to renters, but they might be more prosperous than their bohemian aesthetic indicates. This reverses the common narrative of rich techies from California coming to live in soulless condo developments that will obliterate Austin's charm. YIMBYs are quick to add that many younger renters are working unglamorous service-sector jobs and that small changes in rent prices are particularly onerous for them.

Densification advocates in Austin believe that the city should focus on universal standards of smart urban growth, like public transit and mixed-use urban development, in order to give opportunities for small businesses to thrive in newly built stores that have residential apartments above them, remaking the landscape of strip-malls and highways that dominate Austin and every other Texas city. By focusing on meta planning problems that affect most urbanites, they hope to universalize their mission. However, in a city like Austin, still struggling with segregationist housing policies enacted nearly a hundred years go, this framing is hard to take on.

The YIMBY instigation to "build, baby, build" in order to mitigate soaring housing prices is a delicate issue in Austin, a city that is both racially divided and losing its African American residents at one of the highest rates in the United States.[32] Exactly where new growth goes is of the utmost importance: if it truly fills underused or vacant land, it will be helpful; but if it instead takes advantage of low costs in the predominantly Latino and Black East Austin, it will accelerate a process of gentrification already running at top speed.[33] YIMBYs endorse development as a general concept, but they also use their organizations as vetting agencies to assess good and bad growth in the private sector and to weigh in on planning laws. While YIMBYs are often well-educated professionals advocating for middle-class constituents, they frequently have to organize their efforts around public ballot initiatives. This provides an opportunity to educate people about the social and environmental benefits of living closer together, but it also poses a challenge to their ability to convey complicated urban planning ideas to a broad public and, ultimately, to live with the public's decision on those issues.

Residential Segregation: NIMBY as a Racist Legacy?

Despite Austin's fame as an entrepreneurial paradise with a vibrant cultural sector, it is still a deeply segregated city. When it first created its comprehensive plan in 1928, a key goal was to end the de facto integration of some central neighborhoods that had become racially mixed. This was accomplished by denying municipal services to African American enclaves and then selling that land for redevelopment.[34] The new growth neighborhoods, early suburbs that expanded the size of the city, were protected by restrictive covenants that prevented sale to Black and Latino families. In 1939, then congressman Lyndon Johnson opened the Santa Rita Courts[35] as the first federally funded housing project and received a grant from a New Deal program within the Department of the Interior. It was entirely allocated to Mexican American families. At the time, this seemed like a magnanimous gesture from a city still identified with the racism of Southern Democratic politics. The effect, like many other planning decisions in Austin, was to concentrate Latino and Black families into the city's East Side, an area that was impoverished, ignored by most public services, and beset with environ-mentally degrading land uses.[36] More egregious was the systematic disem-powerment of Black and Latino communities in municipal decision-making through a city council system that elected at-large delegates rather than using a ward system: a decision so successful at reducing minority voters' electoral power that no Black council member was elected until 1971 and no Latino until 1975.[37]

Today, Austin is still a city that is economically and physically divided by Interstate 35, which splits the prosperous West Side from the working-class, and largely Latino, East Side. As a group of researchers led by the sociologist Javier Auyero observe in their book *Invisible in Austin*, behind an economic boom there is extreme inequality. Low-wage workers are pushed further into marginalization by the gig economy: their piecemeal labor is sometimes not enough to pay the bills, even with multiple jobs. High housing costs in Austin have fallen disproportionately on the poor, given that renters have experienced a larger surge in monthly payments than those holding a mort-gage.[38] This burden has only been intensified with the influx of nonminor-ity residents who move to East Austin seeking lower rents, creating more housing competition. The East Side's Latino character and iconic restaurants and bars are appreciated for their genuine food, low prices, and charming straightforwardness. Gentrification of the East Side is proceeding at a gallop because of its central location and inexpensive land prices. However, this is precisely the kind of urban densification that YIMBYs say they would like to avoid and have been accused of encouraging by their opponents.

YIMBY urbanists often use the East Side of Austin as an example of the entrenched NIMBY attitude of the city. They point to redlining and racial exclusion of the city's past as a trend that is carried into the present by NIMBYs who seek to block apartment buildings and lower-income tenants from their neighborhoods (while turning a blind eye to the same type of growth in low-income areas). "Not in My Backyard" may mean environ-mental protection, preservation of community character, and control over congestion today, YIMBYs assert, but it has a pernicious racist legacy that forever stains it. In particular, the 1968 Fair Housing Act banned neigh-borhood segregation but encouraged other less-explicit forms of exclusion through home prices,[39] using economic segregation as a proxy for racial segregation—a practice that worked, given the large and continuing wealth gap between African Americans and whites. As Keeanga-Yamahtta Taylor has recently shown, even after many Black communities were included in homeownership after 1968, it was often done on the basis of "predatory inclusion": creating mortgages that were in increased danger of foreclosure for first-time Black homeowners. All of these factors have created an extremely fraught relationship between African American communities and homeownership, and distrust for state intervention.[40] YIMBYs affirm this assessment and tend to blame entrenched NIMBYism for a continued segregationist mentality in Austin. "It's easier to talk about the buildings than the people," one housing activist told me.[41] Yet, their pro-growth stance has been anything but welcome in Austin's shrinking Black community.

Growth on the East Side of Austin is often easier to accomplish than densification of existing downtown real estate. Some housing is in dismal condition, and few objections are raised when a demolition permit is requested. Rental rates are higher, making it easier to displace people who may have lived in a neighborhood for years but do not have the power accrued from owning a home. Worse yet, many of the teardown projects in East Austin add little or no density to the neighborhood. Tommy Ates, a member of the transit and housing group AURA, who generally supports more housing and is also African American (but not originally from Austin), feels that the city has concentrated on East Austin development because it is "easier than having to deal with rich neighborhood groups." Ates narrated the long and abusive history of urban development in Austin's African American community ending with the comprehensive plan of 2010, which he says "bulldozed community groups" in order to build new apartments on Austin's East Side. Ates fervently hopes the city will change its urban planning laws to allow for new apartments, but he also recognizes that in historically black neighborhoods, there will be little effort to make sure that existing community members can live in those homes:

> African Americans are mostly suspicious of development because of getting screwed over in the past. Elderly residents don't want change, although if you pressed them on it, they would say the current code has destroyed the community. Some see what's happening with their kids and the lack of affordability, but they are mostly on the side of preservationists who have never done anything for them and won't start now.

Ates explained that, in his opinion, historic preservation is a two-edged sword in Austin: it is frequently used not to protect vulnerable and cherished buildings but to maintain the racial and economic status quo of prosperous neighborhoods. He is particularly displeased that some recent planning decisions deprioritized housing in favor of preservation, even if the structures to be protected were not beautiful in any classical sense. In particular, he pointed out the Rosewood Courts housing project, a New Deal–era housing complex for African American Austinites. Despite their pathbreaking legacy, the apartments are graceless, squat brick buildings, yet they are historically protected. Because of Rosewood Courts' heritage status, there is no plan to create more public housing on the site, creating a grim irony for low-income Black residents getting priced out of Austin.[42] Ates sees precedents like these as part of the reason why Austin's African American population is declining, as in other cities with housing affordability crises like Portland and Seattle:[43] "People don't care about the decline in African American population. . . . It's not malicious, it's just uninformed."

For activists like Tommy Ates, history is important—but not at the expense of serving Austin's present Black population, which is leaving the city at an alarming rate. NIMBY thinking is pronounced in cities like Austin, where planning decisions have often devolved to the most local level possible: neighborhood plan contact teams (NPCTs) that evaluate and advise on development proposals, but whose members are mostly homeowners.[44] While the goal is to draw on the nuanced expertise and experiences of actual residents, the unfortunate outcome can be to create an immovable power block.

Many YIMBYs appreciate genuine historic structures as integral visual set pieces in the street-level drama of urban life. Like Jane Jacobs, they celebrate the vernacular density achieved by row houses and small shops, but they also see some preservationist zoning being used as a cudgel to beat back change.[45] In particular, they do not support the creation of entire historic districts, which exist in Austin and make changes difficult because a single home remodeling could alter the neighborhood "feel." Instead, they argue that the protection of historic structures must be made on the basis of the merits of each structure rather than a blanket prohibition on change. This has mostly put them at odds with residents of wealthy neighborhoods filled with nineteenth-century mansions but, at times, also with preservation efforts—such as the Rosewood Courts—that seek to protect ethnic or racial enclaves or vernacular local history.

Those concerned with housing affordability in Austin have far more to fear than preservationists seeking to protect several hundred historic homes: the greater threat comes from displacement brought on by large-scale land developers for both commercial and residential uses. When the tech company Oracle built a riverside campus on the border of East Austin for over one thousand employees, it destroyed low-income housing in order to make office space and new dwellings for its own workers.[46] Like many developers in Austin, the company was quick to build in an area that would be ill equipped to mobilize against development. Susan Somers, a board member of AURA, said that after the ribbon cutting for the new Oracle campus:

> The CEO was totally tone-deaf, in my opinion. He was just like, "People want to be in Austin and we built this in Austin and this was a prairie before." We were just like, "No, this was a low-income apartment complex, bro." He doesn't care. He's like, "My workers are coming in here."

Somers and others worried that without guidance from groups like theirs, housing and new offices would come to the wrong places in Austin. In particular, they felt that Austin would refrain from infilling the downtown, opting instead to build suburban office parks, which are already numerous, or would build in low-income neighborhoods in East Austin. Particularly galling to them was that many low-income neighborhoods in Austin, and elsewhere, already have higher density because of smaller houses and more intergenerational or nontraditional habitation.[47] Stephanie Trinh, the policy advisor to an Austin city councilman, described this paradox in terms of neighborhood political power: "There is already higher density because low-income people live in denser housing and so there's Riverside Apartments; it is already apartments and they are knocking them down and building another apartment. You don't find the NIMBYs in there because it's already low income. People who are renters have no political power, so they were able to do that."

YIMBYs operating in the atmosphere of a characteristically racially divided American city, with white residents on one side of the "tracks" (or highway in this case) and minorities on the other, are well aware of the difficulty of their position. They hope to spark new development in the central city but to avoid neighborhoods that have been previously disadvantaged by urban planning policy. Tommy Ates summed up the feeling in the African American community as bleak: "There has always been a feeling in the Black community that they didn't want us, and now there is a feeling that the segregationists won." Some of the YIMBYs I interviewed found that the politics of housing in formerly segregated communities was too fraught an issue to handle, without appropriation, for a group that skews white and middle class. Encroaching on communities of color should be avoided at all costs, they maintain, including supporting housing rights groups in Black and Latino neighborhoods, for fear of inadvertently turning allyship to agenda-setting.

Anti-gentrification groups in Austin have consistently come together in order to protect neighborhoods' existing racial composition, in contrast to YIMBY groups. In Austin, the group Guadalupe Neighborhood Development Corporation defended a Mexican-American section of East Austin immediately adjacent to the downtown nightlife district by building over one hundred units of affordable housing and Texas's first community land trust.[48] Yet, these efforts on behalf of existing communities often make YIMBYs uncomfortable for three reasons: the idea of a "never changing" demographic goes against their ideas of growth and evolution of urban spaces; they believe that nonprofit or public housing initiatives will never attain scale to tackle affordability; and their membership is largely white and not attuned to the priorities of communities of color. Stanley M. Johnson, an African American YIMBY from Los Angeles who tweets with the handle "Stanley The Black YIMBY," acknowledged that his name choice was a reflection of the YIMBY movement's diversity issues. However, he believes this reticence needs to change in places where African American residents are being priced out, because more housing—negotiated at specific affordability price points—will benefit them and not just newcomers. This, he admits, will require a lot more Black people to engage in the movement and to come to African American neighborhoods and ask people what they would like to see. He conceded that this will be very difficult: it will involve Black density activists not just speaking to African American communities about saying "no" but asking what level of change can be tolerated. As he put it, it will take a holistic approach: "Let's put money aside for a second; let's not look at prices at all. If everything remains equal, from a practical standpoint, how will your neighborhood live? How will it feel?" Those are the questions that he believes the YIMBY movement should ask people but often cannot because it involves some level of compromise and dilution of the existing community, which white activists find very difficult to discuss.

As Somers said of Austin YIMBYs: "We don't want to inhabit or take up the space of people who are advocating for themselves. It's very delicate." In this sense, YIMBYism is housing activism within the "white" center city, while anti-gentrification groups work in neighborhoods of color often at the boundaries of the downtown. YIMBYs see their value added as a dam to keep back gentrification by insisting that more housing be built in the wealthiest central places. Yet, as seen in San Francisco's Mission District, they often cannot help but also weigh in on issues in gentrifying areas. Despite admonitions for restraint, YIMBYs frequently find themselves taking action in neighborhoods that are undergoing gentrification, and in those contexts their supply-side approach to housing politics gets complicated quickly. The bifurcation of the two groups, which ostensibly have similar goals, bespeaks the racial divide in American cities, where being an ally can be so fraught that some shy away from it.

Calling Back the Suburbanites

The Austin YIMBY group AURA was founded in 2013 to advocate for rail transit, and it quickly embraced a number of other causes, particularly housing affordability. Like many YIMBY organizations, it is part grassroots activist group and part policy think tank and provides consulting services on transportation and planning measures. While not a business, the approach to activism is strategic and high-level rather than base-building. AURA searches for political opportunities to push for mass transit and urban density through well-aimed mailing lists, guest editorials, and city government consultation periods rather than general door-knocking. Mass membership is less important than informed membership, although one of the major goals of the group is to educate people about what a new city of higher density and fewer cars could look like. This is a particularly difficult task in Texas, where private property and having a backyard and ample parking are sacrosanct. Showing alternatives to the past also puts YIMBY activists in the uncomfortable position of forsaking the style of urbanism (or in many cases, suburbanism) that came before them, making them an Oedipal force of sorts: denouncing the cities of their parents and grandparents as failures.

In Austin, as in many American cities, getting people back into the downtown serves three distinct purposes: it lessens traffic and creates walkability; its denser spaces create a new kind of community that allows for smaller-footprint businesses and more social life; and—overlooked but tremendously important—it recaptures taxpayers into municipalities rather than suburban districts. The New Urbanist dogma of the 1980s and 1990s was successful in reinventing shopping and entertainment districts, but in order to increase revenue streams, people must actually move back into the city center. AURA member Tommy Ates sees this not just as a way to rejuvenate downtowns that seem hollowed out and unfriendly but as a bid for the very survival of urban governments, which have bled tax dollars to the suburbs since the 1960s: "We have a static zoning code, and that doesn't make a dynamic city. There is an ethical responsibility and a financial responsibility to accommodate more people."

Indeed, YIMBY activists are highly practical in that—while the groups often advocate for more transit, bike lanes, and parks—they do not hold out for hard-to-access federal grants but instead argue that they will expand the tax base. This occurred with the back-to-the-city trend that began in the 1980s,[49] but YIMBYs see this as only a rudimentary start to a change that will be seismic: America, they argue, will go from a suburban country to an urban one in the coming decades. New arrivals to cities are also potential members of nascent political coalition: they will be disproportionately younger and more precarious people who are not homeowners. YIMBYs hope these newcomers will be more likely to approve considerable changes in the built environment, as they will have little vested interest in the existing framework.

The technicalities of where new development should go in central Austin is a major sticking point, not just due to the rapid gentrification of East Austin already discussed, but also because of the penchant for building suburban office parks that make some attempt to be mixed-use development while also being entirely car reliant. One of AURA's first battles was to reduce the number of parking spaces that developers would have to provide. They also sought to eliminate some existing parking: a sacrilegious idea in a city that is both growing in population and extremely limited in public transportation access. In 2015, under intense pressure from neighborhood groups, the city of Austin decided to transform on-street parking to permit spaces designated for residents only. AURA argued that this would effectively subsidize parking for private use and deleteriously impact local businesses. YIMBYs are often anti-parking militants, and they believe that developers will not build structured parking into their buildings unless mandated to, leading to fewer (or no) cars per unit. Going even farther, they argue that if the city eliminates spaces, more people will think twice about driving for every activity. They take up the concept that on-street meter-less parking has historically been a municipal giveaway to car companies and drivers coming at the expense of pedestrians and public transit.[50]

The strategy of ripping out on-street parking often appears like putting the cart before the horse (to use another transport metaphor) for critics who assert that people will not be able to ride transit that does not exist yet. However, YIMBYs stress that Austin is already at a density that should allow for more pedestrians and bikes but that recalcitrant city agencies have not applied the New Urbanist lessons from other cities. Indeed, the suburban mindset is so baked into Austin that many urban neighborhoods lack sidewalks, resulting in high rates of pedestrian fatalities. One particularly tragic example was the death of William Dennis White, killed walking to the hospital to visit his brother, who had been hit by a drunk driver while taking his dog for a stroll only a mile from where White was struck.[51]

AURA has supported a number of new projects that remove parking and make streets smaller, including a plan to radically shrink Guadalupe, the major pedestrian street that runs in front of the University of Texas.

Its brand of urbanism relies on the idea that big cities need small streets in order to make walking inviting and to lessen the sensation of always being on the edge of a roaring and dangerous stream of high-speed steel projectiles. AURA activists find this a hard sell in a place designed around car usage. YIMBYs decry suburbanism as a disorder that limits people's ability to realize practicable solutions because of objections to making neighborhoods too "city-like." Tommy Ates described the attachment to single-family homes, parking, and commuting as all part of why "you can't operate a city on a small-town mentality. They are trying here and it's killing the city." However, to illustrate the extent of transformation needed, he drew on his own family experience: "Urbanity can be scary, and people want the comfort of suburban neighborhoods. My parents would be the same way"—showing that while YIMBYs trumpet the prudence of their ideas, they recognize them as unsettling enough that they may not be able to convince their own parents.

While walking and biking are often touted as easy solutions to car-dependent cities, many places, including Austin, need more complex mass transit plans to truly get the population moving. In western states, the construction of mass transit is often dependent on state bonds that are routinely defeated by conservative voters who are unwaveringly against tax increases. Texas cities will also be dramatically influenced by rising temperatures caused by climate change, making air-conditioned travel a necessity for much of the year. This is a particular problem in Austin, one of the hottest cities in the United States: summer heat is already over 100 degrees Fahrenheit for as many as ninety days a year, making walking and biking all but impossible.

AURA, founded as a transportation advocacy group, has urged the city to create viable public transit, but this has proven a difficult task. In 2014, the group opposed several plans to expand a commuter rail line, arguing that the new routes would not serve a large enough population to make them viable, that tickets were too expensive, and that expansion of bus routes would be quicker and cheaper.[52] Much of its concern was that the state and local political process had drawn out for so long—and through so many backroom meetings—that priorities such as connecting a proposed new medical school were taking precedence over serving the transit needs of existing residents.

Opposing a rail plan was a risky step for a young activist group set up to campaign for alternative transport, but members maintained that the plan offered was "worse than nothing"[53] and the public, desperate for any expansion of Austin's historically neglected mass transit system, should not accept it. The expansion was ultimately unsuccessful in no small part because

AURA convinced pro-transit voters to join with tax-conscious conservatives to bring it down. It then helped pass an ambitious transit bill that connects more populated areas in the 2020 election, making it Austin's first major mass transit infrastructure to be approved in a quarter century. The battle for better mass transit, in true Texas fashion, is still fierce: after the success of the 2020 transit bill, the state has attempted to include widening Interstate 35 to twenty lanes in central Austin as part of "Project Connect" along with rapid bus service and new rail lines: the exact opposite of current planning advice to growing cities.[54]

AURA fulfills a key YIMBY function of a hybrid activist group that combines advocacy with expertise, vetting detailed plans and producing reports that break down complex issues for the public. The political action committee (Let's Go Austin) that supported the rail tried to brand AURA as nothing more than recalcitrant progressives no better than the Tea Party.[55] Despite the bad press, the activists hung on to their belief that a better plan could be forged.

The activists also took issue with the rail project's large stable of real estate backers and publicly decried the involvement of companies whose properties stood to make a profit from enhanced transit access, arguing that light rail should be added to neighborhoods that already have the population to warrant it. In doing so, they showed that while YIMBY groups are generally pro-growth and feel compelled to work with real estate developers, there are limits to their cooperation. Finally, AURA's policy analysis was highly attuned to the economic efficiency of light rail expansion, tailoring it to Texas, where taxpayers' rights arguments are a forceful means to gain attention and command respect from a diverse swath of the political spectrum. However, this approach can be two-sided for densification advocates. On one hand, they argue for market-based forces in real estate to be unleashed, allowing more residential construction. On the other hand, they champion growth in the hearts of existing cities where the infrastructure needed to welcome new residents is extensive, costly, and only viable with significant municipal coordination.

The Missing Middle

A favorite YIMBY theme to sway the unconvinced is the idea of the missing middle. Cities, according to the theme, have done a pretty good job at getting people back into downtowns with new apartment towers and leisure areas packed with smart restaurants, galleries, and even sports arenas.

The problem is what to do with the vast areas that lie between the suburbs and the center of town. These neighborhoods range from postindustrial to gentrifying to low-income to historic to places that look pretty much like any other single-family-home suburb. In eastern cities that developed before World War II, there may be miles of neighborhoods with row houses, triple-deckers, and walk-up apartments, but in many western and Sunbelt cities, the downtown of towers gives way directly to bungalows on large lots. In Austin, 80 percent of the city is zoned only for single-family homes and the minimum lot size is 5,750 square feet.[56] YIMBYs seek to transform these neighborhoods through new zoning that allows for a mix of houses, apartments, and townhouses. In some ways, they hope to make Sunbelt cities more like East Coast cities that evolved without zoning but with natural density based on pre-car mobility. This will, of course, involve knocking down existing houses, raising rooflines that cast shadows, and putting more people into schools and other public services.

The missing middle is not just a critique of the dichotomy between skyscraper-packed downtowns and suburbs with massive minimum lot sizes; it is an indictment of how cities have become polarized economically. In Austin, smart-growth groups that argue for density—such as Evolve Austin, which is sympathetic to YIMBY causes—have argued that housing affordability is a basic issue of equity because the city is losing its middle-class workers and creating less economically diverse neighborhoods. AURA, in supporting the fated CodeNEXT plan, used testimony from ICU nurses at a council meeting to highlight how, without density, critical elements of the workforce would depart.[57] Even at the level of business advocacy, there is a fear that lack of affordable housing in the center of the city will cause Austin to lose the competitive advantage that has propelled it forward in the past two decades. Drew Scheberle of the Austin Chamber of Commerce said: "The competitive advantage we had with downtown Chicago, if you can believe it, is gone. . . . It's not a good thing, and it's a self-created problem."[58] Letting the middle class live within access to all the benefits that thriving downtowns promise is an issue not just of fairness but of canny business thinking: in a service-based economy like Austin, bartenders, club promoters, and chefs make the city run.[59]

Austin is a good example of how even in a meteorically growing city, the development tends to rapidly metastasize outward into low-density suburbs, with only a small area of vertical growth in the very center (or what some describe as an urban density sacrifice zone in chapter 5, dealing with Australian cities). Only the downtown area near the state capitol and corridors of development in South Congress and the riverfront have raised up substantial apartment buildings. Otherwise, growth has been of huge tracts of homes, many of them the stereotypical three-bedroom McMansions, spreading out in every direction but particularly north toward the satellite city of Round Rock. This expansion of the city has created long commutes in order to find spaces that are suitable for a family. Susan Somers, an early member of the activist group AURA, described how her family struggled to stay in the center of the city where new development was aimed primarily at those with very deep pockets who can buy condos, or at students willing to live in badly maintained apartments that turn into noisy house parties every weekend: "It's frustrating . . . my family's basically coming to the realization, like, as far as buying a home, unless something significant changes, our option would be to move way out." This move would disconnect Somers's children from their friends and school, increase her commute, and mean giving up a more vibrant urban neighborhood for a suburban one with fewer businesses and less entertainment and street life. While many Austinites would have previously endorsed the compromise of more square footage in their home and a backyard instead of the bustle of more central neighborhoods, the tide seems to be shifting with millennials. This may be in part to the new influx of people in Austin who come from other parts of the United States, some with more condensed neighborhoods and less emphasis on detached single-family houses.

YIMBY activism in Texas is an uphill battle due to abundant space, which in the past has provided generously sized houses at a cheaper price point than the rest of the United States. Apartment living may be acceptable for college students, but it bears the stigma of low-income life: a choice made by those without many options. Even renting is considered by older and wealthier Austin residents to be somewhat financially irresponsible, given that one cannot accrue value in or modify one's home. Some see it as the choice that people who have been fiscally undisciplined make, despite the fact that it is an increasingly common one for millennials locked out of expensive housing markets in places like Austin. As AURA activist Susan Somers put it: "There is pervasive anti-renter rhetoric in Austin, but you know, we're a majority renter city. I'm a mom of two girls and we rent, and—to listen to some of these people—it's almost like I'm like a child abuser or something." Yet, not only is renting the only option for many but it can also be broadly beneficial: renters have economic mobility to choose new jobs in other locations, they can weather changes in family composition more easily, and they can use their saved assets to pursue other investment options. Many argue that if cities had more renters, the separation between personal equity and neighborhood decision making would provide for more reasonable growth without fears of home devaluation.[60]

When I met another AURA activist, Eric Goff, for lunch in a downtown Austin restaurant, he stood out among the suits as the quintessential mascot for Austin. Big, with hair in a ponytail and a long scraggly beard, Goff was wearing a tie-dyed shirt that had lines of color and paint drips. Despite his appearance, Goff rebuffs some of the conventional slow-growth ideas of those who live by the "Keep Austin weird" motto. He chafes at the complacency of many Austinites who focus on state politics and believe that their island of blue progressivism will enact sensible growth policies: "They figure that Democrats will take care of them and they don't have to really do anything," Goff told me of the typical Austinite. He smells a fair amount of hypocrisy in Austin's bid to control population by limiting home construction in desirable areas:

> Have you heard the "Don't move here" thing? So, it comes from these "Don't move" online discussions about growth, or you see a t-shirt that says, "Don't move here." It's so crazy that we're . . . a sanctuary city that says, "Please, refugees and immigrants, come to America, but don't come here come from somewhere other than here."

In this sense, Goff channels the most popular YIMBY criticism of NIMBY politics: it is just as common among "bleeding heart" liberals as it is with people who wear MAGA hats and care deeply about border security. The desperate scramble to protect home values reveals a kind of left-wing double standard in which empathy is something saved for those who live far away and with whom one does not have to share parking, schools, and hospitals.

Filling in the missing middle inherently means building in neighborhoods with the highest levels of opposition and blessed with abundant resources: neighborhoods with tree-lined streets where residents have garages but could also walk to a nearby café if they choose. Goff laments that in Austin, people who live in neighborhoods like Hyde Park, one of the city's oldest and most stately, are unwilling to embrace new growth even if it only occurs on high-traffic corridors and merely replaces commercial buildings. For too long, he tells me, Austin city government has proposed New Urbanist mixed-use development, but only at the outer fringe of the city. "It's the devil's bargain: we'll build this new thing but it's a separate new city." Rather than retrofitting the city where transit is available, this creates new fringe neighborhoods with pedestrian access within them but with little connectivity to the rest of the city.

YIMBYs believe that blocking the infill of prosperous inner-city neighborhoods leads to two negative outcomes: gentrification and suburban sprawl. In East Austin, with its central location but segregated population, the influx of white newcomers is met with considerable concern. As AURA member Tommy Ates put it: "Before, you couldn't get a pizza delivered in East Austin, and now there is huge housing pressure." YIMBYs largely blame homeowners in affluent neighborhoods for this situation: their desire to maintain their neighborhood makeup and home values has come at the expense of affordable housing. In this sense, YIMBYs are far more sympathetic to developers who are trying to build new housing rather than homeowners who are protecting the existing housing stock. Ates commented that there's a certain pragmatism in this stance and it demystifies the myth of the evil developer: "The biggest voices in the room are the single-family homeowners who hate the greedy developers but don't mind $2 million homes. When you drill down enough, these people will admit that it's all about saving home values." In fact, many YIMBYs in Austin run into a double bind: their pro-growth stance makes housing activists wary of their solutions, which bring in developers, while homeowners dislike them for the same reasons. In some cities this has put wealthy homeowners and poor people in gentrifying neighborhoods on the same side: opposing growth. Yet, the reality is that when both kinds of neighborhoods say "no" to development, one will have to lose in order to increase the housing supply. Almost inevitably, it is the neighborhood with fewer resources.

Austin YIMBYs, like many in the rest of the country, support all new housing as a pressure valve to ease the affordability crisis. This often means greenlighting expensive new apartments first, while projects for lower-income tenants with more rent-controlled units languish in the development stage or go unbuilt. This is what the urban theorist and planner Ananya Roy calls the "All housing matters" fallacy of YIMBY activism:[61] like "All lives matter," which replies to Black Lives Matter with a truism that belittles the urgency of addressing police violence, building market-rate housing diverts important investment from prioritizing not-for-profit housing solutions for the most marginalized. The major divide between "Build more of everything" and "Public housing first" gets at much of the tension between YIMBYs and anti-gentrification activists, but it does not resolve the big questions. First, many YIMBYs agree that public housing, rent control, and even community land trusts should be emphasized, and those in the most need should be the first served. On the other hand, anti-gentrification activists, despite much bluster, do not see private housing markets going away anytime soon and still feel the need to engage in new developments to guarantee some level of affordability. The dichotomized atmosphere between the two movements is quite apparent in cities like Austin. One can usually identify the two groups by their stance on developers: anti-gentrification activists will often reply with some half-kidding version of "Property is theft," while YIMBYs will range between "necessary evil" and "Let's find the good ones." Both groups have been very busy savaging each other online while the status quo has changed little.

For people like Tommy Ates, the driving force in urban development needs to be the construction of apartments and a stop to the single-family homes that characterize Austin: "Everyone sounds sympathetic on the issue of affordable housing, but never at the expense of single-family homes. . . . What we need is conversion of those homes, and that's not happening." This will involve a visible change in many neighborhoods: an influx of people and the construction of new buildings will be disruptive. At the same time, those in East Austin who want to stem gentrification are skeptical of the "trickle down" housing approach in which a handful of new apartments appear in posh places. They believe these attempts will be too little too late to stop massive gentrification and displacement.

Missing-middle policy, in terms of planning high-density cities, is an important tactic that prepares sought-after cities to house a growing population. Yet, politically it is a disaster. New Urbanist programs that rebuilt downtowns depopulated by urban renewal in the 1990s could easily convert industrial spaces, build on parking lots, and knock down some of the ugliest and most soulless office towers to be replaced by somewhat less visually offensive glass apartment towers. This kind of development filled in the "hole" of the urban "donut" and counteracted suburbanization, which expands the city past the donut's edges altogether. Yet, missing-middle growth deals with the substance of the sweet pastry itself: mixing up the ingredients of the already established center city and disrupting the donut. YIMBYs argue that many are dissatisfied with how inner suburban neighborhoods look, especially in western cities. Knocking down tire shops and strip malls to replace them with thoughtful new mixed-use developments should be easy, YIMBYs argue, even if a few admired ranch homes have to go in the process. Yet, the opposition they receive from drivers, homeowners, and those concerned about maintaining the aesthetics of the past—even if that past is the kitsch Americana of drive-through culture[62]—is significant. What's more, they propose legal fixes that empower both the state and developers to build more: a very tough sell in cities where the power of the real estate industry is viewed as a cause of the housing affordability crisis, not as a solution.

Lone Star Urbanism

Austin has established itself as an island of anti-Texas-ness that also happens to be the state capital. While the rest of the state has megachurches, Austin has a Pagan Pride Day. While open carry law allows University of Texas students to bring firearms to class, student protestors in Austin are more likely to be seen with sex toys strapped to their backpacks and buttons advocating "Cocks Not Glocks." The state is known for rustic dry-rub barbeque, but Austin is noted for being the birthplace of the upscale supermarket Whole Foods. Yet, Austin's urban layout is not significantly different from other sprawling Texas cities that have grown quickly in the twenty-first century with near total dependence on the automobile.

Starting during the presidency of the quintessential Texan, Lyndon B. Johnson, federal programs supported highway grants, propped up borrowing for suburban mortgages, and gave tax breaks to office parks strewn off distant highway exits. This enabled suburban economies to flourish while many cities have languished. Austin's rise to both cultural and economic prominence is often narrated as an unequivocal success story, but densification activists see it otherwise. They yearn to break through the single-family-home status quo, and they believe an influx of rent-strained newcomers may be the wedge that makes major change possible. At the same time, Austin's growth—and its rising home prices—threaten to deepen racial inequality through displacement and also through increased stratification between asset-blessed homeowners (who are more likely to be white) and rent-cursed tenants (who are more likely to be Black or Latino). While YIMBYism does not fully account for racial disparities among renters, it has no problem mobilizing the perceived racism of NIMBY urbanism of the last seventy years as a rallying call for change.

5

YIMBYism Goes Global

For seven years in the 2010s, Melbourne was ranked as the most livable city in the world.[1] A robust economy, barely scratched by the 2008 financial crisis,[2] combined with an abundant nightlife and a strong arts sector to pull it out from under the shadow of Sydney, which was Australia's premier city in terms of wealth and population during the twentieth century. Its theater, music, and visual arts cultures are exemplified in dozens of block-long murals tucked into urban laneways, bearing pictures of celebrities, caricatures of politicians, and giant graffiti-style kookaburras and kangaroos. These often-satirical paintings give the city a playful feel, becoming the ubiquitous Instagram backgrounds for visitors and new arrivals. As in most cases, success within the livable city algorithm translates into soaring rents and an urban geography increasingly segmented by class. Melbourne, like most Australian cities, has seen an enormous spike in housing prices: a decade ago only five neighborhoods had a median home price of one million Australian dollars ($740,000 USD) or more, now 121 neighborhoods do.[3] This price jump, which created twenty-four times the number of million-dollar neighborhoods, has also contributed to inequality: the Melbourne homeless population climbed by 11 percent from 2011 to 2016.[4] The coronavirus pandemic has only accelerated the rise in prices as more people take out low-interest mortgages for the most expensive homes possible after living through one of the world's harshest lockdowns. Melbourne's home prices went up by 20 percent just in the year after the coronavirus pandemic began, as new projects to replenish housing stock were stalled due to work restrictions.[5]

The biggest winners of the Melbourne property boom have been home-owners: older people who bought at the right time: when having a mortgage was just a way to get a roof over one's head rather than a potential winning lottery ticket. The losers of the housing bull market are the poor, renters, recent immigrants, and young people. Many have been forced out of the inner suburbs due to high rents and the impossibility of buying. Others have been forced to navigate living in a share house during a pandemic and nego-tiating safety precautions with roommates or extended family.[6] Even those with good jobs and steady incomes are excluded from homeownership. This is, in part, due to the gentrification of inner suburbs that are located within two kilometers of the central business district. Brick row houses with rusted iron balconies that once housed Italian factory workers and newly arrived Cypriot immigrants, in neighborhoods like Fitzroy and Brunswick, now sell for millions of dollars to well-to-do suburbanites hoping to move back into the city. For everyone else, the only option is a place in the sprawling outer suburbs, which are regarded as inconvenient, boring, and sometimes dangerous.

Like in many global cities, Melbourne has seen a status inversion of sub-urbs and the center city.[7] Tract homes with abundant lawns that once lured the middle classes to the edges of cities no longer hold their luster. This is in part because of the growing economic and potentially racial diversity of suburbs, which are now neither homogeneously middle class nor majority white. In Melbourne, suburbanization is a mishmash of shopping centers and single-family homes: ranch houses from the postwar era owned by Anglo Australians stand side by side with new immigrant enclaves. "Milk bars" stocked with basic groceries and homemade meat pies are adjacent to halal butchers and banh mi takeaway shops. The Melbourne suburb of Clayton is a good example: less than 30 percent of the residents were born in Australia, and while a third of the neighborhood is Chinese, it also has significant numbers of Greek, Italian, Vietnamese, Indian, and Malaysian migrants.[8] However, the new diversity of inhabitants has not increased the appeal of suburban life for many. Rather, outer suburbs have frequently faced a downward trajectory with flatlining home values while smaller houses in the inner city see a meteoric rise in price. As in many American cities, this is due in part to lack of investment in public transportation[9] but also to a reconceptualization of outer suburbs as a place for recently arrived immi-grants. In this sense, it mirrors the European understanding of economic and social prestige diminishing as the city extends toward the suburbs, often with a strong correlation with a decreasing proportion of white residents. In

Australia, this does not mean an end to suburbanization—far from it—but it signals that the market for new homes built in the peripheries of cities is determined less by the tastes of the affluent, who seek to flee the melee of urban life, and more by those who simply cannot afford to live elsewhere.

This chapter explores how the concept of Yes in My Backyard activism has gone global. Much of this framing of housing affordability seems uniquely American: it responds to a particular kind of suburbia that the United States implemented in the 1950s and 1960s.[10] It embodies the cultural backlash against suburbias of that era as not just a financial choice but a cultural one.[11] YIMBYism frames new inclusivity on the foundation of past damages: environmentally intensive land use, racially divided neighborhoods, and economically inefficient property development. For density activists, suburbia followed a spatial logic—that created snarled traffic and lackluster residential-only neighborhoods—and it was driven by pernicious ideologies of white flight and hoarding of tax resources. These ideas are quintessentially American and respond to a history of land use that seems uniquely confined to the United States. So how does the concept of YIMBYism travel, and does it retain its same appeal?

This chapter shows how YIMBYism has been adopted as an activist strategy in the United Kingdom and Australia due to the axiomatic power of its name, the attempts of US organizers to create a global brand that brings together disparate groups under one motto, and similar global urban trends of the popularization of city centers due to increased public and private investment. Most of all, the chapter will show how the growth of the YIMBY framing in housing activism is dependent on its "broad tent" appeal that allows for many activists to cooperate despite holding viewpoints that are, at times, directly oppositional. As one Australian density proponent in Melbourne said during a meeting: "Density is a kind of rallying point and it gets people in the room. . . . Once they're there they can sort public/private, townhouse/apartment, carpark or bike racks, and all the rest. . . . Our job is pushing them into that room together."

The YIMBY name has been popularized on social media for a variety of purposes: as an organizational tool for local groups, a forum to skewer NIMBY sentiments, or sometimes just a place to share photos of attractive dense urban life. Sometimes this gives the feeling of YIMBY being a catchall category that includes any conversation about housing or urbanism. The Persian-American Twitter user who runs YIMBY Tehran praised the way the term could instantly attract people to conversations that may have seemed too esoteric in the past. Organizers have begun to use the term outside of the Anglophone world, such as the Twitter group YIMBY Poland. A Polish YIMBY who lives in San Francisco and was inspired by density activism he saw there commented that even though Polish cities are not growing that quickly, they can still take some relevant lessons from the housing struggles in the United States. He also mentioned that in Poland, like so many other countries, skyrocketing urban housing markets in places like Warsaw and Krakow are increasing social and economic divisions between rural and urban citizens.

Sweden has also seen growing interest in YIMBYism despite a fairly robust social housing sector. A YIMBY organizer in Sweden for over ten years understood the utilitarianism of the strategy immediately: "I was walking around the city seeing all these stupid uses of space . . . and suddenly I saw this thing YIMBY that says exactly what I have been thinking. And I said, 'Cool, here is someone who gets it.'" He also said that while many people in the United States may believe that European countries have already won the battle for density, that is often a misperception. Cities like Malmö (which has a population density in the center of just 2,200 per kilometer, compared with other European cities that have ten times that amount[12]) has modernist high-rises but lots of wasted space in between. The Swedish YIMBY, who did not wish his name to be shared because he also works in city planning, said, "If you look at the map you will see that the city is not dense. There are large apartment buildings and between [them] there are vast wastelands." For some European YIMBYs, the movement presented a means to correct the mistakes of mid-century modernism that left large garden spaces (sometimes never planted) between residential areas or that separated housing from shopping. In this sense, it was a philosophy that allowed them to advocate for "filling in" the city. Unlike buildings in American cities, some of the anchoring structures that needed new development around them are hundreds of years old, but nonetheless the philosophy was viewed as comparable.

Global activists, most of whom are in the Anglophone world, endorsed YIMBYism not just because Not in My Backyard is a powerful pejorative in their own cultural contexts but also because they appreciated the optimism and pragmatism of the movement they saw in California and other places. Almost all of them viewed advocating for social housing alone as a losing battle because its benefits were not universal enough to build a large coalition. Additionally, they found design-centered debates too aesthetically focused without enough public policy decisions at stake. Instead, they concentrated on municipal laws. Using simple tools such as Facebook groups, blogs, and small meetings, these international groups formed small cliques of highly educated urbanists who, while they did not create a mass movement for housing, began quietly exerting influence on local councils to build more housing units, develop underutilized land, and put more money into public transit. As another Swedish activist said of the quiet campaign they mounted:

> We don't even have a formal organization. The only thing we have is a blog and a Facebook group. . . . We are focusing less on the NIMBYs and much more on the urban planning system, on the power. We know that they listen to us. They follow our blog. They are afraid of what we are gonna write. . . . We are more like a newspaper. We *do* have power. They prepare for what we are going to write. We know this because emails have leaked from public planning organizations that . . . talk about us as a stakeholder.

As in most iterations of YIMBY activism, internationally it functions not as a mass movement for housing justice but as a new layer of civic infrastructure that places itself between public opinion and planning authorities with a set of skills that translates policy to a larger audience. It seeks to arbitrate both public regulation and private development proposals. Simple online organizing reaches a small but influential group, and many municipalities find it difficult to ignore well-informed activists with professional backgrounds. As Daniel Oleksiuk, a lawyer and founder of Vancouver's Abundant Housing organization said, "There used to be just one guy at public hearings in favor of development." He emphasized that his group was helping Canadians understand density as an ecological asset in a city hemmed in by mountains rather than a capitulation to developers who would sully the city's image as a haven for outdoor activities.

City governments, which often remain skeptical about YIMBYism as a disruptive political platform, nonetheless seek to mollify these groups by including them in the policy-making process as stakeholders, less they should antagonize them and have to endure them as adversaries. As in California, municipal governments in Canada, the United Kingdom, Sweden, and Australia fear the well-crafted meme made by someone who understands zoning and has plenty of time to show up to local council meetings. They also feel the very real pressure of expanding numbers of renters concerned with housing prices. Most of all, they are excited to work with activists who allow them to restart the urban growth machine,[13] with regulated growth, rather than more radical groups who seek only to expand public housing or to block all growth because of gentrification fears.

The United Kingdom: Bribing Homeowners for Density

British housing density groups are not where you would think they would be. As in the United States, most activists are not in the worst-off cities with no sidewalks, where strip malls make up the only commercial areas and houses are widely spaced on half-acre plots. There are no YIMBYs in Slough: the home of the original *Office* television mockumentary where employees sit in a faceless suburban office park all day. Rather, they are in cities that people frequently visit, where they are charmed by their "Europeanness" and bustling centers: Brighton (a capital of LGBTQ culture and a successfully rethought seaside resort), Bristol (a maritime town with no shortage of guidebook hype), and London, Oxford, and Cambridge. Yet, the very popularity of these cities is why housing activism seems so urgent there. For many, middle-class life is a fantasy that can only be lived at the very farthest reaches of the city in a state of outsiderness that estranges residents from the reasons why they came to successful metropolitan areas in the first place. Paul Erskine-Fox, a YIMBY activist in Bristol, shares this sentiment because he and his wife live much farther from the city center than they would have liked: "People feel like they have a relationship with the city because they work or socialize there. . . . They have an economic relationship with Bristol but they can't have the [full] relationship with the city they want to."

This state of being existed for low-income residents for decades as they were banished from downtowns to marginal neighborhoods on the urban periphery.[14] However, it is a very new feeling for middle-class residents. As one British activist said, "People interested in density are often the ones who have done everything right . . . [such as] the university grads with knowledge-sector jobs, but the prices are so high now they feel like they've done something wrong with their lives. . . . They feel depressed about where they have to live and they think it's their own fault." Britain, unlike the United States, has long had a spatial stigma associated with housing on the outskirts of cities: those who cannot afford centrality endure not only long commutes, dreary suburban neighborhoods, and few recreational options but derision for their accents and broader cultural outlook. They are "nearby provincials," as the author V. S. Pritchett mockingly put it: trapped in a suffocatingly quotidian life ripe for satire.[15] More recently, the Booker prize–winning novel *Shuggie Bain* details the complete deterioration of a family that moves from Glasgow social housing to the disconnected and bleak periphery of the city.[16] YIMBY activists are acutely aware of the diminished cultural cachet of suburban living in the United Kingdom compared with more expansive environments like the United States or Australia. This has led them to push for densification with even more ardor.

Erskine-Fox and others from UK YIMBY groups were impressed by the efforts of their American counterparts and the new framing for housing affordability. In particular, they were able to get people animated about zoning issues that previously evoked only groans and yawns. As Erskine-Fox put it, "Our message is, it's time to get as many people as possible involved in the planning process." To this end, he has created a mapping function on the Bristol YIMBY website that shows potential new housing projects and allows users to comment on their impact for the local community. Typical posts read like: "Summit Capital are proposing to re-develop this brownfield site with purpose-built student accommodation, whilst providing high-quality landscaped open space. . . ."[17] The messaging with phrases like "brownfield" and "purpose-built" is not exactly populist—in fact it is mostly for people who already know a lot about city planning—but spatial mapping and info-graphic tools combined with forum comment sections creates an online communication infrastructure to discuss development before it happens. While this may sound trivial, it is a technique that many YIMBY groups expound in order to supplement more predetermined community consulta-tion periods run by developers and local government.[18] In this sense, they seek to make the planning process more deliberative but within a mostly preordained group that has the time and capacity to get involved with spatial issues at a high level of detail.[19]

Like in the United States, part of the function of YIMBY groups inter-nationally has been to facilitate communication with neighbors who previ-ously blocked new developments. YIMBY groups are third-party pro bono consultancies that moderate between community groups, local councils, and developers. However, they are not value neutral: they want new buildings to go *somewhere*, and they believe that "just saying no" should not be an option. "We are asking people to accept that we need to build more homes, and [we are] trying to get them to say where those homes should be built," Erskine-Fox told me. John Myers, the co-founder of the London YIMBY group, summarized their mission in historical terms dating the struggle back to an article published by the preeminent urbanist Peter Hall in the mid-1970s,[20] stating: "Since then, the situation has become drastically worse, and there have been literally hundreds or thousands of reform proposals and nothing has really gone anywhere."

Sam Watling, a YIMBY organizer from the coastal city of Brighton, agreed with my assertion that his density battle was somewhat easier than that faced by a sprawling American city like Phoenix, Arizona, or Houston, Texas. Indeed, some of the neighborhoods that his group would like to become more compact already consist of row houses, which would be an admirable state of affairs for cities west of the Mississippi River, where most housing consists of detached single-family homes, often on large lots.[21] Nor is densification a new idea in the United Kingdom. As early as 1936, George Orwell wrote of the double-edged sword of slum clearance efforts in *The Road to Wigan Pier*:

> When you rebuild on a large scale, what you do in effect is to scoop out the center of the town and redistribute it on the outskirts. This is all very well in a way; you have got the people out of fetid alleys into places where they have room to breathe; but from the point of view of the people themselves, what you have done is to pick them up and dump them down five miles from their work. The simplest solution is flats. If people are going to live in large towns at all they must learn to live on top of one another.[22]

However, despite long familiarity with the necessity of apartment life in the United Kingdom, it still stirs up a sense of class anxiety: of a downward trajectory from house to apartment to council flat, despite Orwell's home-spun planning advice.

Despite the dissimilar housing typology, Watling felt that the idea of YIMBYism was a potent tool in the British and European context. We discussed a member of Parliament near Brighton who insisted on having a million new units of housing built in suburban London while rejecting the construction of two hundred new homes in his own district. Watling made clear that YIMBYism personalizes issues that are often an abstraction while adding a valuable moral component. "It's *my* backyard not *your* backyard . . . and if a project isn't going to work near where you live, there's very little chance of any politician adopting it nationally." Indeed, he and others in the United Kingdom found the siting of new homes to be both a personal sacrifice made for the broader community and a political compromise more politicians would have to make in the future. The problem is, as John Myers from the London YIMBY put it: "Two-thirds of the voters are homeowners and, as far as I know, we have the only government that has an expressed stated policy that home prices should continue to rise. Imagine that being the policy for food or clothing or any other basic need." Activists for housing density, in short, are after a "buck stops here" philosophy with dwellings instead of poker chips, in which members of Parliament finally take responsibility for housing shortages in their own districts.

Much of this discontent also predates the current moment and goes back to the financialization of housing in the 1980s under the Thatcher government. Since Margaret Thatcher sold off council flats to existing tenants, leaving poorer residents more precarious,[23] the expansion of homeownership made asset appreciation of broader interest to a country where renting became less widespread (it went from half the UK in 1979 to less than a third in 2000).[24] For those not fortunate enough to become owners, the private rental market has become more expensive as the available stock of public housing has severely contracted. Compounding the problem, construction has dropped off significantly with a 44 percent decrease in new builds from 1980 until 2014.[25] This has created a rift in the pro-business Conservative Party, in which Tory MPs are split on local control of new development in wealthy areas (to limit new neighbors) alongside maintaining a relationship with construction companies and property developers who are traditional party supporters and are desperate for growth.[26]

As YIMBY adherents point out, there is little appetite for moderating the rise in values or treating housing as a basic commodity, given the middle-class interest in home values. At the same time, the ability to buy is often limited to the previous generation, who obtained mortgages during the Thatcher era. Today, even college-educated workers with good earnings are getting squeezed, particularly in London. For the middle classes, this means that people of age thirty-five to forty-four are three and a half times more likely to rent (in 2017) as they were in 1993. For working-class British tenants, it can mean balancing on the precipice of homelessness.[27]

As in the United States, YIMBY activism in the United Kingdom has sometimes been a fraught mixture between exhorting the public to pay closer attention to urban planning dogma and, at times, challenging the power of the planning profession. On one hand, activists want to incentivize densification of postwar suburbs. On the other hand, they occasionally seek more construction on greenfield sites than the planning profession is comfortable with. Paul Erskine-Fox suggested that the roles might be somewhat reversed between the United Kingdom and the United States: he stated that while people are flocking to the center of cities, that's not where all the new housing should go because of both logistics and consumer preference. He insisted that planners should incentivize densification while also heeding the market: "People still want larger family homes, and most upzoning attempts will not provide for this in crowded downtowns." This rarely means building at the edge of the city but rather in some of its "missing middle" zones that have maintained their value. Yet, finding that land is extremely difficult, and one of the easiest methods is to locate underutilized state-owned land and argue for its development.

Housing activists complained of planning for planning's sake: a kind of vengeful nanny state intent on regulating all changes no matter how minor. John Myers from London noted that there are many detached homes or semi-detached homes within the M25 London ring road and that just densifying these areas with townhouses could "literally more than double London's housing capacity." Despite significant public support, he maintained that the planning profession has not yet responded to this solution because of NIMBYism as well as inertia: "The constraint here is you literally can't add another cubic or square foot to your house without permission from the government, except in extremely limited cases." In this sense, many YIMBYs see their groups as a useful supplement to municipal planners who can deflect public pressure: "We want to create more ways for planners to achieve what they want," said Myers.

Another point of contention is Britain's many greenbelts that provide urban growth boundaries, as in Boulder, Colorado, where cities would otherwise have spilled over in the same kind of uncontrolled suburban sprawl that went on in the United States.[28] While UK YIMBY groups appreciate the historical role of these planning mechanisms, they are skeptical that all land under protection really meets the criteria for high use value in the midst of the national housing crisis. Indeed, the National Housing Federation estimated that 8.4 million people in the United Kingdom were living in unaffordable, insecure, or unsuitable homes.[29] Erskine-Fox, from Bristol, argued this was perhaps the most important issue in the United Kingdom:

> We are trying to build more and more housing in high-density situations but, and this is my opinion, we need to have a review of the greenbelt. . . . We have a lot of green protected land to protect against urban sprawl . . . but there is a lot of land in the greenbelt that doesn't fulfill the purpose and could be used for homes.

As in Colorado, skepticism about the greenbelt was based on unfair commutes for those laboring in Bristol and other cities but forced to travel over an hour by train or bus to reach the city's center. Activists argued that the buffer of an urban growth boundary was no longer functional because of leapfrogging development that has transpired since the 1960s. Additionally, they found environmental benefits to be lacking in some cases because land set aside had not been successfully made into parkland but was simply off limits. Erskine-Fox chalked this up to NIMBYism in many cases: "A lot of the time, the greenbelt doesn't serve that much of a purpose. Quite frankly, it's often because people want a view of it out of their window, and they want to protect the greenbelt because they want to protect their home." Many activists feel that careful consideration of growth boundaries could produce land for new housing while also respecting the general concept. They argue that this has not transpired because what was meant to be a general public good has in some places been used for private advantage by those who bought properties abutting the greenbelt.

The disagreement over the future of UK greenbelts, and particularly the metropolitan growth boundary in London which hugs the orbital M25 highway, is not welcome news to British town planners. Indeed, the intervention of the greenbelt was what conferred power onto the new profession in the early twentieth century.[30] Challenging the sacrosanctity of this tool is akin to disputing the legitimacy of the entire field, which is exactly what some YIMBYs have in mind. Many of those interviewed felt that professional planners had become out of touch with major economic issues such as housing while concentrating on more niche issues. The activists saw their job as refocusing the profession.

One planner who is also a YIMBY supporter described the "rarefication of the field," and "disinclination to experiment." Sam Watling from Brighton called out planners as not necessarily being allies of the YIMBY movement as they frequently are in the United States: "Lots of planners are very skeptical about attempts to simplify the planning system and may oppose things for ideological reasons. They don't want to have their professional power taken away." He also insisted the point of contention was not just about flexibility regarding the greenbelt but about the desire of planners to operate with a blank canvas rather than to engage the messiness of urban densification: "We have fought some bitter battles with town planning agencies that favor new towns over any measure of bottom-up densification," Watling said. In this sense, advocating for limited greenbelt development was not a betrayal of goals to increase density in existing neighborhoods but a compromise to build on *terra nullius* closer at hand rather than on the urban fringe.

British activists endorsed Yes in My Backyard as an umbrella term, but they also worried that it had become divisive because of the zeal of California YIMBYs. "We don't necessarily want all the baggage that comes with it," one London YIMBY supporter said. Yet, most endorsed the positive connotation of the slogan, viewing it as an important reframing of the "cannot" ethos of Not in My Backyard into a rallying cry of "yes, we must." To some, this appeal was community-spirited and about not leaving anyone behind. The

UK housing market has become more financialized and increasingly brutal for those without means. Since 1994, those in the bottom quintile of the working-age population who spend more than a third of their income on housing has increased from 39 percent to 47 percent (in 2018).[31] Now that middle-class activists have taken up the battle for housing affordability, they often use the same language of individual property rights that was successfully deployed during the Thatcher years.

Unlike YIMBYs in the United States, whose talking points emphasize living together in mixed-income communities, some of the British groups have taken a more utilitarian approach that argues for upzoning as a means to maximize property value. As Watling put it in the context of Brighton: "It is basically bribing NIMBYs with their own land value voucher." This more realistic version of densification is based on appeals not to the heart but to the wallet or, as Watling puts it: "We want to make sure that the benefits are concentrated enough that you can basically incentive local homeowners to upzone."

"Bribing owners" is seen as a particularly canny strategy in London where housing prices have reached stratospheric heights. Within the financial capital, prices are based on the city's connection to global financial markets rather than just its primacy in the United Kingdom.[32] London housing is morphologically diverse, but building new high-rises is unpopular given the association with mid-century urban renewal and the creation of council estates with concentrated poverty. "When people think of density they think of towers, and we just don't find that towers win a huge amount of support," said John Myers of the London YIMBY group. Instead he proposed building above row houses to create extra units. This sort of "pop top" can be done structurally but it usually means completing extra stories in a different style: modern boxes that hover above their historic host dwelling in a juxtaposition that many people find parasitic. Myers summarized the public concern over aesthetics:

> If you get two stories of concrete box on top of a Georgian, Edwardian, or a Victorian, everyone around you is gonna scream. So, there has to be some way to address the design concerns. . . . There's just so much old building stock here even if you go further out. Getting people comfortable so that you can add more housing without making it look like something they're not familiar with is really important.

London's blessing and curse is money. "You can literally build a concrete box and you'll make money out of it," Myers commented to explain the well-founded hesitancy of some owners to modify existing neighborhoods. Despite quick and shabby additions, money also provides a strong density incentive to owners. This gives YIMBYs a sweet spot for negotiating with well-heeled homeowners who, in other financial environments, would be more hesitant. Retrofitting a townhouse with more units on the roof is appealing, given the tremendous value of each additional unit, which would not be as tempting in less exorbitantly priced property markets. The average price for a semi-detached or terrace house in a prime London neighborhood like Westminster, Chelsea, or Knightsbridge is between £1.5 million to £2.5 million; however, flats are also worth over £1 million,[33] making the creation of new apartments an attractive option, particularly for long-term residents who may be homeowners but cash poor. Although this intervention is piecemeal and often only adds market-rate units to the housing supply, it still provides a convincing path forward for cities with high prices because, as Myers sees it, even wealthy homeowners want a windfall in order to cope with living in such an expensive city. As he puts it:

> There is so much money to throw around in development that you can literally answer almost any concern you like with profit that will come from development. You can find situations that are win-win. We have a lot on our side to bring people on board: the heritage people, the design people . . . the parks people . . . there are just huge amounts.

The upside for YIMBYs in the United Kingdom is that the organizing work they do is less ideological and more logistical: it is frequently about making the numbers work for specific communities rather than getting those places on board with densification as a basic precept. As Myers commented when considering the US analogy: "The transport-oriented development debate has been won in this country already. We are really just at the point of solving the political constraints."

The practicality of more intensive land use comes at a time of real economic suffering, in which the importance of getting into urban areas with better work opportunities is paramount. As in California, the British YIMBY movement has taken on existential worry about growing regionalism as well. Living in Bristol, Brighton, and London is not just a matter of feeling good in a thriving city but also making a living in a country increasingly riven with regional tensions. In 2017, the average person in Nottingham had a disposable after-tax income of only £12,445 (approximately $16,150 USD) while Londoners enjoyed average annual earnings of £46,288 ($60,150 USD).[34] Not being able to access housing in better-off cities has meant that people are locked out of mobility, instead resigned to stay in de-industrialized towns with stagnant or falling wages.

With this decline, worsened by austerity following the 2008 economic crisis, a new kind of cultural animus has formed as part of the identity of failing cities and towns. Much sociological research has centered on how the feeling of being left behind relative to London—with its connections to Europe and the world—has added to a sense of nationalism fueling the successful Brexit referendum.[35] Several YIMBY activists argued this was true, but understanding the phenomenon simply as pride for downtrodden municipalities did not get at the full picture. "People shut out of opportunity have often voted to leave the EU, and that hasn't necessarily been part of the debate—which I want to make it," Sam Watling stated. He insisted that it is not just people who do not earn enough but those who cannot get a foothold somewhere else in the country. For those invested in the project of YIMBYism, Brexit was not just a backlash against Europeanization but a cry for help from citizens with lessened mobility: those unable to take advantage of open borders in continental Europe but also incapable of renting a flat in London, Oxford, or anywhere else with higher wages.

Outback Suburbia

Australia has been commended for internationalizing its economy in ways that allowed it to weather the financial crisis of 2008, but the country now faces an existential dilemma based on both trade and immigration. Australia's finances are inextricably bound to China, not just as a major supplier of raw materials—mined in the vast center of the continent—but also through direct foreign investment, including wealthy Chinese real estate speculators snapping up properties in major cities.[36] In 2015–16, the Australian government approved $47.3 billion AUD in Chinese investment, $32 billion of which was in real estate.[37] This has created a sizable portion of the Australian real estate sector designed specifically for Chinese nationals, most notably high-density inner-city skyscrapers that tower above the late Victorian row houses that define Australian cities.

At the same time, the issue of suburban violence in areas with large migrant populations has exploded within Australian politics, particularly in Melbourne. The issue was largely manufactured as a campaign talking point in 2018 by the conservative Liberal Party to smear Victoria's Labor government as soft on crime. News outlets widely reported a wave of violence perpetrated by "African gangs" in the outer Melbourne suburbs, leading to a hardening of views around refugee resettlement as well as a growing fear of the suburban periphery.[38] While the crime stats remain mostly a fantasy, Australians—who have a much stricter immigration and refugee regime than the United States and Europe—are receptive to nativist flag-waving. For a country with so much space, xenophobia is most visible in the arena of urban housing, and there is a real sense of scarcity when it comes to sheltering those who are urban newcomers.

During the coronavirus pandemic of 2020, the right-wing nationalist politician Pauline Hanson commended the city of Melbourne for locking down only public housing projects on the edge of the city (and not nearby single-family homes) because the residents were "drug addicts" and "alcoholics" who had not bothered to learn English, adding: "they are from war torn countries . . . they know what it is like to be in tough conditions."[39] In Melbourne, these opinions are not just voiced by ultranationalists during plague times, but they simmer in more mundane periods and reflect how people see the city's outer neighborhoods that host more public and low-income housing. This translates to anxiety over a future in which the city is composed of a wealthy Chinese center (downtown towers), an unaffordable Australian middle (gentrified inner suburbs), and a "dangerous" African/South Asian periphery (the exurban fringe), creating a telling pie chart of contemporary racial fears.

This section explores how YIMBYism has become an important framing for Australian housing activists, particularly millennials fighting to inhabit "missing middle" zones of cities nestled between skyscraper-packed central business districts and more sprawling outer suburbs. It shows how migration has played an oversized role in the conversation around housing shortages but also, potentially, offers a solution in furnishing new models of cohabitation based on density from European and East Asian cities. The ways migrants have used Australian cities—first Southern Europeans in the 1960s and later East Asians in the 1980s until today—have challenged the hegemonic logic of suburbanization as the realization of the "Australian Dream."

In Melbourne, Southern European migrants often took over the iron-columned terrace homes of their Anglo forebears and embraced neighborhood street life and small markets in communities that exist to this day. While second-generation Greek and Italian migrants have often moved to single-family homes in more dispersed suburbs, the mixed commercial and residential infrastructure they created in the inner city is still enjoyed by new, often younger and more affluent residents. Similarly, heavily East Asian neighborhoods in Melbourne number in the dozens and forms of urbanism common to Chinese cities—such as apartment living and central produce and fish markets—abound. Indeed, Melbourne is one of the few wealthy cities to have a multi-block fish, meat, and vegetable market (Queen Victoria Market) in the very epicenter of the city, where locals have vociferously resisted redevelopment plans that do not keep its unique function as a purveyor of fresh food.[40]

YIMBY activism has become a means not just to petition for broader zoning laws that incorporate different land uses but also more welcoming cities that include people of different ethnic and economic backgrounds. Yet, at the same time, the promise of substantial new housing development bringing newcomers to central neighborhoods where immigrants already struggle with affordability creates a paradox. South European and Asian cities are increasingly valued as models for Australian urbanism, but the creation of those spaces threatens less-resourced immigrant communities with displacement.

The Terrace House and the Tract Home: Changing Land Use in Melbourne

Most Australian cities sprawl out into the vast landscape like their counterparts in Nevada and California. Despite the country's British history, there has always been a desire to emulate American material success. While cities like Sydney and Adelaide began with row houses organized around high streets with shopping, they quickly lost most of their European-style density in the postwar period as the automobile became the main means of transportation and the landscape offered abundant space for suburban expansion. As more people moved off cattle stations and farms to work in manufacturing and clerical jobs, Australian cities constructed vast tracts of suburban freestanding homes, often stretching into fire-prone bushland.

In 1954 the chief urban planner of Los Angeles told a Melbourne audience that "our cities must be built around the necessity for the car," and they wholeheartedly agreed with him.[41] The subsidies that had previously served to fund trams and municipal rail were diverted to highway construction, even by Labor Party governments who represented more inner-city working-class constituents without automobiles.[42] The eminent Australian urbanist Graeme Davison observed that by the late 1960s, the Labor Party leader and future prime minister Gough Whitlam "realized that the so-called 'mortgage belt' was where the party's electoral future would be decided." In this sense, the proliferation of ranch homes with swimming pools into the parched outskirts of Adelaide or the river floodplains of Brisbane modeled the American trend of suburbanization as a new frontier that conquered nature through human ingenuity.[43]

Outward growth was based not just on consumer desires and cheap lending rates but also on the Aussie/American shared sense of manifest destiny. As the architect and critic Robin Boyd wrote in his 1960 satire *The Australian Ugliness*—a thorough takedown of the country's urban aesthetics and nouveau riche prosperity—suburbanization was a form of pioneering: "Less romantic than the first . . . since it involves factories and subdivisions instead of sheep, gold, and the limitless acreages of bush."[44] For Boyd, the landscape was already irrevocably marred in the 1960s with ill-planned housing mushrooming from every hilltop. As he wrote of Wollongong, near Sydney: "The suburbs' stealthy crawl like dry rot eating into the forest edge . . . more trees being bulldozed from yellow clay of the housing developments, as if the estate-agents and builders are determined to make all the coast match the now-barren, windswept sands of Botany Bay."[45] Yet, housing in this era was still a middle-class right, and Boyd's assessment of suburbs has always betrayed a hint of classism when it comes to the aesthetic critique. He deemed the pink lawn flamingos and plaster columns on brick bungalows in far-flung Sydney to be delusions of American prosperity: "The essence of Australian suburban life is unreality: frank and proud artificiality. . . . But it is the city's bastion against the bush." Suburbia was a defensive line against Australia's existential enemy: its harsh natural environment. It also played into the foundational myth of successful conquest, in which Europeans subdued a fearsome terrain that was often hostile to their health and well-being.

The industrial labor force in the cities of the 1960s was becoming more diverse, with new immigrants from Greece, Italy, and Yugoslavia. Australia took in 214,304 from Greece alone between 1947 and 1972, referring to these immigrants as "New Australians," a moniker never used for previous Anglo-Saxon or Irish migrants.[46] Anglo-Australians living in first-generation suburbs were often newly middle-class homeowners who, like their American counterparts, sought ethnically homogeneous neighborhoods to match their recent prosperity. First-generation Anglo (and Irish) homeowners who migrated to the suburbs were frequently replaced by Southern European migrants who took over their terrace homes in central locations, leading to anxiety about the deterioration of the inner city into immigrant "ghettos" in the 1960s.

By the end of the 1960s, Australia had become a destination not only for Southern Europeans but also for Asians previously barred by the White

Australia policy, a racist measure meant to halt the migration of Chinese immigrants in the early twentieth century that was not expunged from federal law until 1973. Both Southern European and Asian immigrants originally clustered in highly populated urban areas, and they often remade them into more thriving mixed-use neighborhoods. These districts, close to the commercial core, were soon filled with mom-and-pop restaurants, produce markets, variety stores, butchers, bakers, and delicatessens. This also had an impact on how people used downtowns. The center of Melbourne, uninhabited for a generation aside from government buildings and a dull stretch of office towers, saw a surge in cafés, starting with Italian espresso bars on Collins Street near the State Parliament, which led to it being dubbed "the Paris End" in the late 1950s. A generation later, Vietnamese and Chinese entrepreneurs added smaller-scale retail to central business districts, enlivening them for those wishing not only to work in the center but to live there full-time.

Immigrant patterns of land use—first Southern European and then Asian—helped to jump-start the process of inner-city gentrification, showing that central neighborhoods could once again be desirable. Graeme Davison observed how this completely realigned the Australian perception of space, creating bourgeois rather than working-class downtowns: "neighborhoods which were once 'dense' and 'overcrowded' now become 'compact' and 'fine-grained,' their unwelcome 'promiscuity' becomes an attractive 'sociability,' their threatening 'cosmopolitanism' a mature 'sophistication.'"[47] This also had much to do with the mellowing of ethnic prejudices as immigrant neighborhoods became more defined by first-generation Australians who opened businesses that combined their ancestral cultures with Australian characteristics: Italian bakeries with biscotti and lamington cake; Macedonian *burek* shops with heaps of sausage rolls for the midday rush of construction workers. These businesses often infused life into inner suburbs as well as the central business district, creating a cosmopolitan mélange that represented the "New Australia" to non-urbanites encountering widespread ethnic diversity for the first time.

In the sixty years since *The Australian Ugliness* was published, the outer suburbs have lost much of their appeal: the housing stock is older, new highways have not reduced traffic, and migration has challenged some white Australians' views of what made suburbia appealing. Yet, by the early twenty-first century, the new popularity of central urban neighborhoods had created problems: new housing is not being built at a sufficient rate, particularly not higher-density apartment buildings. Those seeking density can only find it in a small number of high rises built for Chinese investors and students in the busiest downtown locations, while neighborhoods directly abutting these towers are nearly flat: filled with row houses and the occasional six-unit apartment complex (dubbed "six-packs").[48]

Australians fetishize homeownership like their American counterparts. It is seen as a major step toward successful adulthood. Once, buying a fixer-upper in neglected urban neighborhoods was easy due to widespread economic growth and high wages, even for unskilled workers. Yet, by the 2000 Sydney Olympics, Australian cities were ascendant with new fortunes being made from real estate transactions.[49] As in other developed countries, real estate increasingly makes up an outsized portion of the economy.[50] Investment incentives, such as "negative gearing," which allows those who own multiple homes to write off losses from additional properties on their place of residence, creates a market in which people with means are encouraged to buy several properties while those without are left stranded with homeownership as a distant dream. The increased financialization of homeownership has created a middle class obsessed with rising home values (most Australian newspapers, including Melbourne's *The Age,* publish weekly real estate supplements that are one of their most widely read sections[51]). However, the increase in home values has also created anxiety among renters and those locked out of homeownership, creating fertile conditions for YIMBYism to attract Australian followers.

Having Your Toast and Eating it Too: Millennials in Melbourne

In 2017, the Australian real estate mogul Tim Gurner, a millennial, took his generation to task. He argued that Australia's housing affordability crisis is due to young people's failure to save their money: their future mortgage down payments are simply frittered away on "smashed avocado [toast] for $19 and four coffees at $4 each."[52] Aside from exhaustion with millionaires lecturing the middle class on thrift, aggrieved Australians were quick to point out that even forgoing tens of thousands of toasties would not produce the funds for a mortgage in big global cities.[53] Worse yet, it is exactly this age group that has seen unprecedented casualization of their work and stagnant pay despite Australia's robust economy and fortuitous geopolitical placement near rising China.

The existential anxiety of Melbourne's housing market is not just a generational tussle over how much new housing to put up and where it should go. Melbourne's downtown skyline is filled with steel pillars born aloft by cranes to make apartment towers with names like Prima Pearl, Eureka Tower, and Australia 108 (108 stories tall). Yet, few Melburnians are reassured that high-rises will help affordability because new units are often at the luxury end of the market and are clustered in the central business district, where taller height limits apply. Melbourne's central business district is viewed by many as an area solely for Chinese buyers, creating a parallel housing market. Australians are generally unaccustomed to apartments and prefer to live outside of the densest areas of the city. Local newspapers have reported[54] for years on the city's downtown being awash with Asian capital and new foreign residents: often students taking advantage of their parents' purchase while completing a degree. While many Australians are cognizant of their country's increasing dependence on Chinese funds, they also resent intrusion into an already tight real estate market, especially when stories of empty investment properties abound.[55] As in cities such as Vancouver, the families from abroad who live in downtowns are often not considered "real" residents, with commenters sometimes even questioning their kinship ties with terms like "astronaut families" and "parachute children": xenophobic put-downs similar to "anchor baby."[56]

While Australians have been accustomed to East Asian migration for two generations—with each major city containing multiple Chinese and Vietnamese neighborhoods—many previously viewed these immigrants as workers in low-wage jobs until the 1990s. The transition of Asian immigrants from an unseen labor force "behind the kitchen door" to front-and-center consumers of luxury goods (and the highest bidders at apartment auctions) has been shocking for older Australians. Billboards advertising real estate to Asian buyers have been defaced[57] with signs saying "Australia is not Asia," while "No Chinese Allowed" signs have been put up at Australian universities by neo-Nazi groups. The sense of white grievance is strong in rural areas but also in less-affluent suburbs. Indeed, the far-right Australian senator Pauline Hanson told Parliament in 1996 that "we are in danger of being swamped by Asians. They have their own culture and religion, form ghettos and do not assimilate"; yet she is from suburban Brisbane, not rural Queensland.[58] Just like suburban Trump voters, many people on the edges of the city feel they have been pushed out by foreigners with money, who are assisted by the immigration policies of progressives who care more about letting in new people than about supporting struggling compatriots.

The larger migration trend in Australian cities is similar to the trajectory in the United States: as inner-city neighborhoods have gentrified, outer suburbs have become comparably cheaper and more diverse. While the

Levittown ranch homes of Long Island are increasingly filled with Latino families, the 1960s bungalows of suburban Sydney and Melbourne are home to Sri Lankan, Sudanese, Vietnamese, and Afghan immigrants. Just between 2011 and 2016, the Melbourne suburb of Box Hill went from 26.7 percent people of Chinese ancestry to 35.4 percent.[59] Box Hill is an example of an area where a wave of relatively wealthy migrants from mainland China have successfully increased density by attracting overseas capital and changing zoning laws to allow taller buildings. More common are exurban neighborhoods, like Dandenong, Broadmeadows, and Sunshine, in which deteriorating suburban homes from the 1970s are being sold or rented to lower-income residents who face long commute times. Outer neighborhoods have also become zones where it is easier to place new social housing projects, to give grants for subsidized housing, or to temporarily settle refugees. This has led to an identity crisis for some of the older residents who moved to Melbourne's edges at the same time as diversity rose (or perhaps in response to the rise) within the city center in the 1970s and 1980s.

Outer suburbs are portrayed as both boring and violent. An article[60] about Melbourne's "ignored, discounted" western edges in the newspaper *The Age* was commented on by one reader who felt that "the only way to see the western suburbs is by flying over them, preferably at night." Antipathy toward far-flung suburbs comes from urbanites who tsk-tsk the life of strip malls and drive-throughs and, more ominously, from nativists who see them as not white enough. Starting in 2017, a central issue in Melbourne politics has been a full-blown moral panic around immigrant crime in the more affordable outer suburbs, where Sudanese gangs supposedly roam with impunity, harassing and beating their Australian neighbors.[61] Like the claim made by the US ambassador to the Netherlands that there are "no-go zones" in Dutch cities[62] where politicians are burned alive, the issue of immigrant crime in Melbourne is largely a fantasy despite some real issues with assimilation and joblessness.[63] Frequent alarmist headlines about African gangs prowling the streets of western Melbourne also ignore the very real concerns of immigrants themselves, who often live with little hope of upward mobility. Crime on the periphery of the city has racialized entire areas of Melbourne, such as the western suburb of Sunshine, leaving a permanent sense of stigma for new Australian residents who grow up there.[64] As one popular preacher said of these areas: "I think they [parents] need to pack them up and send them back—let them experience 3 to 6 months of real life in a war torn country. . . . It will teach them respect—they'll be begging their families to bring them back to Australia."[65] In this sense, the less dense edges of the city are viewed as places that are veering out of reach of the authorities as well as deviating from mainstream Australian culture.

Housing precarity in the United States and Australia can often become a moral judgment against nonowners. Those who rent are frequently assumed to be either unreliable sorts or those living in public housing towers. Tim Gurner's jibe about avocado toast and millennials draws on the prevailing logic that those who cannot lock down a mortgage by their thirties have done something wrong. Melbourne has not reached the full-blown housing disaster of San Francisco, where tremendous rents have forced working people to sleep in caravans or commute for three hours. It is far more a crisis of the middle class that is increasingly shut out of homeownership. Yet, little is being done to correct the problem. New buildings for renters owned by a single owner/manager are so uncommon that they have a special name, "build-to-rent," as if the concept were some kind of novel urban innovation that previous developers were unable to contemplate with the limited technologies of the past. However, as prices rise in Melbourne, the arithmetic is changing. Inner neighborhoods have started building almost 50 percent of their new homes as apartments, with increasing attention to small-footprint stores that can be reached without a car.[66]

The Last Bastion of Central Affordability: Melbourne's Footscray Neighborhood

Melbourne's charismatic streets of terrace homes that formerly housed Southern European immigrants and originally had only a backyard privy have been entirely gentrified. Houses often cost between one and three million Australian dollars. This means that many urbanites have been pushed to less-wealthy and more nonwhite suburbs. One such place is the suburb of Footscray, a mix of commercial, residential, and light industrial buildings clustered around a large Vietnamese and Chinese produce market. The neighborhood is contained within the administrative district of Maribyrnong and separated from Melbourne's central business district by a tributary of the city's major river, the Yarra, and a two-kilometer jumble of highways, railroad tracks, and a container port. One has to either take the train one stop to the west of the major regional station or navigate snarled truck traffic coming from the cargo terminal and a mass of rail crossings by bike or car.

For over thirty years, Footscray has been a bastion of affordability for Vietnamese, Indian, and Chinese immigrants, who make up nearly 30 percent of the population. More recently, its convenient train access has led to significant gentrification by younger people, particularly artists and those working in culture industries. As one low-income artist told me, "It makes a lot of sense because it is one of the few places with affordable accommodation and large former factory spaces that are appealing to artists." As in many places experiencing arts-based gentrification,[67] the climate of concentrated creativity—with bungalow backyards housing sculpture workshops and suburban white picket fences displaying handmade ads for poetry readings—has drawn a plethora of younger renters. The largest population group is twenty-five- to twenty-nine-year-olds,[68] and the youthful energy is palpable in the commercial main street where upstart galleries and performance spaces sit adjacent to discount laksa vendors and Filipino minimarts. At the same time, the proximity of this haven of affordability has not gone unnoticed by homebuyers. Just in the years 2017 and 2018, housing prices rose by over 20 percent in Footscray, sending the average cost of a three-bedroom home from $700,000 AUD to $940,000 AUD.[69]

Housing activists have mobilized in several ways to protect neighborhoods like Footscray both for their cultural amenities and for their affordability, but little can be done without expanding the existing housing stock. This includes providing newly built housing with affordability commitments from developers, protecting the numerous public housing sites in the suburb, and, potentially, expanding the stock of nonprofit state-financed social housing. On its face, this should be a fairly simple task, given the large number of garages, light manufacturing buildings, and underused parcels of land owned by the Victorian State Government. Yet, locals often feel that they have reached a saturation point when it comes to changes in the built environment, and they have resisted new development vociferously. Some of this has been promulgated by affordability activists themselves, who feel that new housing will exacerbate gentrification. Yet, densification activists have taken a different approach. They hope to retain Footscray's relative affordability, cultural diversity, and arts economy all while welcoming new residents and green-lighting more construction—a delicate balance that many locals, who are skeptical of property developers as a whole, are hesitant to endorse.

Five years ago, residents with backgrounds in urban planning started a group in Footscray inspired by American YIMBYism called YIMaBY: "Yes, In Maribyrnong's Backyard!" to address new construction. They eventually renamed it Housing AIM (Affordable, Inclusive, Maribyrnong) and started holding meetings, eventually attracting local council funding for community engagement events. Kate Breen, a co-founder, said that she was originally interested in making the group while reading online comments about new development. "People are recognizing that development is happening but not resulting in housing they can afford," she said. This was creating a sense of anger, but simultaneously many people were stopping projects that could also have been beneficial.

Breen was inspired to start the group while reading Facebook posts about plans to open a boardinghouse in the neighborhood, all of which were against it. Yet, reading through the posts she saw comments such as "[W]rong location but aren't we an inclusive community? Can't these people live somewhere?" This, she decided, was an ideal opening for "YIMBY type goals even when people were still saying no." As with many YIMBY groups, she felt that the average Australian clinging to housing affordability at the edge of the city was practicing wishful thinking, believing that development would never come to *their* backyards. YIMBYism, Breen believes, "needs to tell people that their neighborhoods *will* be developed. And they need to work out what a good outcome will be. Don't go in [with] anti-development as your banner. Figure out what you want. . . . Building nothing is not an option."

Housing AIM meetings were often held in a handsome central Maribyrnong office space over cups of tea and biscuits. There was a beguiling mix of urban planning jargon and affecting personal stories of single mums living in Footscray because of its affordability but now threatened by displacement. At one meeting, a woman said that her situation was even worse than that of social housing residents because she could not apply for state housing due to waiting times that can stretch for years, nor could she afford rent: "In some ways social housing residents . . . have won the lottery while single mothers, like me, are getting forced out," she said. Other meetings, which were well attended primarily by women, focused on how being an affordable neighborhood in a city experiencing a housing crisis was actually a curse: "[There is the] idea that housing in Maribyrnong is relatively affordable and that makes it less of an issue. . . . In fact, that makes it more important to protect it because people in this neighborhood really need it and can't afford to lose it," one attendee said. Many who were involved in these groups saw affordable housing as the last thing they had left and, without it, their lives would become unbearably precarious. At one meeting, an older man said: "It's important to communicate the essence of being on the precipice. . . . The moment a community is perceived as affordable in the current market is the end. . . . It won't be affordable anymore." Having lost well-paid work or experienced addiction, domestic violence, or separation, many low-income residents stated that their home, rented at below-market cost, was their only anchor in an increasingly unrecognizable and hostile city.

YIMBY groups in the Melbourne suburbs have taken a different approach than densification activists in other cities: they support new development as long as it has an affordability mandate. Thus, they are quite particular about what gets built. Much of this comes from working in a slightly different space than YIMBYs in London, San Francisco, or Boulder: they are protecting one of the city's last proximate working-class neighborhoods rather than demanding access to a wealthier neighborhood. Footscray housing activists have also moved to support novel public housing schemes that bring together disparate partners. They were instrumental in securing community support for eight locations on a Maribyrnong four-lane highway that will host fifty-eight movable small homes.[70] This project was widely objected to because the units will be made available to those experiencing homelessness—a classic NIMBY consternation. The small homes that the unhoused people will be given are subsidized through a special below-market contract called a "peppercorn lease," in this case an agreement between the state highway authority (VicRoads) and a nonprofit housing provider (Launch Housing). The agreement is not permanent because, for the time being, the state is merely lending the land for affordable housing in anticipation of taking it back for future road widening. Despite its temporary use, the project was ill regarded by neighbors who disliked the idea of low-income formerly homeless residents. Fear of those who had been homeless created significant backlash. As one resident put it in a guest editorial: "We believe that housing a large number of people in such close proximity, in such tiny spaces has potential to create and amplify social issues."[71]

Much of the work that Housing AIM did was to smooth the way for the project, explaining the need for housing for the economically vulnerable (particularly given that many facing homelessness in Victoria are older women who have suffered domestic violence[72]). After facing much skepticism, Breen said, "We were able to generate a bit of a community groundswell . . . more people to publicly put their hand up and go to council processes and to say, 'I'm actually here to support affordable housing and here is why.' We didn't have any 'buts.'" People got on board because the nonprofit organization shared the stories of those facing housing precarity, and local residents began to understand the extent of the crisis: they saw people like themselves. As one person working in the homelessness sector (not for the partner organization) said, "It's good that people are becoming more sympathetic and learning more about the crisis. . . . At the same time they also know how limited resources are. . . . They know this will be the 'model' homeless . . . the grandmas and such." That said, the project utilizes an easily replicated formula for quickly adding new housing stock: building on public land that is not being used. Researchers at the University of Melbourne have confirmed that many of these spaces are already available in prime locations. As in California, this land is frequently co-located with transit, delivering a double win of more housing and better access to mass transit. Indeed, using this "lazy land" could help to narrow the gap between Melbourne's plan to build 4,700 affordable housing units between 2017 and 2022 and the estimated need for 164,000 more homes.[73]

Melbourne's urban density activists have focused on traditionally vulnerable populations such as those with precarious housing, refugees, and aboriginal people, but they also are increasingly concerned with young people. "A lot of people my age are pretty much one gig away from not being able to make rent, and they are very worried about ever getting to settle somewhere permanently without getting priced out," an early twenties Footscray artist told me. Kate Breen confirmed that "for young people, homeownership is looking increasingly unlikely in any middle-ring suburb of an Australian city." Footscray, which is six kilometers from the city center, is one of the last nearby suburbs with good transit options with a weekly rent of under $400 AUD. However, Breen added that rents have not yet gotten to the level of unaffordability as American cities, which is exactly the concern. When Australia's millennial and Generation Z renters are suddenly confronted with a crisis of overall affordability and not just the impossibility of homeownership, then housing will truly become a matter of middle-class existential fear.

At a public forum sponsored by Housing AIM, in which Footscray residents told harrowing stories of their experiences with homelessness, Kate Breen passed out heavy stock paper with a cut-on-the-dotted-line drawing of a coffin. The coffin had a small window in its center and said: #everybodyshome. It came with an array of cut-out pets and furniture that people could fill their "home" with. The event mixed individuals describing their economic insecurity in the heart of one of the world's wealthiest cities with architects dissecting new housing proposals and teaching the audience what to look for when it comes to affordability mandates from local councils' negotiations with builders. For many young and low-income Australians, including those who attended the meeting, the development of new affordable housing is not coming fast enough. Their situation feels like the macabre joke of the meeting's conversational prop: a coffin waiting for them. Most of the speakers at the event emphasized their middle-classness until they were deprived of housing, and then they told heart-wrenching stories about their lives disintegrating, including one woman recounting her first night sleeping rough on a bench just two blocks from the home she had shared with an abusive partner.

Melbourne-based YIMBYs celebrate two facts that are often lamented: people still work overwhelmingly in the downtown and must commute to the center, and homeownership is decreasing. Most people are still credulous about urban density for those very reasons. Homeownership is the backbone of Australian middle-classness and the downtown is a place where people are forced to drive into during the chaos of rush hour traffic that they have little affinity for. Yet, for YIMBYs, the central business district maintains cohesion and a more vertical urban form while renting increases mobility and gives voice, on development issues, to those with different priorities than homeowners protecting their investments. More and more, it seems that a bit of generational stigma may be a useful organizing tool for avocado-toast eaters and working-class suburbanites to come together and develop a political identity based on renting. Like the United States—where many are increasingly willing to question the regressive home mortgage interest deduction tax credit that favors homeowners with no relief for the renting poor—Australia may be having a moment in which the supposed sacredness of homeownership is being rethought. YIMBYism plays an increasingly visible role in this conversation by giving people an alternative image of what urban life could look like beyond the patchwork of suburbs strung together by highways that currently defines Australian cities.

Brisbane: "Flat White Urbanism"

In YIMBY circles, the avocado toast insult was a turning point. By twinning lifestyle and lack of homeownership, it provided an easily subverted symbol. Indeed, many dedicated YIMBY activists have added an avocado emoji to their Twitter handles to show just where they stand on the debate. Lifestyle shaming was a particularly galvanizing taunt because cafés that serve avocado toast are emblematic of what densification activists want to see in their cities: "third places" where people can meet, work, and relax away from their shared or small apartments.[74] The sociability of coffee shops and brunch restaurants may not cut across class lines but, for YIMBYs, they are a much better start than single-family homes with gates and private backyards. In Australia, this shift has been particularly important because the service economy of cafés, bars, tourism, and performance spaces has grown exponentially in the past twenty years: by 2018 three out of four Australian workers worked in the service sector.[75] While "flat white urbanism"[76] has been disparaged by some as a hipster—and sometimes greenwashing—facade for real estate developers to use in order to encourage growth, many YIMBYs are content with it as an alluring piece of coffee-focused propaganda to get people out of car-dependent low-density suburbs.

There are dedicated YIMBY groups in Melbourne and Brisbane as well as affiliated housing organizations that support densification and new development in other Australian cities. Many of these groups also have environmental concerns. Cities like Adelaide and Melbourne have sprawled so far that they have endangered agricultural supply chains by taking over farmland, leaving entire regions without food sovereignty in the event of crises such as droughts (which are frequent).[77] What's more, out-of-control suburbanization has been a major risk factor for wildfires.[78] Despite the warnings of fire management officials, Australian cities have built out into the bush, where homes are threatened by intensive blazes such as those of 2019–2020 that destroyed over 16 million acres of land and hundreds of homes across the country.[79]

In Brisbane, the architect and urban consultant Natalie Rayment started the group Queensland YIMBY to encourage more development in her city. Brisbane has no shortage of growth, in her opinion, but a dearth of smart development. The city is semi-tropical, located around several bends in the eponymous river. It grew exponentially during the 1980s, often into low-lying areas at risk of flooding.[80] While the downtown has been filled in with office towers, the city remains dispersed. The region's characteristic house from one hundred years ago is "The Queenslander:" a Victorian cottage on stilts with a weather-beaten rusted roof of corrugated iron. This type of housing respected the challenging heat and flood-prone environment, while new construction has been less sensitive. Brisbane's horizontal growth has rolled out in every direction with single-family homes in suburbs reaching up and down Moreton Bay on the Coral Sea to the western hills of Flinders Peak. While the city continues to grow steadily with 50,000 new residents annually (with a population of 2.5 million in 2019),[81] few of those residents are moving to inner suburbs. Most settle for long commutes from sprawling satellite cities.

Rayment is encouraged by the Queensland State Government's belated recognition of density as a key challenge but feels that there are still a lot of cultural stumbling blocks. "Lots of people support the YIMBY philosophy until they don't," she said. Apartments mean lower property values to many Queenslanders, as well an imported lifestyle at odds with what they see as comfortable living. As in other Australian cities, the apartment is regarded as a form of housing stock primarily for immigrants and unsuitable for the native born. As a Brisbane architect told me, "I keep trying to convince clients to subdivide their lots and build townhouses, but they won't do it despite the profit potential because they can't imagine not living in a 'real home.' . . . So when you introduce the idea of apartments 'stacked up on top of each other' . . . they just don't see that as a place to live."

Rayment, in her work as a YIMBY organizer, has attempted to make new development of apartments more palatable to people who grew up in single-family homes. Yet, she finds that task immensely difficult. In her advocacy work, she stresses that getting people comfortable even with small two- or three-story apartment buildings can be a challenge. "People go to the nth degree" when it comes to this issue, she said: "they want 3D shadow renderings even on short buildings." While many people do not live surrounded by traditional "timber 'n' tin" Queenslander houses, they are still skeptical of demolishing single-family homes to create density in ways that YIMBYs favor.

Despite the fact that Brisbane has seen an economic boon from tourism in the nearby Gold Coast and the internationalization of property markets, many people hold on to their sense that more housing will fundamentally challenge people's sense of community and their ability to raise their families. As one resident told a local newspaper in reference to a new apartment building: "The current plan of 49 units with access via the very short dead-end Nuttall St into an already very congested Lytton Rd beggars belief. Do we have to wait until a child is injured (at the nearby school crossing) or worse?"[82] Yet, despite this near hysteria, the site is a vacant lot in a mixed commercial and residential area in the heart of the city: the Bulimba neighborhood that juts into the Brisbane River like a mini-peninsula. This viewpoint also envisions a future of car use alone despite the fact that Bulimba has a rapid ferry service eight blocks from the development site as well as a bus stop with four routes just a block away. The objection is akin to a Brooklynite arguing that fifty apartments is something that should only be built in Manhattan.

Rayment and other density advocates in Brisbane are not surprised by opposition, even to modest proposals for more development. Oftentimes those fighting against apartments are the beneficiaries of living in the city's sweet spot between the Brisbane central business district and the outer suburbs farther from the river. People who live in neighborhoods like West End, Milton, and Albion have houses with driveways, but they also have access to city buses. They can easily reach the downtown and its charismatic river

walk jammed with tourists, or they can enjoy the quiet of sparsely populated neighborhoods. When it comes to sharing their space with others, they
show little interest. "One of the big issues is getting people behind density
that is not high-rises," Rayment said. Her group advocates to local councils
to approve small apartment buildings and duplexes in desirable "missing
middle" neighborhoods, but it is these buildings that people have the most
issues with. "Let high-rises happen but leave the rest the hell alone," is what
Rayment said of Brisburnians. She reiterated that many see apartments as
something for foreign buyers and feel that this type of dwelling should be
confined to the heart of the city.

It is relatively common in Australian cities to believe that the central business district can be built up ad infinitum but vernacular attempts to increase
density—which do not involve construction cranes—are more destructive.
Part of this thinking comes from the divide between the downtown as a
purely work and entertainment space and inner suburbs as neighborhoods
where each house has a history. Although the central business district was
indeed a mixed-use district before World War II, it lost that feeling with a
period of urban renewal that closely aligns with the American experience
(1950s to 1980s). Many believe that if new immigrants or anyone else wants
to do the "peculiar thing" of moving to the downtown, let them, and build
as many high-rises as they want. However, if they complain about the lack
of inner-suburban housing stock, they are out of line. The Brisbane architect
Greg Vann explained this to me as a particularly interesting paradox because
many suburbanites feel left behind, with much of the Queensland tax revenue going to fund transportation, leisure spaces, and infrastructure exclusively in inner-city Brisbane. In this sense, business districts with skyscrapers
or former industrial areas are seen as sacrifice areas where abundant amounts
of housing can be located, but once suburban taxpayers are asked to fund
the transport, parks, and other amenities that make these neighborhoods
viable they balk. Part of this is also a class issue: newly built apartments in
the center are not cheap (they are the lowest rate of any major Australian
city but still cost $500 AUD/week in rent for a two-bedroom apartment).[83]
Those living in the outer suburbs are frequently indignant that they will
have to help pay for inner-city improvements they will not live near and
will seldom visit.

Fractured municipal governance, like in Melbourne, has also been a
challenge. Local councils control building approval and—in lieu of more-
centralized city government—they are more likely to capitulate to NIMBYistic
demands. As soon as an application is advertised, communities can lodge an

objection and go to court for about a thousand dollars. Rayment is convinced that much of this comes from a kind of initial shock rather than careful contemplation of the plans. "People get spooked by giant announcement signs," she notes, and the mandatory public announcements with architectural renderings serve as a rallying point for property owners. As in the United States, local governance is good for those who seek to stop development and affordable housing. It is also, often, a tug-of-war between more-centralized regional government, of the state of Queensland, seeking to enact a plan to build up housing stock and local municipalities that fight to stop construction or displace it elsewhere. Cities like Brisbane are particularly fraught examples because they must answer calls to address affordability but also need to prepare for the more existential threats of climate change, most notably sea rise and bushfires. Adhering to the status quo of suburban development is not only irresponsible but dangerous, as new homes are built in urban floodplains, coastal areas exposed to sea rise, or the exurban periphery where nearby bushland makes fires a growing threat. Densification, as unpalatable as it is to many residents, may be the only way for the city to consolidate risk.

International Densification and the YIMBY Brand

The international diffusion of YIMBY groups may have more to do with an opportune moment to address housing affordability than a truly transnational network of activists. While groups in Australia, the United Kingdom, and the United States attend some of the same conferences and share materials and strategies online, they address fundamentally local issues, supporting individual projects. All of those involved abroad spoke about not just the simplicity of the idea of collective responsibility for the broader "backyard" but also the San Francisco origins of the movement. The Bay Area connection gave ideas about density a new flair of tech-oriented practicality but also communicated the urgency of the issue. All of the international organizers said that San Francisco's housing crisis was much more pressing than their own and, seeing things go so wrong there, lent a sense of immediacy to their organizational efforts. "All you need to do is mention San Francisco and people listen," a Melbourne participant said.

At the same time, other longtime affordability activists found the movement to be too name-based and sometimes imbued with the same kind of tech "solutionism" that Silicon Valley app engineers use when designing tools to address social problems.[84] "I really think it's all in the name, and that's the big problem," a housing activist who has worked on maintaining and expanding social housing in London said. She did not believe that YIMBYs were the naive "dupes"[85] of the real estate industry, just that "they've made a good slogan, . . . taken hold of some pretty commonsense ideas, gotten their brand around, . . . and what's next? I just don't see what is next and I'm not sure they do either." However, YIMBYs abroad and in the United States defended both their lack of ideological guidelines for members and their loose mission, most often describing their supporters as renters and younger people rather than those struggling financially. Reframing densification as a means to create urban happiness focuses on mobility and lifestyle rather than class, wagering that these issues may seem more inclusive.

Indeed, many densification activists abroad have strategically avoided a class-based framing because of past failures to mobilize people around preserving social housing or extending housing subsidies. "More housing for poor people or cheaper housing for poor people never really worked. . . . Margaret Thatcher knew that and that's how she won so big with council house privatization," an activist from Manchester told me. Yet, densification activists often feel that they can sneak in a progressive policy that helps the most precarious first while discussing design and zoning. In Melbourne's Footscray neighborhood this was certainly the case, and it was generally truer of international YIMBY groups than American chapters. Perhaps this is not just because Americans tend to trust the free markets more but also because British, Australian, and Swedish cities have more social housing, which has fared better in terms of providing safe, comfortable lodging than in the United States.

While international YIMBY groups are still far too small to begin thinking about running their own candidates for office or using housing as part of a larger political platform, they do seek to prod local governments into action. In this sense, the movement—despite what it sometimes claims—is a means not to disempower "high-handed" urban planners but rather to redirect their regulatory efforts. Instead of blocking construction with zoning, the groups hope that planners will take a more active role in shaping the carrying capacity of each neighborhood. While they seek to represent renters, they also want to put pressure on state governments to fund new mass transit. In countries like the United States and Australia, regional trains and urban trams and buses have been ignored for generations, but new interest from more-affluent young urbanites has created intense pressure on elected officials. In 2018, the premier (governor) of Victoria ran and won on a platform of creating new rail lines in Melbourne as his key reelection issue, committing the city to finally build a circle line that connects outer suburbs to each other as well as to the center. Likewise, in the United Kingdom, much of the rail system has been renationalized to acknowledge the mass subsidies provided by the state and to lower consumer costs. The relationship between density activists and the state is complex, but overall, YIMBY groups hope to interject their own priorities into institutions either as policy or through elected members in order to keep their goals alive and well for years to come.

In many international cities, housing affordability has also become the means to measure the competence of the state to address complex issues. Activists see themselves as standing by to see if market-based solutions will yield results and are prepared for more radical means if they are disappointed. "For now, I say go the developer route, but who knows? One day we may have the army building homes for bushfires or something else," one Melbourne activist told me, in reference to the devastating 2019–2020 fires. Creating more dense housing at affordable rental or mortgage prices seems to be a threshold responsibility for governments solving twenty-first-century problems. Indeed, because the issue is so perennial, many fret that if it cannot be addressed, then governments have no chance of tackling more existential urban issues such as water scarcity, higher temperatures, or rising sea levels. Yet, many YIMBYs feel that if they can get a jump start on densification now, as a means to expand the housing stock and control prices, this infrastructure will help to solve future problems: especially environmental threats posed by climate change that may necessitate a contraction of existing cities in order to maintain habitability.

Conclusion

Density in Times of Plague

In August of 2020, a woman in a white suit jacket and a man in a blue blazer sat soberly in their Missouri living room speaking virtually to the Republican National Convention in support of President Donald Trump's reelection. "What you saw happen to us could just have easily have happened to any of you who are watching from quiet neighborhoods around our country," the woman, Patricia McCloskey, said. Her husband, Mark McCloskey, continued recounting how an "out-of-control mob" of "Marxist" "revolutionary" activists surrounded their home while they protected it with firearms. Patricia McCloskey then added a surprising urban planning non sequitur:

> They're not satisfied with spreading the chaos and violence into our communities. They want to abolish the suburbs altogether by ending single-family home zoning. This forced rezoning would bring crime, lawlessness, and low-quality apartments into now thriving suburban neighborhoods.[1]

The activists marching outside of the McCloskeys' Saint Louis mansion were taking part in a Black Lives Matter protest, but the couple used their national spotlight to denounce higher-density development. For YIMBY activists, this was shocking but not surprising. It tied together what they have been saying for nearly ten years: NIMBY objections to building apartments are connected to racial fears, unwillingness to share resources, and an ugly history of equating lower-income urbanites with crime and lawlessness. This is particularly true in Saint Louis, one of America's most racially and economically divided cities, with an ugly history of suburban-ization as an answer to growing inequality.[2] The McCloskeys' rabid defense of their house—a seventeen-room Italian palazzo revival[3]—illustrates the disturbing link between those who support "stand your ground" laws and single-family-home zoning.

The McCloskeys' beliefs are emblematic of what YIMBYs say they are up against when it comes to changing zoning codes, densifying neighbor-hoods, and expanding the stock of affordable housing in American cities. This is not to say that the McCloskeys represent the mainstream, but they are closer to other more moderate defenders of low-density suburbia than one would think upon first glance. Like other NIMBYs, the McCloskeys resort to calling those in favor of multifamily housing radical *sans-culottes* intent on destroying all norms of private property. In reality, ending single-family zoning is largely in line with the interests of real estate developers, store owners, and many others. The barriers to creating more compact cities are not just technical; they are ideological and deeply ingrained at that.

In the summer of 2020, advocates for density had a far more existential crisis on their hands: the stigmatization of density due to the still-raging coronavirus.[4] Cities once again were riven with fear. Some Americans were worried that protest movements would bring crime and disorder, but they were in the minority.[5] The majority were apprehensive about sharing cities with others for epidemiological reasons. A new kind of NIMBYism has arisen not because of crowded schools, traffic, and lack of parking but due to fears of human proximity spreading the deadly microbes that cause COVID-19. These fears were also present in other places besides the United States where people were navigating new urban fears. One candidate in Melbourne's 2020 council elections wrote in her main pitch to voters: "The coronavirus pandemic has proven beyond doubt that high rise and dense populations are not safe and not healthy . . . despite residents' opposition and evidence in support of low density living, free standing homes, trees and vegetation keep disappearing."[6] If, as YIMBYs are fond of saying, density is destiny then newly upzoned cities are potentially in trouble.

Little actual science backs up new concerns around housing density and the spread of the coronavirus.[7] Naturally, someone living in Idaho with few neighbors will be safer than an apartment dweller in downtown Boston, but the majority of Americans live in suburbs, not rural ranches. They still need to buy groceries, see the doctor, and, if they cannot work from home, go to their jobs, making contamination risk more evenly distributed between cities and suburbs.[8] What's more, wealthy and highly populated cities like San Francisco, Seattle, and Denver are often the places that have the best disease tracking infrastructure and local healthcare systems. However, this has not stopped many from proclaiming an "end to the city" or a rebirth of suburban life.[9] Some of this is undoubtedly true: people working from home want larger spaces, backyards, and distance from their neighbors during a pandemic.[10] These desires also mesh with ongoing trends of flexible work hours, casualization of the workforce, and telecommuting.[11] However, for density activists, the COVID-19 pandemic has not been a colossal setback but a new opportunity.

The loneliness of housebound people "sheltering in place" during the coronavirus pandemic reinforced the need to create stimulating, attractive, and supportive neighborhoods. As people were locked into their homes and their immediate neighborhoods for months, the quality of those environments came under renewed scrutiny.[12] Many cities began to expand their bike paths and exercise areas.[13] In cities like Melbourne, where residents were confined to one-hour walks within five kilometers of their homes for nearly three months during a second outbreak of the virus, citizens petitioned for more cycling infrastructure[14] as well as increased recreational spaces in exurban areas. As YIMBYs have long argued, in most cities it is precisely the wealthy neighborhoods (where homeowners are most reticent about adding new residents) that have the best parks and other recreational opportunities in close proximity. New sprawling suburbs are often ill equipped for alternative transit and underendowed with communal green spaces. These disparities became even more glaring during the coronavirus pandemic when people were locked into the areas surrounding their homes without the broader set of resources of the city as a whole.

On a more sociological level, the coronavirus pandemic has called into question ideas about cohabiting space and neighborliness.[15] Many YIMBYs push the notion that density is not just about creating affordability but about reviving a lost ethos of shared space, community connections, and mutual aid. While these values may be a bit quixotic when attached to the simple construction of new apartments, the pandemic has shown the need for them: from getting groceries for elderly residents, to distributing homemade facemasks, or even the solidarity of applauding medical workers from a balcony at 7:00 p.m. YIMBYs may have lofty goals for cities that seem idealistic, and frankly rather bourgeois—when most people are just trying to make rent or hold on to their mortgage—but they also are fundamentally optimistic about urbanites' ability to collectively solve problems rather than run away to a bunker in Montana when things get tough. There is also some hope that the coronavirus crisis will produce larger outlays of funding from the federal government that, given the political will, can be directed into socially purposeful economic stimulus such as a green jobs program, mass transit infrastructure, or the construction of subsidized high-density housing.

The epidemiological and financial crises of COVID-19 have also refocused attention on housing affordability. The fallout from the pandemic may produce a mortgage default crisis like the one precipitated by the 2008 financial crash. Indeed, 20 percent of renters in Los Angeles struggled to pay on time during the pandemic,[16] and at one point in early 2021, 19 percent of renters nationally were behind on payments.[17] Unlike in the 2008 crisis, it will be much harder for fiscal conservatives to blame those with precarious housing for their misfortune by claiming that they reached beyond their means. The newly vulnerable will include everyone who worked in the tourism and hospitality industries: thousands of former flight attendants, waiters, and museum workers will face eviction. If they seize the moment, they will be able to form a block of endangered residents who concretely demonstrate that the housing crisis has jumped scales from largely affecting the poor to now jeopardizing the middle class (a classic YIMBY talking point). With adequate organizing, the newly housing precarious (but formerly middle class) may further add to the ranks of YIMBY activists, potentially pushing for similar goals of more housing construction. However, in this schema, the role of subsidized and even public housing may be far greater than density activists campaigned for in the past if private markets deteriorate.[18]

For years, housing activists of both the anti-gentrification and the YIMBY variety tried to dramatize how rising rents were pricing out working-class people. San Francisco was the prototypical example: while tech workers streamed in, janitors, waiters, cops, and schoolteachers were forced out. Workers who ran the basic services of the Bay Area still performed their jobs, but they were severed from the neighborhoods they provided for, compelled to become "super-commuters" as the region's center and periphery became segmented by class.[19] Now, with the experience of the pandemic, a new language has been deployed to describe what they do and its social importance: they are essential workers.

Providing more affordable housing to essential workers can be a first step in recognizing their labor, rather than just clapping, congratulating them at the checkout counter, and writing gushing editorials. Nurses, supermarket workers, ambulance drivers, and many others must be able to live in the communities they serve—not because it enables them to still go to work when there is an emergency but because it recognizes them as indispensable members of the community who cannot be asked to perform some of the most taxing jobs while also struggling to afford housing, often far away from their job sites.[20] Obviously, affordable housing is only one aspect of treating these workers with the respect they deserve. Increasing wages would be both more effective and long overdue. However, co-locating essential workers close to their workplaces would say a lot about what kind of cities we want to live in, and it would be a small but important step in dismantling the class divisions that have emerged within urban spaces. The concept of the essential worker also dramatizes arguments about neighborhood economic diversity that housing activists have been making for decades: in order to share a collective future, people of different incomes must live close enough together to recognize that they are part of a shared community.

Density as Destiny

Throughout this book, I have argued that urban density activism is providing a new template for the broader fight to create affordable housing in American cities. It has also been suggested that YIMBY groups are promoting a new framing within the housing debate: concentrating on supply-side mechanisms, working with (not against) developers, and emphasizing the rights of middle-class newcomers to wealthy cities. These activists contend that middle-class urbanites should pressure wealthier neighborhoods to accept new residents while allowing working-class neighborhoods to maintain autonomous organizations that preserve low-income communities and safeguard them against gentrification. They uphold the legitimacy of their separate cause insisting that different socioeconomic spheres of the city can also have separate forms of activism. They also believe that American cities have reached a stage of inequality that has hollowed out the middle class, making their lives more similar to working-class precarity despite steady incomes, college degrees, and intergenerational wealth transfers.

YIMBYism, while born in San Francisco, has attained global reach. It has had political successes as well as significant backlash, not just from those in expensive homes afraid of "radicals" seeking to "abolish the suburbs," but much more substantiated attacks from communities of color and grassroots activist groups. Municipal YIMBY groups have been accused of activist astroturfing, misrepresenting the major issue as one of construction alone, and interloping into low-income communities. They have been labeled as a Trojan horse for developers who endanger the environment and challenge historic preservation. At the same time, YIMBYism has been extremely successful in making density into a mainstream issue no longer communicated in architecture schools alone. Through canny slogans and wry memes, ideas like "build more of everything" and "the missing middle" have gone from the hinterlands of wonky urbanist thought to the center of debates about municipal progress. They have spurred immediate action on the part of new allies like In God's Backyard: a group of churches building affordable housing on their property. While this activism has succeeded in educating a large audience about city planning through community meetings, online forums, and local politics, it is still very much a technocratic insider's game for the highly educated. Yet, this specialization has brought impressive legislative successes such as the long-awaited jettisoning of single-family zoning in some American cities,—most notably Minneapolis, which became the first city to entirely eliminate it in 2019.

In the preceding chapters, I have suggested that YIMBY activism is meeting a certain ideological and rhetorical demand that was previously underserved. Members are dissatisfied with income inequality in cities, but for the most part, they pursue capitalist solutions to the housing crisis. They see a state role for transit, coordination of growth, and managing environmental resources, but they eschew the idea that local or state government will become large-scale landlords or developers. Depending on whom one asks, YIMBYs are either underambitious in their vision of decommodifying the housing market or clear-eyed about what is possible in the current moment of lackluster governance at the state and national level.

Given the challenges of housing affordability exacerbated by the economic impact of the coronavirus pandemic, gross inequality, and damage from hurricanes, wildfires, and other climate-change-related events, the moderation of the YIMBY movement may prove to be its greatest vulnerability. At a moment when housing policy should be rethought in order to deal with incomparable threats, the centrist free-market approach of simply allowing upzoning and more building permits may be useful but inconsequential. More troublingly, this strategy may miss out on using a political opportunity[21] that would allow far more long-sighted control of the built environment, restructuring the ability of state and federal government to take advantage of a crisis to buttress climate change risks and decommodifying housing. Indeed, given the level of national trauma associated with imperiled housing—from mass dislocations of fires like the Camp Fire in California (2018) or Hurricane Maria (2017) in Puerto Rico—Americans may be ready to rethink zoning, single-family homes, and even private ownership if it means gaining more security. In this sense, YIMBYs, while not necessarily opposed to pioneering housing solutions, could be forfeiting the moral authority and political will of the moment to create measures like community land trusts, co-ops, and public housing. Given their internal conflicts between market-based and regulatory impulses, they may also have trouble summoning the will to call for a strong state role in mandating density, including using eminent domain, tearing down exurban areas, and building new social housing.

Downsizing the City

The densification of American cities has been promoted as a means to make housing affordable and to allow more people to live in successful neighborhoods. It stresses that places with good transit, beautiful streets filled with interesting architecture, and abundant parks are hard to come by and must remain open to new residents. The subtext is that cities should stop building greenfield suburbia because these areas expand the city beyond reasonable boundaries, overtaxing municipal services and necessitating lengthy commutes for the "privilege" of living in boring and often shoddily built subdivisions. Given enough accrued political power, densification activists would make the creation of new sprawl extremely difficult, and they would attempt to pack in more housing for all except the most far-flung neighborhoods. Many would like to see cities shrink down from their existing boundaries in order to concentrate growth on places with mass transit and some agglomerated services (stores, hospitals, schools, and entertainment facilities). However, cities may need to reduce their size for more pressing reasons.

Cities that have stretched out along coastlines or crept up mountainsides are in grave danger of becoming victims of climate change. Each year the California wildfire season lasts longer into autumn and incinerates more land, often very close to cities. In 2019, record-breaking conflagrations destroyed homes in central Los Angeles, even reaching the doorstep of the Getty Museum.[22] In 2020, those fires became still worse, carpeting the entire American West in smoke and soot. Urban areas near forests that have experienced more drought and higher temperatures must rethink their development pattern. No more can they allow homes to be built up mountaintops with "fingers" of forest between them. Similarly, coastal cities like Miami, Baltimore, and New Orleans, face ever more fearsome storms that bring destructive flood waters due to rising sea levels. These cities, and many more, must rethink their designation of floodplains as well as consider how many times residents should be allowed to rebuild their beachfront houses with federal and state financial assistance. Already, insurance companies are stepping in where the government has failed to respond, supplying an actuarial assessment of climate change while many American politicians dither and deny.[23] The concept of managed retreat is gaining traction to protect cities from the ocean[24] but it may also have the positive effect of spurring densification.

As cities face the idea of downsizing, for both economic and environmental reasons—such as in Detroit—the prospect of increased regional inequality grows. What if the Sunbelt, which attracted so many people in the past half century, starts to rapidly depopulate due to higher temperatures, drought, and flooding? Where will these people be rehoused, and will it provoke a new form of regionalism in which wealthier cities effectively close their doors to American climate refugees? In Paolo Bacigalupi's dystopian novel *The Water Knife*, western states mobilize militias to fight each other over the water rights of the Colorado River while turning away impoverished and thirsty Texans fleeing from their overheated cities. The science fiction story contains more than a kernel of truth as cities face very different climate futures and the possibility of expansion and contraction of entire regions has entered the popular conversation.[25] This future also gets at the heart of saying "yes" to the city: will urbanites in more temperate places have the solidarity necessary to let in millions of new residents, or will they invent derisive regional monikers and tell them to beat it?[26]

At the same time as climate change forecasts have led to widespread pessimism about the future of American cities and the possibilities of sharing scarce resources, some activists see this moment as potentially transformative. By viewing resources as finite and bound by geographic realities rather than arbitrary political borders, policymakers may have to finally grapple with long-deferred regional issues. Housing will, of course, be on the top of that list. YIMBY activists hope that the climate crisis will finally create regional plans for providing housing that promote non-carbon-based mobility, higher-density housing, and mixed-use neighborhoods. The so-called twenty-minute city, in which people live within twenty-minute commutes using alternative or mass transit, is a true possibility with more condensed urban footprints.[27] At the same time, it will take government intervention that minimizes the role of private developers and potentially provokes the ire of cost-cutting libertarians as well as small-government conservatives concerned with overreach. This new reality will fracture the existing coalition of density activists attracted to the YIMBY movement, but it may add new allies from larger environmentalist groups.

While YIMBY activism has, until now, focused on middle-classness (and its imperiled status in the New Gilded Age),[28] its future may have to move on from the creation of successful neighborhoods to the promotion of a decarbonized planet. The technocratic solutions offered by YIMBYism that focus on public-private options led by for-profit developers is underwhelmingly ambitious in an era of such rapid and alarming changes to the environment and American governance. However, this does not mean that the movement's future is in jeopardy. Far from it. Instead, teaching people how to live together—efficiently, compromising between self-interest and community well-being, and striving to create realistic urban policy—is more important than ever. Density activists use the neighborhood and city as a social and political laboratory for broader changes, activating the previously complacent to speak up. If they continue to do so, they may indeed build a political coalition around urban planning issues. This new party will be wonky and detail oriented. It will be less grassroots and more technocratic. Yet, it also might reintroduce an appreciation for expertise into debates about urban policy rather than raw emotion and simply saying "no."

METHODOLOGICAL APPENDIX

Much has been written about the history of Not in My Backyard thinking in urban planning and urban history. Many would argue that the term has become hollow from overuse. However, as a cultural sociologist interested in how people draw on urban forms to discuss contemporary politics, I am not one of those people. I believe that the epithet NIMBY still carries a stinging resonance for those whom it is directed at. That was a major reason that I was drawn to the housing movement of YIMBYism, organized as a rebuke to homeowners who fought against growth in their neighborhoods. This book began in 2016 with a media analysis of the proliferation of the word "YIMBY" in an attempt to determine what people meant by it and how it helped them shape new kinds of activism. I quickly discovered that the prodigious amount of information available on social media, newspapers, city council minutes, and blogs was useful but did not fully express why the movement has grown so quickly or why participants found it so different from housing affordability campaigns of the past. For this reason, the book draws on four varieties of data that are set in conversation with each other to understand what contemporary density activism is and the legacies of land use that it responds to: I use social media data and online conversations about development, ethnographic observation of activist meetings, archival research on municipal history, and—most of all—sixty-five in-depth interviews with YIMBY activists in sixteen cities spread over five countries.

The book examines the Yes in My Backyard movement as a distinctly middle-class urban social movement that has formed dozens of independent groups in the United States in the past ten years. Broadly, these groups fight for housing affordability in the same way that other urban activists have for decades. However, unlike anti-gentrification groups, they are determinedly pro-growth and they are less interested in preserving, or creating, public housing. I show how YIMBY groups became vocal advocates for compact metropolises and mixed-use (residential and commercial) development using data from over five dozen interviews with housing activists in US,

British, Canadian, Swedish, and Australian cities. The interviews were conducted from 2017 to 2020, using YIMBY organization websites, Facebook pages, newspaper articles, in-person and online meetings, and Twitter accounts for recruitment. The informants were from a variety of housing groups focused on renters, and they embodied an ideological range from socialist to libertarian. For the most part, YIMBYs were highly educated professionals, and the vast majority interviewed for the project were millennials (born between 1980 and 2000). Those who were not millennials stated that the issue of housing is often framed as a generational divide because of the importance of dramatizing what the future city should look like. Of the YIMBY participants interviewed, 29 percent had formal training in urban planning or architecture. Every YIMBY activist interviewed had attended university and many had graduate degrees, confirming a general lack of class diversity within the movement.

Long Format Interviews

Members of YIMBY groups were recruited using a snowball sampling methodology: asking interviewees to recruit further participants. However, I attempted to control for sampling that emphasized agreement and friendship among group members by having participants suggest someone they had encountered with very different views from their own. This often included people that they had disagreed with online within housing affordability discussions specific to their city or neighborhood. I also sought to broaden the study away from the cities that are the focus of chapters (Austin, Boulder, San Francisco, and Melbourne) by speaking with YIMBYs in other cities in order to strip away some of the place-specific factors that informants often concentrated on. These interviews frequently lasted for over an hour and used a semi-structured technique that covered key issues such as the participants' stance on affordable housing, zoning reform, and activist tactics, while leaving space for them to bring up their own favorite topics. Often this created some fortuitous surprises, such as when many of my UK informants were excited to talk about the history and future of the London greenbelt and conflicts between housing activists and environmentalists without knowing that this was a major interest of mine and the focus of chapter 3 on Boulder, Colorado.

Another means of understanding local development pressures outside of the YIMBY narrative was a smaller sample of homeowners and anti-growth activists whom I interviewed in five American cities (Austin, Boston,

Denver, San Francisco, and New York). This sample of twenty-one members of neighborhood groups who oppose new housing construction was useful in reconstructing recent debates over specific proposed apartment buildings as well as teasing out some of the online rancor that developed around issues that YIMBY groups were active in. These participants were recruited, in the five American cities, by contacting people from websites of homeowners' associations or anti-growth groups, via Twitter or from community meetings. Most often, interviewees coalesced around specific permitting processes (zoning approval) or local referendums on growth.

Neighborhood groups have a long history in the United States, where they often start as social networks organized by email list servers to create a greater sense of community. However, they frequently take up activist causes, using their membership to appeal to the local planning board or city council. These groups most frequently are formed to protect home values or environmental quality, or to limit traffic. Some of these groups also may sponsor a neighborhood watch that patrols local streets and liaisons with the police. This smaller subset of activists interviewed for this book were always homeowners and most were over the age of fifty. The majority subscribed to the generational view of housing density: saying they saw larger buildings as out of character with their communities. They worried apartments could potentially bring new residents who did not "share the neighborhood's values" or were not "invested in the upkeep of their properties." For all interviews, original names are used, given that many of the activists are identifiable and have very active social media profiles. In the cases in which informants did not want to be named, they are simply referred to in general terms rather than using a pseudonym.

Urban Archives

YIMBY activism is quite a new phenomenon: at less than ten years old, it is an example of a rapidly growing social movement propelled by social media. Its catapulting from digital spaces to local organizing in multiple American cities and then to several (mostly) Anglophone countries shows the speed of online organizing. However, in every location where groups were formed, densification activists responded to local conditions, particularly laws and municipal practices that made the construction of multifamily dwellings more difficult than building single-family homes. In order to capture the historical trends that were being reacted to, I drew on secondary sources as well as archival data from Australia, the United Kingdom, and the United

States. To assemble this data I enlisted research assistants to comb through planning board and city council reports, internal municipal documents on growth and housing, and newspaper accounts of construction controversies. Archival sources were utilized the most systematically to explain the construction of Boulder's greenbelt and to illustrate the no-growth trend in that city that began in the late 1960s. Chapter 3 not only uses hundreds of archival documents to show the long history of aversion to population growth, but it also draws on numerous oral history accounts of how this sentiment was codified into local laws.

Social Media Data

YIMBYism got its start in the San Francisco Bay Area. It responds to the influence of the tech industry in that region, while many of the activists in local chapters work in the same sector. Many seek to mitigate the influence of their employers (on property markets), while drawing on social media marketing practices to popularize their activist cause. Organizing occurs through Facebook groups, and debates are held on Twitter, Reddit, and other platforms. For this book, I examined more than 2,000 individual posts (and their responses) related to the YIMBY movement while also collecting 238 articles from local and national journalism sources on density activism. Using a team of research assistants, I coded tweets based on their theme (community opposition to apartments, missing-middle densification, parking, transit, and gentrification).

I also used online data as a means to recruit interview subjects. Reviewing members' substantial online presences before speaking with them was a useful tool to hone my questions and to get a base sense of their opinions on crucial topics. It also allowed me to track conflicting ideologies within the movement—such as how much affordable housing should be contained within new construction ventures—in real time and to follow disputes. Most of all, this gave me the ability to track developments in the United States over a three-year period while I taught sociology classes in Melbourne, Australia. Being "away from the action" was a logistical challenge that made scheduling my interviews during frequent trips to the United States tricky, but it also gave me the quintessential experience of YIMBY activism: as an ongoing war over policy details fleshed out on Twitter. At first this seemed ethereal to me. Yet, as I came to know many of those involved in online debate on a daily basis, it enriched my data as well as converted me from an ethnographer bent on being present in physical space to one who recognizes intense depth in the intricate arguments people have about urban spaces on social media. The complementary relationship between interviews and social media data allowed me to track controversies as they arose and to use a longitudinal approach to the development of the activist groups that better conveys how they matured.

Participant Observation of Housing Affordability Organizers

Given the international scope of this project and the presence of so many density activists scattered across the United States, it was not possible to create a multi-sited ethnography that would do justice to each location. Rather, I attended meetings in the United States, but the majority of the participant observation used in the study took place in Melbourne where I went to activist and council meetings from 2017 until 2020. I participated in these meetings as an observer but also sometimes offered my opinions as an urbanist or as an apartment renter, or both. While some Australians in these groups experienced more acute housing insecurity, many were the modal YIMBY: white, middle class, under forty years old, well educated, and opinionated about urban planning. I am all of those things too and my status as a stereotypical YIMBY made me fit in well. That said, fitting in is not always a good thing and I attempted to constantly interrogate my sympathy for densification with the viewpoints of anti-growth activists.

One helpful aspect of my ethnographic dynamic is that I am not Australian, giving me a modicum of outsider status. Given my accent and fairly recent arrival in the country, I could ask very basic questions about land use and the cultural relationship with single-family homes from a range of people. Being (and playing) the curious outsider, allowed me to ask people fundamental questions about aboriginal land rights, the expansion of cities into greenfield territory, and fire management that have become somewhat taboo in the Australian context and immediately draw-upon contentious political agendas. By mobilizing my newness in the country, I was able to ask informants to explain things that most people are presumed to already have an opinion on and often avoid in order to minimize conflict.

Through attending meetings in many different districts in Melbourne, I was able to see how those concerned about housing interacted with local councils and how they made use of Victoria's abundant mechanisms to participate in urban policy from an early stage. Like in the United States, Melbourne is characterized by an immense fracturing of jurisdictions with thirty-one inner-city neighborhoods having their own councils. This added to a diversity of approaches within the broader region that was on display in meetings with local activists. Unlike the United States, the state of Victoria is still the major source of urban regulation and financing, making it the ultimate arbiter of affordable housing policy. Meeting with state officials working in planning and government allowed me to measure the effectiveness of density activists by observing the extent to which their ideas informed new policy.

Last, I was drawn into Australian YIMBYism (in Brisbane and Melbourne) through my role as an urban policy scholar who is able to comment on proposed projects. This was at first uncomfortable because it put me in the same shoes as those I was studying: offering unsolicited advice about growth in cities. Unlike my informants, I did not give impassioned speeches at council meetings and planning boards, but between 2017 and 2020, I did offer my perspective in private: effectively mirroring the influence work that YIMBYs take part in. The attempts of density activists to model their activism on think tanks or shadow government agencies is interesting for those of us who study social movements and are used to "bodies in the streets" rather than "boots in the boardroom." Yet, it also points to two growing trends: activism that engages in deep education on complex processes (climate change, supply chains, water supply, etc.) and the meme-ification of issues into bite-sized digital morsels that can be shared. One trend is deeply earnest and shows the need to command an audience's sustained attention; the other is snarky and lightning quick. Watching YIMBYs offer both of these sources of information simultaneously was fascinating in real time. Sometimes it seemed that there was a hoped-for target audience of people who wanted to become experts in transportation planning, sustainable design, or zoning; other times there seemed to be an admission that contemporary activism depends on online provocation. In both instances, I sought to engage in open-minded conversation with my interlocutors, and by the end, I had learned tremendously from them.

Introduction

1. Sophocles, *Oedipus at Colonus*, trans. Francis Storr (New York: Open Road Media, 2014).

2. John R. Logan and Harvey L. Molotch, *Urban Fortunes: The Political Economy of Place* (Berkeley: University of California Press, 1987).

3. With some exceptions due to economic hardship in which landowners try to attract problematic environmental uses in order to bring increased capital for risk. For a study of hydraulic fracturing, see Colin Jerolmack, *Up to Heaven and Down to Hell: Fracking, Freedom, and Community in an American Town* (Princeton, NJ: Princeton University Press, 2021).

4. Ted Steinberg, *American Green: The Obsessive Quest for the Perfect Lawn* (New York: W. W. Norton, 2006).

5. Vicki Been, "City NIMBYs," *Journal of Land Use & Environmental Law* 33, no. 2 (2018): 217–50.

6. Robert Fogelson, *Bourgeois Nightmares: Suburbia, 1870–1930* (New Haven, CT: Yale University Press, 2007).

7. Thomas Sugrue, *The Origins of the Urban Crisis: Race and Inequality in Postwar Detroit* (Princeton, NJ: Princeton University Press, 2014).

8. Richard Rothstein, *The Color of Law: A Forgotten History of How Our Government Segregated America* (New York: Liveright, 2017).

9. Vicki Been shows that NIMBY thinking has also moved from suburbia to inner-city neighborhoods. She also demonstrates how the sentiment has proliferated among renters who, without property at stake, still fear that new development will price them out of their chosen neighborhood due to drastic rent increases. Vicki Been, "City NIMBYs." *Journal of Land Use & Environmental Law* 33, no. 2 (2018): 217–50.

10. Richard Florida, *The New Urban Crisis: How Our Cities Are Increasing Inequality, Deepening Segregation, and Failing the Middle Class—and What We Can Do about It* (New York: Basic Books, 2017).

11. Been, "City NIMBYs," 238–40.

12. Whitney Airgood-Obrycki, Ben Demers, Solomon Greene, et al. "Renters' Responses to Financial Stress during the Pandemic," Joint Center for Housing Studies of Harvard University, Cambridge, MA, 2021, https://www.jchs.harvard.edu/sites/default/files/research/files/harvard _jchs_renter_responses_covid_airgood-obrycki_etal_2021.pdf.

13. "Tracking the COVID-19 Recession's Effects on Food, Housing, and Employment Hardships," Center for Budget and Policy Priorities, Washington, DC, August 9, 2021, https://www .cbpp.org/research/poverty-and-inequality/tracking-the-covid-19-recessions-effects-on-food -housing-and.

14. Trivess Moore and David Oswald, "Why Did the Miami Apartment Building Collapse? And Are Others in Danger?" *Conversation*, June 25, 2021, https://theconversation.com/why-did -the-miami-apartment-building-collapse-and-are-others-in-danger-163425.

15. Louis Wirth, "Urbanism as a Way of Life," *American Journal of Sociology* 44, no.1 (1938): 14.

16. "San Francisco's Housing Crisis Needs Political Will," *Financial Times*, November 9, 2019, https://www.ft.com/content/d618987a-021f-11ea-be59-e49b2a136b8d.

17. Adam Brinklow, "SF Might Finally Have Gained More New Homes than People in 2019," *Curbed,* December 23, 2019, https://sf.curbed.com/2019/12/23/21035307/san-francisco-population-2018-2019-housing-gains-california-department-finance.

18. Matthew E. Khan, "The Environmental Impact of Suburbanization," *Journal of Policy Analysis and Management* 19, no. 4 (2000): 569–86; William B. Meyer, *The Environmental Advantage of Cities: Countering Commonsense Antiurbanism* (Cambridge, MA: MIT Press, 2013).

19. UN Sustainable Development Goals, "Transforming Our World: The 2030 Agenda for Sustainable Development," accessed December 2, 2020, https://sustainabledevelopment.un.org/post2015/transformingourworld.

20. Malte Steinbrink "'We Did the Slum!'—Urban Poverty Tourism in Historical Perspective," *Tourism Geographies* 14:2 (2012): 213–34, 213.

21. Robert E. Park and Ernest W. Burgess, *The City: Suggestions for Investigation of Human Behavior in the Urban Environment* (Chicago: University of Chicago Press, 1967 [1925]), 53.

22. Mitchell Duneier, *Ghetto: The Invention of a Place, the History of an Idea* (New York: Farrar, Straus and Giroux, 2017).

23. Wirth, "Urbanism as a Way of Life," 15.

24. For a discussion on density and political mobilization, see Colin McFarlane, "The Force of Density: Political Crowding and the City," *Urban Geography* 41, no. 10 (2020): 1310–17.

25. Ibid, 48.

26. Georg Simmel, *Simmel on Culture: Selected Writings*, ed. Mike Featherstone (London: Sage, 1997), 176.

27. Jane Jacobs, *The Death and Life of Great American Cities* (New York: Penguin, 2020 [1961]).

28. Max Holleran, "Bright Lights, Small Government: Why Libertarians Adore Jane Jacobs," *New Republic*, November 23, 2016, https://newrepublic.com/article/138071/bright-lights-small-government.

29. Jane Jacobs, *Vital Little Plans: The Short Works of Jane Jacobs,* ed. Samuel Zipp and Nathan Storring (New York: Random House, 2016).

30. Emily Talen, "Sense of Community and Neighborhood Form: An Assessment of the Social Doctrine of New Urbanism," *Urban Studies* 36, no. 8 (July 1999): 1361–79.

31. Andres Duany, Elizabeth Plater-Zyberk, and Jeff Speck, *Suburban Nation: The Rise of Sprawl and the Decline of the American Dream* (New York: North Point Press, 2000).

32. Svetlana Boym, *Architecture of the Off-Modern* (Princeton, NJ: Princeton Architectural Press, 2009).

33. Neil Smith "New Globalism, New Urbanism: Gentrification as Global Urban Strategy," *Antipode*, 34, no. 3 (2002): 427–50.

34. Emily Badger and Quoctrung Bui, "Cities Start to Question an American Ideal: A House with a Yard on Every Lot," *New York Times,* June 18, 2019, https://www.nytimes.com/interactive/2019/06/18/upshot/cities-across-america-question-single-family-zoning.html.

35. For the British example, see John Boughton, *Municipal Dreams: The Rise and Fall of Council Housing* (New York: Verso, 2018). For more on the American divestment in public housing, see Sudhir Venkatesh, *American Project: The Rise and Fall of a Modern Ghetto* (Cambridge, MA: Harvard University Press, 2002).

36. Stephen J. K. Walters, *Boom Towns: Restoring the Urban American Dream* (Stanford, CA: Stanford University Press, 2014).

37. Vicki Been, Ingrid Gould Ellen, and Katherine O'Regan, "Supply Skepticism: Housing Supply and Affordability," *Housing Policy Debate* 29:1 (2019): 25–40.

38. Andrés Rodríguez-Pose and Michael Storper, "Housing, Urban Growth and Inequalities: The Limits to Deregulation and Upzoning in Reducing Economic and Spatial Inequality," *Urban Studies* 57, no. 2 (February 2020): 223–48.

39. Tom Agnotti and Sylvia Morse (eds), *Zoned Out! Race, Displacement and City Planning in New York City* (New York: Terreform, 2016); Andrejs Skaburskis, "Filtering, City Change and the Supply of Low-priced Housing in Canada," *Urban Studies* 43, no. 3 (2006): 533–58.

40. Been, "City NIMBYs."

41. Nils Kok, Paavo Monkkonen, and John M. Quigley, "Land Use Regulations and the Value of Land and Housing: An Intra-metropolitan Analysis," *Journal of Urban Economics* 81 (2014): 136–48; Stuart S. Rosenthal, "Are Private Markets and Filtering a Viable Source of Low-Income Housing? Estimates from a 'Repeat Income' Model," *American Economic Review* 104, no. 2 (2014): 687–706.

42. Xiaodi Li, "Do New Housing Units in Your Backyard Raise Your Rents?" NYU Furman Center Working Paper, December 16, 2019, https://blocksandlots.com/wp-content/uploads/2020/02/Do-New-Housing-Units-in-Your-Backyard-Raise-Your-Rents-Xiaodi-Li.pdf.

43. Jake Wegmann and Karen Chapple, "Hidden Density in Single-Family Neighborhoods: Backyard Cottages as an Equitable Smart Growth Strategy," *Journal of Urbanism: International Research on Placemaking and Urban Sustainability* 7, no. 3 (2014): 307–29.

44. Been, Ellen, and O'Regan, "Supply Skepticism."

45. Gianpaolo Baiocchi and H. Jacob Carlson, "What Happens When 10 Million Tenants Can't Make Rent?" *New York Times*, March 3, 2021, https://www.nytimes.com/2021/03/03/opinion/affordable-housing-federal-agency.html.

46. Manuel B. Aalbers, "The Variegated Financialization of Housing," *International Journal of Urban and Regional Research* 41, no. 4 (2017): 542–54; Brett Christophers, "How and Why U.S. Single-Family Housing Became an Investor Asset Class," *Journal of Urban History*, July 2021, https://doi.org/10.1177/00961442211029601.

47. Martine August and Alan Walks, "Gentrification, Suburban Decline, and the Financialization of Multi-family Rental Housing: The Case of Toronto," *Geoforum* 89 (2018): 124–36.

48. Esther Sullivan, *Manufactured Insecurity: Mobile Home Parks and Americans' Tenuous Right to Place* (Berkeley: University of California Press, 2018).

49. Tim Logan, "Two Gatherings, Two Visions for Fixing Boston's Housing Crisis," *Boston Globe*, September 20, 2018, https://www.bostonglobe.com/business/2018/09/20/two-gatherings-two-visions-for-fixing-boston-housing-crisis/aB9HnRP3QGmSHxM07bV8WI/story.html.

50. A version of this chapter appeared as the article Max Holleran, "Millennial 'YIMBYs' and Boomer 'NIMBYs': Generational Views on Housing Affordability in the United States," *Sociological Review* 69, no. 4 (2021): 846–61, https://doi.org/10.1177/0038026120916121.

51. Doug McAdam and Hilary Boudet, *Putting Social Movements in Their Place: Explaining Opposition to Energy Projects in the United States, 2000–2005* (Cambridge: Cambridge University Press, 2012).

52. Robert Fishman, *Urban Utopias in the Twentieth Century: Ebenezer Howard, Frank Lloyd Wright, Le Corbusier* (Cambridge, MA: MIT Press, 1982).

53. Joshua Long, *Weird City: Sense of Place and Creative Resistance in Austin, Texas* (Austin: University of Texas Press, 2010).

54. Sharon Zukin, *Naked City: The Death and Life of Authentic Urban Places* (New York: Oxford University Press, 2009).

Chapter 1: The Bay Area and the End of Affordability

1. Lawrence Ferlinghetti, "In Golden Gate Park That Day . . . ," *Coney Island of the Mind* (New York: New Directions, 1958).

2. Alison Isenberg, *Designing San Francisco: Art, Land, and Urban Renewal in the City by the Bay* (Princeton, NJ: Princeton University Press, 2017).

3. Fred Turner, *From Counterculture to Cyberculture: Stewart Brand, the Whole Earth Network, and the Rise of Digital Utopianism* (Chicago: University of Chicago Press, 2008).

4. Clayton Howard, "Building a 'Family-Friendly' Metropolis: Sexuality, the State, and Post-war Housing Policy," *Journal of Urban History* 39, no. 5 (2013): 941.

5. Howard, "'Family-Friendly' Metropolis," 947.

6. Turner, *From Counterculture to Cyberculture*.

7. Adam Brinklow, "San Francisco Market Rents Soar up to 105 Percent above Average," *Curbed San Francisco*, October 2, 2019, https://sf.curbed.com/2019/10/2/20895578/san-francisco -median-rents-market-census-september-2019.

8. Michael D. Shear, Thomas Fuller, and Peter Baker, "San Francisco to Get Environmental Violation for Homeslessness, Trump Says," *New York Times,* September 18, 2019, https://www .nytimes.com/2019/09/18/us/politics/trump-san-francisco-homeless.html.

9. Benjamin Schneider, "The Dirty Truth about San Francisco's Sidewalks," *CityLab*, August 2, 2018, https://www.citylab.com/equity/2018/08/san-franciscos-sidewalk-poop-problem/566621/.

10. Alec MacGillis, *Fulfillment: Winning and Losing in One-Click America* (New York: Farrar, Straus, and Giroux, 2021).

11. This term was originally used by Bill DeBlasio in his campaign for New York City mayor but is applicable to most large and expensive American cities.

12. Conor Dougherty and Andrew Burton, "A 2:15 Alarm, 2 Trains and a Bus Get Her to Work by 7AM," *New York Times*, August 17, 2017, https://www.nytimes.com/2017/08/17/business /economy/san-francisco-commute.html.

13. Christin Ayers, "San Jose Median Home Price Drops $1.2 Million," CBS SF Bay Area, April 23, 2019, https://sanfrancisco.cbslocal.com/2019/04/23/san-jose-median-home-price -drops-slightly-1-2-million/.

14. Sarah Holder, "The Cities Where Job Growth Is Outpacing New Homes," *CityLab*, September 10, 2019, https://www.bloomberg.com/news/articles/2019-09-09/the-cities-where-job -growth-is-outpacing-new-homes.

15. Blanca Torres, "Housing's Tale of Two Cities: Seattle Builds, S.F. Lags," *San Francisco Business Times*, April 28, 2017, https://www.bizjournals.com/sanfrancisco/news/2017/04/28/san -francisco-seattle-housing-production-pipelines.html.

16. John Baranski, *Housing the City by the Bay: Tenant Activism, Civil Rights, and Class Politics in San Francisco* (Stanford, CA: Stanford University Press, 2019).

17. Victoria Fierce, "YIMBY Socialism," *Medium*, April 22, 2017, https://medium.com/@ tdfischer_/yimby-socialism-704e6cb4007c.

18. Deepa Varma, "The Big Lie about California's Housing Crisis," *San Francisco Chronicle* July 27, 2017, https://www.sfexaminer.com/opinion/the-big-lie-about-californias-housing-crisis/.

19. Laura E. Ferguson, "A Gateway without a Port: Making and Contesting San Francisco's Early Waterfront," *Journal of Urban History* 44, no. 4 (2018): 610.

20. John R. Logan and Harvey L. Molotch, *Urban Fortunes: The Political Economy of Place* (Berkeley: University of California Press, 2007).

21. Tony Robinson, "Gentrification and Grassroots Resistance in San Francisco's Tenderloin," *Urban Affairs Review* 30, no. 4 (March 1995): 487.

22. Nikil Saval, *Cubed: The Secret History of the Workplace* (New York: Anchor, 2015).

23. "San Francisco City and County Census," *Bay Area Census*, accessed June 2020, http:// www.bayareacensus.ca.gov/counties/SanFranciscoCounty70.htm.

24. "Bay Area Census, Historical Data" *Bay Area Census*, accessed June 2020, http://www .bayareacensus.ca.gov/historical/corace.htm.

25. Louise Nelson Dyble, "The Defeat of the Golden Gate Authority: A Special District, A Council of Governments, and the Fate of Regional Planning in the San Francisco Bay Area," *Journal of Urban History* 34, no. 2 (January 2008): 293–95.

26. Quoted in Baranski, *Housing the City by the Bay*, 147.

27. Baranski, *Housing the City by the Bay*.

28. Isenberg, *Designing San Francisco*, 325.

29. Paul Goldberger, "Transamerica Building: What Was All the Fuss About?" *New York Times*, March 2, 1977, https://www.nytimes.com/1977/03/02/archives/transamerica-building-what-was-all-the-fuss-about.html.

30. Baranski, "Housing the City by the Bay," 134.

31. Howard, "'Family-Friendly' Metropolis," 944.

32. "Brown Assails Prop. 14 as 'Cudgel of Bigotry,'" *Los Angeles Times*, October 8, 1964, p. 18.

33. Carol Hager and Mary Alice Haddad, *Nimby Is Beautiful: Cases of Local Activism and Environmental Innovation around the World* (New York: Berghahn, 2015).

34. Conor Dougherty, *Golden Gates: Fighting for Housing in America* (New York: Penguin, 2020).

35. Jeffrey I. Chapman, *Proposition 13: Some Unintended Consequences* (Sacramento, CA: Public Policy Institute of California Report, 1998).

36. Alex Schafran, "Origins of an Urban Crisis: The Restructuring of the San Francisco Bay Area and the Geography of Foreclosure," *International Journal of Urban and Regional Research* 37, no. 2 (March 2013): 663–88.

37. Richard E. DeLeon. "The Urban Antiregime: Progressive Politics in San Francisco," *Urban Affairs Quarterly* 27, no. 4 (June 1992): 561–62.

38. DeLeon, "Urban Antiregime," 563.

39. Robinson, "Gentrification and Grassroots," 498.

40. John Stehlin, "The Post-Industrial 'Shop Floor': Emerging Forms of Gentrification in San Francisco's Innovation Economy," *Antipode* 48, no.2 (2016): 480.

41. Jathan Sadowski, *Too Smart: How Digital Capitalism Is Extracting Data, Controlling Our Lives, and Taking Over the World* (Cambridge, MA: MIT Press, 2020).

42. Keller Easterling, *Extrastatecraft: The Power of Infrastructure Space* (New York: Verso, 2016).

43. Nikhil Annand, Akil Gupta, and Hannah Appel (eds.), *The Promise of Infrastructure* (Durham, NC: Duke University Press, 2018).

44. Susan Leigh Star and Karen Ruhleder, "Steps toward an Ecology of Infrastructure: Design and Access for Large Information Spaces," *Information Systems Research* 7, no. 1 (1996): 111–34.

45. Sharon Zukin, *Naked City: The Death and Life of Authentic Urban Places* (New York: Oxford University Press, 2011).

46. Neil Smith, *The New Urban Frontier: Gentrification and the Revanchist City* (New York: Routledge, 1996).

47. Baranski, *Housing the City by the Bay*, 199.

48. Simon Marvin and Stephen Graham, *Splintering Urbanism: Networked Infrastructures, Technological Mobilities and the Urban Condition* (New York: Routledge, 2001): 215.

49. Adam Brinklow, "More Than 60 Percent of SF Renters Have Rent Control, Says City," *Curbed San Francisco*, July 12, 2018, https://sf.curbed.com/2018/7/12/17565192/housing-needs-trends-report-rent-control-san-francisco.

50. "Consumer Expenditures for the San Francisco Area: 2017–18," Western Information Office, US Bureau of Labour Statistics, accessed June 2020, https://www.bls.gov/regions/west/news-release/consumerexpenditures_sanfrancisco.htm.

51. Joe Matthews, "'Protecting Community Character' Is a Governing Philosophy That's Hurting Californians," *Desert Sun*, December 28, 2018, https://www.desertsun.com/story/opinion

/columnists/2018/12/28/protecting-community-character-philosophy-divides-california-joe
-mathews-column/2434731002/.

52. Ibid.

53. Julian Mark, "How the Developer of SF's 'Historic' Laundromat Quietly Won," *Mission Local*, February 4, 2019, https://missionlocal.org/2019/02/how-the-developer-of-sfs-historic
-laundromat-quietly-won/; https://www.reddit.com/r/yimby/comments/jspagh/are_memes
_welcome_here/.

54. Tim Redmond, "Nimbys, SFBARF, and a Clueless Writer at the NY Times" *48 Hills*, April 23, 2016, https://48hills.org/2016/04/nimbys-sfbarf-clueless-writers-ny-times-2/.

55. Ben CS, "Tim Redmond and the Selfishness of the Old and Rich," *Medium*, April 27, 2016, https://medium.com/@fonssagrives/tim-redmond-and-the-selfishness-of-the-old-and-rich
-2e938e13ba01.

56. Redmond, "Nimbys, SFBARF, and a Clueless Writer."

57. Japonica Brown-Saracino, *A Neighborhood That Never Changes: Gentrification, Social Preservation, and the Search for Authenticity* (Chicago: University of Chicago Press, 2009).

58. Erin McCormick, "Rise of the Yimbys: The Angry Millennials with a Radical Housing Solution," *Guardian*, October 2, 2017, https://www.theguardian.com/cities/2017/oct/02/rise-of
-the-yimbys-angry-millennials-radical-housing-solution.

59. Erin McElroy and Andrew Szeto, "The Racial Contours of YIMBY/NIMBY Bay Area Gentrification," *Berekeley Planning Journal* 29 (2017): 7–46.

60. Scott Beyer, "Nativism: The Thread Connecting Progressive NIMBYs with Donald Trump," *Forbes*, November 30, 2016, https://www.forbes.com/sites/scottbeyer/2016/11/30
/nativism-is-the-thread-connecting-progressive-nimbys-with-donald-trump/#b34c0f414ede.

61. Conor Dougherty, *Golden Gates: Fighting for Housing in America* (New York: Penguin, 2020).

62. Angela Nagle, *Kill All Normies: Online Culture Wars from 4chan and Tumblr to Trump and the Alt-Right* (London: Zero Books, 2017).

63. Reddit comment, R/YIMBY, 2017, https://www.reddit.com/r/oakland/comments/73tcu5
/rise_of_the_yimbys_the_angry_millennials_with_a/.

64. Matt Levin, "'Yes in My Backyard' Movement, YIMBY, Grows as Bay Area Housing Tightens," *WBUR*, August 8, 2018, https://www.wbur.org/hereandnow/2018/08/08/yimby-bay-area
-housing-regulations.

65. "Zucchini Rebuttal," YouTube, June 26, 2017, https://www.youtube.com/watch?v
=Rqxxg3sFt24.

66. Marty Branagan, "The Last Laugh: Humor in Community Activism," *Community Development Journal* 42, no. 4 (2007): 470–81.

67. Trisha Thanani, "SF Supervisors Reject Housing Complex That Would Cast Shadow on SoMA Park" *San Francisco Chronicle*, April 9, 2019, https://www.sfchronicle.com/politics/article
/SF-supervisors-reject-housing-project-that-would-13755026.php#photo-17201635.

68. Ellie Anzilotti, "Welcome to Housing Twitter, the Shoutiest Debate on the Internet," *Fast Company*, August 29, 2019, https://www.fastcompany.com/90384931/welcome-to-housing
-twitter-the-shoutiest-debate-on-the-internet.

69. Åsa Wettergren, "Fun and Laughter: Culture Jamming and the Emotional Regime of Late Capitalism," *Social Movement Studies* 8, no. 1 (2009): 1–15.

70. Richard Schragger, *City Power: Urban Governance in a Global Age* (New York: Oxford University Press, 2016).

71. "CASA Compact," Committee to House the Bay Area, January 2019, https://mtc.ca.gov
/sites/default/files/CASA_Compact.pdf.

72. Mary Jo Bowling, "Housing Activists Say Sue the Suburbs, Starting with Lafayette," *Curbed San Francisco*, September 4, 2015, https://sf.curbed.com/2015/9/4/9923852/housing-activists
-say-sue-the-suburbs-starting-with-lafayette.

73. Jared Brey, "The YIMBY Group That Is Suing Small Cities," *Next City*, August 15, 2019, https://nextcity.org/daily/entry/the-yimby-group-that-is-suing-small-cities.

74. Nancy Raquel Mirabal, "Geographies of Displacement: Latina/os, Oral History, and The Politics of Gentrification in San Francisco's Mission District," *Public Historian* 31, no. 2 (2009): 7–31; S. Easton, L. Lees, P. Hubbard, and N. Tate, "Measuring and Mapping Displacement: The Problem of Quantification in the Battle against Gentrification," *Urban Studies* 57, no. 2 (2020): 286–306.

75. Reddit comment, R/YIMBY, 2020, https://www.reddit.com/r/LandlordLove/comments /il6rwm/yimby_is_an_astroturfed_movement_in_support_of/.

76. Conor Dougherty, *Golden Gates: Fighting for Housing in America* (New York: Penguin, 2020).

77. Loretta Lees, "Gentrification and Social Mixing: Towards an Inclusive Urban Renaissance?" *Urban Studies* 45, no. 12 (2008): 2449–70.

78. Joe Rivano Barros, "Artist vs. Artist: Recent Tenants Fight Eviction from Inner Mission," *Mission Local*, July 23, 2015, https://missionlocal.org/2015/07/artists-vs-artists-deal-between -inner-mission-and-developer-jeopardized-by-recent-tenants/.

79. Sarah Tan, "S.F. Planning Panel Approves 'Beast on Bryant' Development," KQED, June 3, 2016, https://www.kqed.org/news/10976875/s-f-planning-department-approves-beast-on-bryant -development.

80. John Elberling, "What We Won—and Lost—with the Beast on Byrant," *48 Hills*, June 5, 2016, https://48hills.org/2016/06/won-lost-beast-bryant/.

81. Joe Eskenazi, "Developer's 'I Am Not a Monster' Ad Blitz Makes Few Friends," *Mission Local*, September 18, 2017, https://missionlocal.org/2017/09/developers-i-am-not-a-monster-ad -blitz-makes-few-friends/.

82. Ibid.

83. Ibid.

84. Laura Waxmann, "Tensions over Mission District Gentrification Flare at Hearing on 16th Street Project," *San Francisco Examiner*, February 8, 2019, https://www.sfexaminer.com/news /tensions-over-mission-district-gentrification-flare-at-hearing-on-16th-street-project/.

85. Tim Redmond, "Chilly Reception for the New Monster in the Mission Plan," *48 Hills*, February 8, 2019, https://48hills.org/2019/02/chilly-reception-for-the-new-monster-in-the -mission-plan/.

86. Brock Keeling, "The 'Monster in the Mission' Is Officially Dead," *Curbed San Francisco*, February 24, 2020, https://sf.curbed.com/2020/2/24/21151617/monster-in-the-mission-deal -update-dead-sf.

87. Theda Skocpol and Vanessa Williamson, *The Tea Party and the Remaking of Republican Conservatism* (New York: Oxford University Press, 2016). This provides an alternative account of how some new social movements are evolving to move directly into electoral politics but also shows how these movements, like YIMBYs, are often not of the purely grassroots variety and frequently have wealthy institutional underwriters.

88. McCormick, "Rise of the Yimbys."

89. "Beverly Hills Getting First New Apartments in 21 Years," USC Lusk Centre for Real Estate, Los Angeles, March 17, 2003, https://lusk.usc.edu/news/beverly-hills-getting-first-new -apartments-21-years.

90. Erin Baldassari, "Sen. Wiener Wants to Abolish Single-Family-Only Neighborhoods in California," KQED, March 9, 2020, https://www.kqed.org/news/11805850/sen-wiener-wants-to -abolish-single-family-only-neighborhoods-in-california.

91. Henry Grabar, "Why Was California's Radical Housing Bill So Unpopular?" *Slate*, April 20, 2018, https://slate.com/business/2018/04/why-sb-827-californias-radical-affordable-housing-bill -was-so-unpopular.html.

92. Benjamin Ross, "A Tangle for the Anti-Development Left," *Dissent*, March 14, 2018, https://www.dissentmagazine.org/online_articles/california-sb-827-yimby-housing-transit -gentrification.

93. Dan Brekke, "It's SB 827, the Sequel: Weiner Introduces Revamped Bill to Spur Housing Near Transit," KQED, December 4, 2018, https://www.kqed.org/news/11709817/its-sb-827-take -2-wiener-introduces-revamped-bill-to-require-more-housing-near-transit.

94. Patrick Range McDonald, "Selling Out California: Scott Wiener's Money Ties to Big Real Estate," Housing Is a Human Right, March 29, 2019, https://www.housinghumanright.org/selling -out-california-scott-wiener-money-ties-to-big-real-estate/.

95. Ibid.

96. Jenna Chandler, "California Transit Density Proposal SB 50 on Pause until 2020" *Curbed Los Angeles*, May 16, 2019, https://la.curbed.com/2019/5/16/18628217/senate-bill-50-status-postponed.

97. Alissa Walker, "The Real Reason California's Upzoning Bill Failed," *Curbed*, February 7, 2020, https://www.curbed.com/2020/2/7/21125100/sb-50-california-bill-fail.

Chapter 2: Millennial YIMBYs and Boomer NIMBYs

1. Ben Sasse, *The Vanishing American Adult: Our Coming-of-Age Crisis—and How to Rebuild a Culture of Self-Reliance.* (New York: Macmillan, 2017).

2. Malcolm Harris, *Kids These Days: Human Capital and the Making of Millennials* (New York: Little, Brown, 2017).

3. Adam Okulicz-Kozaryn and Rubia R. Valente, "No Urban Malaise for Millennials," *Regional Studies* 53, no. 2 (2019): 195–205.

4. Jung Choi, Jun Zhu, Laurie Goodman, Bhargavi Ganesh, and Sarah Strochak, "Millennial Homeownership: Why Is It So Low and How Can We Increase It?" Research report, Urban Institute, 2018, accessed January 2019, https://www.urban.org/sites/default/files/publication/98729 /millennial_homeownership_0.pdf.

5. Karen Zraick, "San Francisco Is So Expensive, You Can Make Six Figures and Still Be 'Low Income,'" *New York Times*, July 30, 2018, https://www.nytimes.com/2018/06/30/us/bay -area-housing-market.html.

6. Anya Kamenetz, *Generation Debt: How Our Future Was Sold Out for Student Loans, Bad Jobs, No Benefits, and Tax Cuts for Rich Geezers—And How to Fight Back* (New York: Riverhead, 2006).

7. Veikko Eranti, "Re-visiting NIMBY: From Conflicting Interests to Conflicting Valuations," *Sociological Review* 65 (2017): 285–301.

8. Richard Schragger, *City Power: Urban Governance in a Global Age* (New York: Oxford University Press, 2016).

9. Peter Ganong and Daniel Shoag, "Why Has Regional Income Convergence in the U.S. Declined?" *Journal of Urban Economics* 102 (2017): 76–90.

10. Enrico Moretti, *The New Geography of Jobs* (New York: Mariner Books, 2013).

11. Richard Florida, *The New Urban Crisis: How Our Cities Are Increasing Inequality, Deepening Segregation, and Failing the Middle Class—and What We Can Do about It* (New York: Basic Books, 2017).

12. Dan Woodman and Johannah Wyn, "Class, Gender and Generation Matter: Using the Concept of Social Generation to Study Inequality and Social Change," *Journal of Youth Studies* 18 (2015): 1402–10.

13. Joan Williams, *White Working Class: Overcoming Class Cluelessness in America.* (Cambridge, MA: Harvard Business Review Press, 2017).

14. Greg Martin, *Understanding Social Movements* (New York: Routledge, 2015).

15. Robert Fishman, *Bourgeois Utopias: The Rise and Fall of Suburbia* (New York: Basic Books, 1987).

16. Dolores Hayden, *Building Suburbia: Green Fields and Urban Growth 1820–2000* (New York: Vintage, 2004).

17. Thomas Sugrue, *The Origins of the Urban Crisis: Race and Inequality in Postwar Detroit* (Princeton, NJ: Princeton University Press, 2014).

18. William Julius Wilson, *The Truly Disadvantaged: The Inner City, the Underclass, and Public Policy* (1987; repr. Chicago: University of Chicago Press, 1990).

19. David I. Kertzer. "Generation as a Sociological Problem," *Annual Review of Sociology* 9 (1983): 125–49.

20. Joshua Bloom and Waldo Martin, *Black against Empire: The History and Politics of the Black Panther Party*, George Gund Foundation Imprint in African American Studies (Berkeley: University of California Press, 2016).

21. Setha Low, *Behind the Gates: Life, Security, and the Pursuit of Happiness in Fortress America* (New York: Routledge, 2004).

22. Sugrue, *The Origins of the Urban Crisis: Race and Inequality in Postwar Detroit*.

23. Robert Fogelson. *Bourgeois Nightmares: Suburbia, 1870–1930* (New Haven, CT: Yale University Press, 2007).

24. Richard Rothstein. *The Color of Law: A Forgotten History of How our Government Segregated America* (New York: Liveright, 2017).

25. Low, *Behind the Gates.*

26. Sugrue, *Origins of the Urban Crisis.*

27. US Census Bureau Quick Facts, 2019, https://www.census.gov/quickfacts/fact/table/w estporttownfairfieldcountyconnecticut,fairfieldcountyconnecticut,bridgeportcityconnecticut /PST045219.

28. Brian McCabe, *No Place Like Home: Wealth, Community, and the Politics of Homeownership* (New York: Oxford University Press, 2016).

29. Low, *Behind the Gates.*

30. Eranti, "Re-visiting NIMBY."

31. McCabe, *No Place Like Home.*

32. Ulrich Beck, *Risk Society: Towards a New Modernity* (London: Sage, 1992).

33. Steven Conn, *Americans against the City: Anti-urbanism in the Twentieth Century* (New York: Oxford University Press, 2014).

34. Sharon Zukin, *Naked City: The Death and Life of Authentic Urban Places* (New York: Oxford University Press, 2009).

35. Saskia Sassen, *Cities in a World Economy* (New York: Sage, 1994).

36. Zukin, *Naked City.*

37. Jane Jacobs, *The Death and Life of Great American Cities* (New York: Vintage, 1991).

38. Florida, *New Urban Crisis.*

39. Meagan M. Ehlenz, Deirdre Pfeiffer, and Genevieve Pearthree, "Downtown Revitalization in the Era of Millennials: How Developer Perceptions of Millennial Market Demands Are Shaping Urban Landscapes," *Urban Geography* 41, no. 1 (2020): 79–102.

40. Markus Moos, "From Gentrification to Youthification? The Increasing Importance of Young Age in Delineating High-Density Living," *Urban Studies* 53, no. 14 (2016): 2903–20.

41. Choi et al., "Millennial Homeownership."

42. Richard Fry, "Gen X Rebounds as the Only Generation to Recover the Wealth Lost after the Housing Crash," Pew Research Center, 2018, http://www.pewresearch.org/fact-tank/2018/07/23 /gen-x-rebounds-as-the-only-generation-to-recover-the-wealth-lost-after-the-housing-crash/.

43. Reid Cramer, "Framing the Millennial Wealth Gap: Demographic Realities and Divergent Trajectories," New America Report, 2016, https://www.newamerica.org/millennials/reports /emerging-millennial-wealth-gap/framing-the-millennial-wealth-gap-demographic-realities-and -divergent-trajectories/.

44. David Owen, *Green Metropolis: What the City Can Teach the Country about True Sustainability* (New York: Riverhead Books, 2010).

45. Nick Gallent, "Re-connecting 'People and Planning': Parish Plans and the English Localism Agenda," *Town Planning Review* 84, no. 3 (2013): 371–96.

46. Martin, *Understanding Social Movements*.

47. Ibid.

48. Katherine VanHoose and Federico Savini, "The Social Capital of Urban Activism: Practices in London and Amsterdam," *City* 21, no. 3–4 (2017): 293–311.

49. Harris, *Kids These Days*.

50. Alan France and Steven Roberts, "The Problem of Social Generations: A Critique of the New Emerging Orthodoxy in Youth Studies, *Journal of Youth Studies* 18 (2015): 215–30.

51. Stephen Halebsky, "Explaining the Outcomes of Anti-superstore Movements: A Comparative Analysis of Six Communities," *Mobilization* 11, no. 4 (2006): 443–60.

52. Eric Klinenberg, *Palaces for the People: How Social Infrastructure Can Help Fight Inequality, Polarization, and the Decline of Civic Life* (New York: Crown, 2018).

53. Elijah Anderson *The Cosmopolitan Canopy: Race and Civility in Everyday Life* (New York: W. W. Norton, 2011).

54. Martin, *Understanding Social Movements*.

55. Logan and Molotch, *Urban Fortunes*.

56. Wilson, *The Truly Disadvantaged*.

57. McCabe, *No Place Like Home*.

58. France and Roberts, "The Problem of Social Generations."

59. Conn, *Americans against the City*.

60. Daniel Aldana Cohen, "A Green New Deal for Housing," *Jacobin*, February 8, 2019, https://www.jacobinmag.com/2019/02/green-new-deal-housing-ocasio-cortez-climate.

61. Martin, *Understanding Social Movements*.

62. Williams, *White Working Class*.

63. Japonica Brown-Saracino, *A Neighborhood That Never Changes: Gentrification, Social Preservation, and the Search for Authenticity* (Chicago: University of Chicago Press, 2010).

64. Fry, "Gen X Rebounds."

65. Imogen Tyler, "Classificatory Struggles: Class, Culture, and Inequality in Neoliberal Times," *Sociological Review* 63, no. 2 (2015): 493–511.

66. Sasse, *Vanishing American Adult*.

67. Harris, *Kids These Days*.

68. France and Roberts, "The Problem of Social Generations."

69. For a similar discussion around flood mapping and the fairness of transitioning away from coastal areas for older homeowners, see Rebecca Elliott, *Underwater: Loss, Flood Insurance, and the Moral Economy of Climate Change in the United States* (New York: Columbia University Press, 2021).

70. Richard Sennett and Jonathan Cobb, *The Hidden Injuries of Class* (New York: W. W. Norton, 1972).

71. Brown-Saracino, *A Neighborhood That Never Changes*.

Chapter 3: Between a Rock and a Greenbelt

1. "Bikes in Boulder," City of Boulder, Colorado, accessed June 2020, https://bouldercolorado.gov/goboulder/bike.

2. Michael Roberts, "Only in Boulder: Almost a Decade of Pet Guardianship," *Westword*, March 30, 2009, https://www.westword.com/news/only-in-boulder-almost-a-decade-of-pet-guardianship-5906222.

3. Zillow data, https://www.zillow.com/boulder-co/home-values/.

4. Marc Perry, "Population Growth in the 1990s: Patterns within the United States," *Population Research and Policy Review* 21, no. 1/2 (April 2002): 55–71.

5. City of Boulder, Open Space and Mountain Parks, Department Information, https://bouldercolorado.gov/osmp/department-information-and-osmp-history.

6. John Grindrod, *Outskirts: Living Life on the Edge of the Green Belt* (London: Sceptre, 2017).

7. Housing Colorado, "Paycheck to Paycheck: Colorado Report—May 2019," https://cdn.ymaws.com/www.housingcolorado.org/resource/resmgr/paycheck_to_paycheck_report/Paycheck_to_Paycheck_May_201.pdf.

8. This language is not entirely new, but YIMBYs have mobilized it for the millennial generation. Density has always been a prime concern in urban planning. See Colin McFarlane, "De/re-densification," *City* 24, no. 1–2 (2020): 314–24.

9. David Owen, *Green Metropolis: What the City Can Teach the Country about True Sustainability* (New York: Riverhead, 2009).

10. Dorceta Taylor, *The Rise of the American Conservation Movement: Power, Privilege, and Environmental Protection* (Durham, NC: Duke University Press, 2016).

11. Peter Dauvergne, *Environmentalism of the Rich* (Cambridge, MA: MIT Press, 2016).

12. Richard C. Schragger, *City Power: Urban Governance in a Global Age* (New York: Oxford University Press, 2016).

13. Grindrod, *Outskirts*, 147.

14. Stanley Buder, *Visionaries and Planners: The Garden City Movement and the Modern Community* (New York: Oxford University Press, 1990).

15. Peter Hall and Colin Ward, *Sociable Cities: The Legacy of Ebenezer Howard* (New York: Wiley, 1999).

16. Buder, *Visionaries and Planners*.

17. Steven Conn, *Americans against the City: Anti-urbanism in the Twentieth Century* (New York: Oxford University Press, 2014).

18. Joseph L. Arnold, *The New Deal in the Suburbs: A History of the Greenbelt Town Program, 1935–1954* (Columbus: Ohio State University Press, 1971).

19. Phoebe Cutler, *The Public Landscape of the New Deal* (New Haven, CT: Yale University Press, 1985).

20. Kenneth T. Jackson, *Crabgrass Frontier: The Suburbanization of the United States* (New York: Oxford University Press, 1987).

21. Mike Davis, *Ecology of Fear: Los Angeles and the Imagination of Disaster* (New York: Vintage, 1999).

22. Grindrod, *Outskirts*.

23. Franklin R. Moore, "Proprietary Patterns," *South Boulder Creek: A Feasibility Study* (1968), pamphlet in Carnegie Local History Library, Boulder, CO.

24. Robert Gottlieb, *Forcing the Spring: The Transformation of the American Environmental Movement* (Washington DC: Island Press, 2005).

25. City of Boulder, *Lessons from the Greenbelt Program* (1971), pamphlet in Carnegie Local History Library, Boulder, CO.

26. "The Greenbelt: How Much Is Enough?" *Daily Camera*, May 14, 1987.

27. Andrew Needham, *Power Lines: Phoenix and the Making of the Modern Southwest* (Princeton, NJ: Princeton University Press, 2014).

28. Conn, *Americans against the City*.

29. The site dates back to 1898 and features a public performance venue. It is part of the Chautauqua movement, a community cultural enrichment program that spread across the United States in the late nineteenth century.

30. Bob McKelvey, 2002, Oral History Project, Carnegie Local History Library, Boulder, CO.

31. Taylor, *Rise of the American Conservation Movement.*

32. Robyn Eckersley, *The Green State: Rethinking Democracy and Sovereignty* (Cambridge, MA: MIT Press, 2004).

33. Ruth M. Wright, 1978, Oral History Project, Carnegie Local History Library, Boulder, CO.

34. "Greenbelt Conference Planned," *Town and County Shopper,* June 22, 1967.

35. Boulder, *Lessons from the Greenbelt Program.*

36. "Greenbelts Committee Endorses Charter Change," *Daily Camera,* September 23, 1969, 10.

37. "Greenbelt Offer Rejected by Lack of Council Action," *Daily Camera,* October 16, 1968.

38. "Open Space Concept Wins Council Support," *Daily Camera,* November 22, 1968.

39. "Greenbelt Offer Rejected by Lack of Council Action," *Daily Camera,* October 16, 1968.

40. Feasibility study (1968), Greenbelt File Archive, Carnegie Local History Library, Boulder, CO.

41. "Greenbelt Program in Grave Trouble," *Daily Camera,* May 2, 1974.

42. Gottlieb, *Forcing the Spring.*

43. Alison Bashford, *Global Population: History, Geopolitics, and Life on Earth* (New York: Columbia University Press, 2014).

44. The major exception to this are several housing towers built by the University of Colorado, which utilized its status as a state institution to override local planning laws in a unilateral decision that angered local residents.

45. Clay Evans, "25 Years Later, Boulder Is at a Turning Point," *Daily Camera,* January 28, 1996, 1.

46. "The Greenbelt: How Much Is Enough?" *Daily Camera,* May 14, 1987.

47. Gottlieb, *Forcing the Spring.*

48. Mary Riddel, "Housing Market Dynamics under Stochastic Growth: An Application to the Housing Market in Boulder, Colorado," *Journal of Regional Science* 40, no. 4 (2000): 771–88.

49. Katharine J. Jackson, "The Need for Regional Management of Growth: Boulder, Colorado, as a Case Study," *Urban Lawyer* 37 no. 2 (2005): 299–322.

50. See Max Besbris, *Upsold: Real Estate Agents, Prices, and Neighborhood Inequality* (Chicago: University of Chicago Press, 2020).

51. "Renter Cost Burdens, Metropolitan and Micropolitan Areas," Joint Center for Housing Studies, Harvard University, 2016, https://www.jchs.harvard.edu/ARH_2017_cost_burdens_by_metro.

52. Paul Danish, "Boulder's Insane Densification," *Boulder Weekly,* April 16, 2015, https://www.boulderweekly.com/opinion/danish-plan/boulderrsquos-insane-densification/.

53. While bus transit exists to connect suburbs with Boulder, it is not well used, and the Regional Transportation District (Boulder-Denver Bus and Rail System) has experienced problems maintaining ridership, opening new rail lines, and keeping competitive pricing (Boulder has some of the highest public transit costs in the United States). Angela Evans, "RTD Says Frequent Riders Should Pay the Highest Prices," *Boulder Weekly,* April 25, 2019, https://www.boulderweekly.com/news/rtd-says-frequent-riders-should-pay-the-highest-prices/.

54. "Boulder's Growth: A Succinct History," Livable Boulder, accessed June 2020, http://livableboulder.org/boulders-secret-limited-growth/boulders-growth-a-succinct-history/.

55. Kriston Capps, "14 Incredible Objections to a Single Boulder Housing Development," *Bloomberg CityLab,* January 7, 2016, https://www.citylab.com/equity/2016/01/14-incredible-objections-to-a-single-boulder-housing-development/422724/.

56. Eric Budd, "Boulder Could Enshrine Class and Race Exclusion into Its City Charter," *Articulate Discontent,* October 19, 2015, https://ericmbudd.wordpress.com/2015/10/19/boulder-could-enshrine-class-and-race-exclusion-into-its-city-charter/.

57. "Latinos in the 2016 Election: Colorado," Pew Research Center, 2016, https://www.pewresearch.org/hispanic/fact-sheet/latinos-in-the-2016-election-colorado/.

58. Chelsea Castellano and Eric Budd, "Boulder Can Choose Compassion over Exclusion," *Boulder Weekly*, November 24, 2021, https://www.boulderweekly.com/opinion/boulder-can -choose-compassion-over-exclusion/.

Chapter 4: Exclusionary Weirdness

1. Mary Patillo, *Black on the Block: The Politics of Race and Class in the City* (Chicago: University of Chicago Press, 2007); Japonica Brown-Saracino, *A Neighborhood That Never Changes: Gentrification, Social Preservation, and the Search for Authenticity* (Chicago: University of Chicago Press, 2009).

2. Sharon Zukin, *Naked City: The Death and Life of Authentic Urban Places* (New York: Oxford University Press, 2009).

3. James Howard Kunstler, *The Geography of Nowhere: The Rise and Decline of America's Man Made Landscape* (New York: Simon and Schuster, 1994).

4. Ferdinand Tönnies, *Tönnies: Community and Civil Society* (New York: Cambridge University Press, 2012); Max Weber, *Economy and Society*, vol. 2 (Berkeley: University of California Press, 1978).

5. Eric Klinenberg, *Heat Wave: A Social Autopsy of Disaster in Chicago* (Chicago: University of Chicago Press, 2002); Rebecca Solnit, *A Paradise Built in Hell: The Extraordinary Communities That Arise in Disaster* (New York: Penguin, 2009).

6. Sylvie Tissot, *Good Neighbors: Gentrifying Diversity in Boston's South End* (New York: Verso, 2015).

7. Patrick Sharkey, *Stuck in Place: Urban Neighborhoods and the End of Progress toward Racial Equality* (Chicago: University of Chicago Press, 2013), 60.

8. Benjamin Ross, *Dead End: Suburban Sprawl and the Rebirth of American Urbanism* (New York: Oxford University Press, 2014), 30.

9. Rachel Feit, "The Ghost of Developers Past," *Austin Chronicle*, May 25, 2012, https://www .austinchronicle.com/food/2012-05-25/the-ghost-of-developers-past/.

10. Will Anderson, "Austin's Population Keeps Popping; Here's How Many People Are Added Each Day," *Austin Business Journal*, March 22, 2018, https://www.bizjournals.com/austin/news /2018/03/22/austins-population-keeps-popping-heres-how-many.html.

11. "Imagine Austin," City of Austin, TX, accessed June 2020, http://www.austintexas.gov /department/imagine-austin.

12. Matt Largey, "A Word about Your Responses to Our CodeNEXT Language Story," KUT 90.5 Radio, December 14, 2017, https://www.kut.org/post/word-about-your-responses-our -codenext-language-story.

13. Aubrey Byron, "CodeNEXT or None, Austin Has an Identity Crisis," *Strong Towns*, September 17, 2018, https://www.strongtowns.org/journal/2018/9/17/codenext-or-none-the-code -in-austin-is-undeniably-broken.

14. Syeda Hasan, "Austin City Council Votes Unanimously to Scrap CodeNEXT," KUT 90.5 Radio, August 9, 2018, https://www.kut.org/post/austin-city-council-votes-unanimously-scrap -codenext.

15. Heather Way, Elizabeth Mueller, and Jake Wegmann, "Uprooted: Residential Displacement in Austin's Gentrifying Neighborhoods and What Can Be Done about It?" report, University of Texas at Austin Center for Sustainable Development, 2018.

16. Joshua Long, *Weird City: Sense of Place and Creative Resistance in Austin* (Austin: University of Texas Press, 2010).

17. Richard Lloyd, *Neo-Bohemia: Art and Commerce in the Postindustrial City* (New York: Routledge, 2010).

18. Zukin, *Naked City*, 3.

19. Corrie Maclaggan, "Austin's Black Population Leaving City, Report Says," *New York Times*, July 17, 2014, https://www.nytimes.com/2014/07/18/us/austins-black-population-leaving-city-report-says.html.

20. Richard Florida, *The Rise of the Creative Class* (New York: Hachette, 2019).

21. Long, *Weird City*.

22. "The Economic Impact of the Creative Sector in Austin," Record Industry Association of America, 2020, https://www.riaa.com/reports/the-economic-impact-of-the-creative-sector-in-austin/.

23. William Scott Swearingen, *Environmental City: People, Place, Politics, and the Meaning of Modern Austin* (Austin: University of Texas Press, 2010).

24. Jed Kolko, "Seattle Climbs but Austin Sprawls: The Myth of the Return to Cities," *New York Times*, May 22, 2017, https://www.nytimes.com/2017/05/22/upshot/seattle-climbs-but-austin-sprawls-the-myth-of-the-return-to-cities.html.

25. Florida, *Creative Class*.

26. Long, *Weird City*.

27. F. Steiner, "Envision Central Texas," in *Emergent Urbanism: Evolution in Urban Form, Texas*, ed. S. Black, F. Steiner, M. Ballas, and J. Gipson (Austin: University of Texas, School of Architecture, 2008); Reid Ewing and Shima Hamidi, "Measuring Sprawl 2014," *Smart Growth America*, April 2014, https://www.smartgrowthamerica.org/app/legacy/documents/measuring-sprawl-2014.pdf.

28. Way, Mueller, and Wegmann, "Uprooted," 88.

29. Elizabeth Findell, "Latest Debate about Merits, Demerits of CodeNEXT Hits Usual Points," *Austin American Statesman*, May 30, 2018, https://www.statesman.com/news/20180530/latest-debate-about-merits-demerits-of-codenext-hits-usual-points.

30. David Harvey, *Rebel Cities: From the Right to the City to the Urban Revolution* (New York: Verso, 2012).

31. "Imagine Austin Population and Jobs Forecast," City of Austin, TX, accessed June 2020, https://data.austintexas.gov/stories/s/Imagine-Austin-Population-and-Jobs-Forecast/j5a7-yk8d/.

32. Eric Tang, "Those Who Left," UT Report, https://liberalarts.utexas.edu/iupra/_files/pdf/those-who-left-austin.pdf.

33. Neil Smith, *The New Urban Frontier: Gentrification and the Revanchist City* (New York: Routledge, 1996).

34. Andrew Busch, "Building 'A City of Upper-Middle-Class Citizens': Labor Markets, Segregation, and Growth in Austin, Texas, 1950–1973," *Journal of Urban History* 39, no. 5 (September 2013): 975–96.

35. Mike Clark-Madison, "What's Wrong with Public Housing?" *Austin Chronicle*, August 21, 2001, https://www.austinchronicle.com/news/2001-08-31/82842/.

36. Eliot M. Tretter, "Contesting Sustainability: 'SMART Growth' and the Redevelopment of Austin's Eastside," *International Journal of Urban and Regional Research* 37, no. 1: 297–310.

37. Cecilia Ballí, "What Nobody Says about Austin," *Texas Monthly*, February 2013, https://www.texasmonthly.com/politics/what-nobody-says-about-austin/.

38. Javier Auyero (ed.), *Invisible in Austin: Life and Labor in an American City* (Austin: University of Texas Press, 2015).

39. Ross, *Dead End*, 95.

40. Keeanga-Yamahtta Taylor, *Race for Profit: How Banks and the Real Estate Industry Undermined Black Homeownership* (Chapel Hill: University of North Carolina Press, 2019).

41. Auyero, *Invisible in Austin*.

42. Ken Herman, "What's Next for Rosewood Courts," *Statesman*, April 13, 2018, https://www.statesman.com/news/20180413/herman-whats-next-for-rosewood-courts.

43. Tang, "Those Who Left."

44. Nick Barbaro, "Public Notice: Planning for Better Plans," *Austin Chronicle*, November 18, 2016, https://www.austinchronicle.com/news/2016-11-18/public-notice-planning-for-better-plans/.

45. Jane Jacobs, *The Death and Life of Great American Cities* (New York: Random House, 2011).

46. Michael King, "Ambiguous Oracle: Company's New Austin Campus Displaces Longtime Residents," *Austin Chronicle*, December 29, 2015, https://www.austinchronicle.com/daily/news/2015-12-29/ambiguous-oracle-companys-new-austin-campus-displaces-longtime-residents/.

47. Peter Tatian, G. Kingsley, Joseph Parilla, and Rolf Pendal, "Building Successful Neighborhoods," What Works Collaborative, April 2012, https://www.urban.org/sites/default/files/publication/25346/412557-Building-Successful-Neighborhoods.PDF.

48. Way, Mueller, and Wegmann, "Uprooted," 57.

49. Derek Hyra, "The Back-to-the-City Movement: Neighbourhood Redevelopment and Processes of Political and Cultural Displacement," *Urban Studies* 52, no. 10 (August 2015): 1753–73.

50. Ross, *Dead End*.

51. Kate McGee, "One Mile and One Week Apart, Two Brothers Meet Similar Fates Walking in Austin" KUT 90.5 Radio, May 10, 2016, https://www.kut.org/post/one-mile-and-one-week-apart-two-brothers-meet-similar-fates-walking-austin.

52. "Why Austin's 'Rail Fail' in 2000 Still Resonates Today," KUT 90.5 Radio, October 1, 2014, https://www.kut.org/transportation/2014-10-01/why-austins-rail-fail-in-2000-still-resonates-today.

53. Eric Goff, "Is the Prop1 PAC running a campaign for Republican Rail?" *Aura: An Austin for Everyone*, October 21, 2014, https://www.aura-atx.org/is_the_prop_1_pac_running_a_campaign_for_republican_rail.

54. Henry Grabar, "The 20-Lane Highway Texas Wants to Force through Austin," *Slate*, October 19, 2021, https://slate.com/business/2021/10/austin-texas-interstate-35-expansion-20-lanes.html.

55. Goff, "Is the Prop1 PAC running a campaign."

56. Aubrey Byron, "CodeNEXT or None," *Strong Towns*, September 17, 2018. https://www.strongtowns.org/journal/2018/9/17/codenext-or-none-the-code-in-austin-is-undeniably-broken.

57. Aura: An Austin for Everyone (@AURAatx), "In the next 25 years, 650 square miles of currently rural area will be paved over to become suburban and urban," Twitter, June 18, 2018, https://twitter.com/AURAatx/status/1008706679691673600.

58. Brandon Formby, "Austin Group Aims to Reframe Debates around City's Growth, Development," *Texas Tribune*, April 12, 2017, https://www.texastribune.org/2017/04/12/austin-group-wants-reframe-debates-around-citys-growth-development/.

59. Elizabeth Megan Shannon, "Quantifying the Impacts of Regulatory Delay on Housing Affordability and Quality in Austin, Texas" (master's thesis, University of Texas at Austin, 2015), https://repositories.lib.utexas.edu/handle/2152/32194.

60. Brian McCabe, *No Place Like Home: Wealth, Community and the Politics of Homeownership* (New York: Oxford University Press, 2016).

61. Ananya Roy, quoted in an interview with Jay Caspian Kang, "Want to Solve the Housing Crisis? Take Over Hotels," *New York Times*, August 19, 2019, https://www.nytimes.com/2021/08/19/opinion/housing-crisis-hotels.html?smid=url-share.

62. Denise Scott Brown, Robert Venturi, and Steven Izenour, *Learning from Las Vegas: The Forgotten Symbolism of Architectural Form* (Cambridge, MA: MIT Press, 1977).

Chapter 5: YIMBYism Goes Global

1. Calla Wahlquist, "Melbourne 'World's Most Livable City' for Seventh Year Running," *Guardian*, August 16, 2017, https://www.theguardian.com/australia-news/2017/aug/16/melbourne-worlds-most-liveable-city-for-seventh-year-running.

2. Michael Stutchbury, "The Luckiest Country," *World Policy Journal* 28, no. 1 (2011): 41–51.

3. Craig Butt and Jamie Brown, "Melbourne House Prices: Million-Dollar Suburbs Mapped," *Domain*, August 5, 2017, https://www.domain.com.au/news/melbourne-house-prices-milliondollar-suburbs-mapped-20170805-gxpxwr/.

4. "Homelessness Statistics," Homelessness Australia, accessed June 2020, https://www.homelessnessaustralia.org.au/about/homelessness-statistics.

5. "The Impact of COVID-19 on Australia's Residential Property Market," KPMG Economics, 2021, https://assets.kpmg/content/dam/kpmg/au/pdf/2021/covid-impact-australia-residential-property-market.pdf.

6. Kate Raynor and Laura Panza, "The Impact of COVID-19 on Victorian Share Households," University of Melbourne Hallmark Research Initiative for Affordable Housing, 2020, https://research.unimelb.edu.au/__data/assets/pdf_file/0028/165934/The-impact-of-COVID-19-on-Victorian-share-households.pdf.

7. Roger Keil, *Suburban Planet: Making the World Urban from the Outside In* (New York: Wiley, 2017).

8. "How Diverse Is My Suburb?" *SBS News*, accessed June 2020, https://www.sbs.com.au/news/interactive/how-diverse-is-my-suburb.

9. Glen Searle and Crystal Legacy, "Australian Mega Transport Business Cases: Missing Costs and Benefits," *Urban Policy and Research* 37, no. 4 (2019): 458–73.

10. Lizabeth Cohen, *Saving America's Cities: Ed Logue and the Struggle to Renew Urban America in the Suburban Age* (New York: Farrar, Straus and Giroux, 2019).

11. Setha Low, *Behind the Gates: Life, Security, and the Pursuit of Happiness in Fortress America* (New York: Routledge, 2004); and Dolores Hayden, *Building Suburbia: Green Fields and Urban Growth, 1820–2000* (New York: Pantheon Books, 2003).

12. Thomas Brinkhoff, "City Population, Malmö," accessed June 2020, https://www.citypopulation.de/en/sweden/skane/1280__malm%C3%B6/; Alasdair Rae, "Europe's Most Densely Populated Square Kilometres—Mapped," *Guardian*, March 22, 2018, https://www.theguardian.com/cities/gallery/2018/mar/22/most-densely-populated-square-kilometres-europe-mapped.

13. John Logan and Harvey Molotch, *Urban Fortunes: The Political Economy of Place* (Berkeley: University of California Press, 2007).

14. Loïc Wacquant, *Urban Outcasts: A Comparative Sociology of Advanced Marginality* (London: Polity, 2007).

15. Quoted in Paul Theroux, "The Last Man of Letters," *New York Times Books*, May 25, 1997, https://archive.nytimes.com/www.nytimes.com/books/97/05/25/bookend/bookend.html.

16. Douglas Stuart, *Shuggie Bain* (New York: Grove, 2020).

17. Bristol YIMBY website, via Wayback Machine, https://web.archive.org/web/20190509135600/https://bristolyimby.com/.

18. Samuel Stein, *Capital City: Gentrification and the Real Estate State* (New York: Verso, 2019).

19. This is more or less in contrast to new ideas of participation from radical planning that calls for reinvigorating democratic practices through planning activities without the rancor that is often displayed in front of planning councils. YIMBY activists, on the other hand, are comfortable with the adversarial nature of planning meetings and attempt to use that atmosphere to their own benefit; Andy Inch, "Ordinary Citizens and the Political Cultures of Planning: In Search of the Subject of a New Democratic Ethos," *Planning Theory* 14, no. 4 (2015): 404–24.

20. Peter Hall, "The Containment of Urban England," *Geographical Journal* 140, no. 3 (1974), pp. 386–408.

21. Emily Badger and Quoctrung Bui, "Cities Start to Question an American Ideal: A House with a Yard on Every Lot," *New York Times*, June 18, 2019, https://www.nytimes.com /interactive/2019/06/18/upshot/cities-across-america-question-single-family-zoning.html ?searchResultPosition=2.

22. George Orwell, *The Road to Wigan Pier* (Manchester: Macmillan, 2021).

23. Andrew Gamble, *The Free Economy and the Strong State: The Politics of Thatcherism* (London: Palgrave Macmillan, 1988); Bob Jessop, "New Labour or the Normalization of Neo-liberalism?" *British Politics* 2, no. 2 (2007): 282–88.

24. Alan Holmans, "Historical Statistics of Housing in Britain," Cambridge Centre for Housing & Planning Research, November 2005, https://www.cchpr.landecon.cam.ac.uk/Research/Start -Year/2005/Other-Publications/Historical-Statistics-of-Housing-in-Britain.

25. "Housing and Home Ownership in the UK," Office for National Statistics, January 22, 2015, https://www.ons.gov.uk/peoplepopulationandcommunity/populationandmigration /internationalmigration/articles/housingandhomeownershipintheuk/2015-01-22.

26. Robert Booth, "Tory MPs Back Plan to Give People a Vote on New Housing in Their Areas," *Guardian*, October 25, 2021, https://www.theguardian.com/society/2021/oct/24/tory -mps-back-plan-to-give-people-a-vote-on-new-housing-in-their-areas.

27. "Living Longer: Changes in Housing Tenure over Time," *Office for National Statistics*, February 10, 2020, https://www.ons.gov.uk/peoplepopulationandcommunity /birthsdeathsandmarriages/ageing/articles/livinglonger/changesinhousingtenureovertime#wh at-would-be-the-implications-of-an-increase-in-older-people-renting-privately.

28. Although in many areas, including London, the greenbelt continues to protect public land, but growth has gone far beyond it.

29. "Housing Crisis Affects Estimated 8.4 Million in England," *BBC News*, September 23, 2019, https://www.bbc.com/news/uk-49787913.

30. Stanley Buder, *Visionaries and Planners: The Garden City Movement and the Modern Community* (New York: Oxford University Press, 1990); Marco Amati and Makoto Yokohari, "The Establishment of the London Greenbelt: Reaching Consensus over Purchasing Land," *Journal of Planning History* 6, no. 4 (2007): 311–37.

31. Department for Work and Pensions, *Households Below Average Income, 1994/95–2017/18* [data collection], 13th ed. (UK Data Service 2019), SN: 5828, http://doi.org/10.5255/UKDA-SN -5828-11.

32. Saskia Sassen, *The Global City: New York, London, Tokyo* (Princeton, NJ: Princeton University Press, 2013).

33. "House Price Statistics," UK House Price Index, accessed April 2020, https://landregistry .data.gov.uk/app/ukhpi/browse?from=2019-03-01&location=http%3A%2F%2Flandregistry.data .gov.uk%2Fid%2Fregion%2Fkensington-and-chelsea&to=2020-03-01.

34. "Regional Gross Disposable Household Income: 1997 to 2017," Office for National Statistics, May 22, 2019, https://www.ons.gov.uk/economy/regionalaccounts /grossdisposablehouseholdincome/bulletins/regionalgrossdisposablehouseholdincomegdhi /1997to2017#what-was-the-average-disposable-household-income-in-your-local-area.

35. Philomena Murray and Alex Brianson, "Rethinking Britain's Role in a Differentiated Europe after Brexit: A Comparative Regionalism Perspective," *JCMS: Journal of Common Market Studies* 57 (2019): 1431–42.

36. Stutchbury, "Luckiest Country."

37. Su-Lin Tan, "Chinese Investment in Real Estate Grows to \$32b: FIRB," *Australian Financial Review*, May 9, 2017, https://www-afr-com.eu1.proxy.openathens.net/property/chinese -investment-in-real-estate-grows-to-32bn-firb-20170509-gw0sla.

38. John Budarick, "Media Outlets Are Racialising Melbourne's 'African Gang' Problem," *ABC News*, August 2, 2018, https://www.abc.net.au/news/2018-08-01/media-outlets-racialising -african-gang-problem-melbourne/10060834.

39. Ben Graham, "Pauline Hanson Axed from Channel 9 after Towers Rant," News.com.au, July 6, 2020, https://www.news.com.au/entertainment/tv/morning-shows/drug-addicts-pauline -hanson-blasts-melbourne-tower-residents-for-not-learning-english/news-story/f0e4e53ce6851 698382d1f99ed29b171.

40. Besha Rodell, "Melbourne Haggles over the Future of Its Most Popular Market," *New York Times*, June 12, 2017, https://www.nytimes.com/2017/06/12/dining/queen-victoria-market -melbourne-australia.html.

41. Graeme Davison, *City Dreamers: The Urban Imagination in Australia* (Sydney: New South Books, 2016).

42. Paul Mees and Lucy Groenhart, "Travel to Work in Australian Cities: 1976–2011," *Australian Planner* 51, no. 1 (2014): 66–75.

43. Kenneth T. Jackson, *Crabgrass Frontier: The Suburbanization of the United States* (New York: Oxford University Press, 1987); Neil Smith, *The New Urban Frontier: Gentrification and the Revanchist City* (New York: Routledge, 1996).

44. Robin Boyd, *The Australian Ugliness* (Melbourne: Text Publishing, 2012), 93.

45. Ibid., 100.

46. Joy Damousi, "Assimilation in Modern Australia," in *Memory and Migration in the Shadow of War: Australia's Greek Immigrants after World War II and the Greek Civil War* (Cambridge: Cambridge University Press, 2015): 73–74.

47. Davison, *City Dreamers*.

48. Jana Perković, "Six-Pack Living: Type Street Apartment," *Assemble Papers*, accessed June 2020, https://assemblepapers.com.au/2019/07/16/six-pack-living-type-street-apartment/.

49. Frank Bongiorno, *The Eighties: The Decade That Transformed Australia* (Melbourne: Black Inc. Books, 2017).

50. Ian W. McLean, *Why Australia Prospered: The Shifting Sources of Economic Growth* (Princeton, NJ: Princeton University Press, 2012).

51. Lindsay Bennett, "Weekend Newspaper 'Renaissance': Domain Magazine Hits Record 1.6m Readers" *AdNews*, August 29, 2017, https://www.adnews.com.au/news/weekend-newspaper -renaissance-domain-magazine-hits-record-1-6m-readers.

52. Sam Levin, "Millionaire Tells Millennials: If You Want a House, Stop Buying Avocado Toast," *Guardian*, May 16, 2017, https://www.theguardian.com/lifeandstyle/2017/may/15 /australian-millionaire-millennials-avocado-toast-house.

53. Linda Qiu and Daniel Victor, "Fact-checking a Mogul's Claims about Avocado Toast, Millennials and Home Buying," *New York Times*, May 15, 2017, https://www.nytimes.com/2017 /05/15/business/avocado-toast-millennials.html.

54. Simon Johanson, "Chinese Investors Are Pushing into Melbourne and Sydney," *The Age*, October 11, 2014, https://www.theage.com.au/business/chinese-investors-are-pushing-into -melbourne-and-sydney-20141010-113q7x.html.

55. Simon Johanson, "Up to Half of Chinese Buyers Leave Apartments Vacant," *The Age*, August 22, 2017, https://www.smh.com.au/business/companies/up-to-half-of-chinese-buyers -leave-apartments-vacant-20170822-gy1n5p.html. This problem is pronounced in the US as well: see Jake Wegmann, "Residences without Residents: Assessing the Geography of Ghost Dwellings in Big U.S. Cities," *Journal of Urban Affairs* 42, no. 8 (2020): 1103–24.

56. Alanna Boyd, *Astronaut Families and Parachute Children: The Cycle of Migration of Chinese Business Migrants in Melbourne* (unpublished master's thesis, University of Melbourne, 2005); Val Colic-Peisker and Ling Deng, "Chinese Business Migrants in Australia: Middle-Class

Transnationalism and 'Dual Embeddedness,'" *Journal of Sociology* 55, no. 2 (June 2019): 234–51; David Ley, *Millionaire Migrants: Trans-Pacific Life Lines* (New York: Wiley, 2010).

57. Heidi Han, "Chinese-Australian Real Estate Billboard Defaced with Anti-Asian Posters in Sydney," *SBS Mandarin*, February 23, 2017, https://www.sbs.com.au/language/english/chinese -australian-real-estate-billboard-defaced-with-anti-asian-posters-in-sydney.

58. "Pauline Hanson's 1996 Maiden Speech to Parliament: Full Transcript," *Sydney Morning Herald*, September 15, 2016, https://www.smh.com.au/politics/federal/pauline-hansons-1996 -maiden-speech-to-parliament-full-transcript-20160915-grgjv3.html.

59. "2016 Census QuickStats—Box Hill (Vic)," Australian Bureau of Statistics, accessed June 2020, https://quickstats.censusdata.abs.gov.au/census_services/getproduct/census/2011 /quickstat/SSC20168; https://quickstats.censusdata.abs.gov.au/census_services/getproduct /census/2016/quickstat/SSC20312?opendocument.

60. Ceridwen Spark, "Ignored, Discounted, Not Taken Seriously: This Is Life in Melbourne's West," *Sydney Morning Herald*, January 8, 2018, https://www.smh.com.au/opinion/ignored -discounted-not-taken-seriously-this-is-life-in-melbournes-west-20180108-h0exoh.html.

61. Kathy Lord, "Sudanese Gangs a 'Real Concern' in Melbourne, Prime Minister Malcolm Turnbull Says," *ABC News*, July 17, 2018, https://www.abc.net.au/news/2018-07-17/sudanese -gangs-real-concern-in-melbourne-malcolm-turnbull-says/10002556.

62. "Trump's Ambassador to Netherlands Finally Admits 'No-Go Zone' Claims," *BBC News*, January 12, 2018, https://www.bbc.com/news/world-europe-42671283.

63. Calla Wahlquist, "Is Melbourne in the Grip of African Crime Gangs? The Facts behind the Lurid Headlines," *Guardian*, January 3, 2018, https://www.theguardian.com/australia-news /2018/jan/03/is-melbourne-in-the-grip-of-african-gangs-the-facts-behind-the-lurid-headlines.

64. Luke Henriques-Gomes, "South Sudanese Australians Report Racial Abuse Intensi- fied after 'African Gangs' Claims," *Guardian*, November 4, 2018, https://www.theguardian.com /world/2018/nov/04/south-sudanese-australians-report-abuse-intensified-after-african-gangs -claims.

65. "Gun-toting Preacher Says Deport Sudanese Gangs," *Sunshine Coast Daily*, September 6, 2018, https://www.sunshinecoastdaily.com.au/news/gun-toting-preacher-says-deport-sudanese -gangs/3513789/.

66. Victorian Department of Planning, "Housing Development Data 2005 to 2016—Metropolitan Melbourne," accessed September 2020, https://www.planning.vic.gov.au/ __data/assets/pdf_file/0022/250726/Metro-Melbourne-HDD-2016.pdf.

67. Sharon Zukin, *Loft Living: Culture and Capital in Urban Change* (New Brunswick, NJ: Rutgers University Press, 1989); Richard Lloyd, *Neo-Bohemia: Art and Commerce in the Postin- dustrial City* (New York: Routledge, 2010).

68. "2016 Census QuickStats: Footscray," Australian Bureau of Statistics, accessed June 2020, https://quickstats.censusdata.abs.gov.au/census_services/getproduct/census/2016/quickstat /SSC20929.

69. "Suburb Profile: Footscray," *Domain*, accessed June 2020, https://www.domain.com.au /suburb-profile/footscray-vic-3011.

70. "Building More Social Housing in Melbourne's West," Office of the Premier of Victo- ria, accessed June 2020, https://www.premier.vic.gov.au/building-more-social-housing-in -melbournes-west/.

71. Kate Russell, "Two Sides of the Coin—The Launch Housing Project Debate (Pt. 1)," *Westsider*, May 11, 2017, https://thewestsider.com.au/two-sides-of-the-coin-the-launch-housing -project-debate-part-one/.

72. Sharon Bradley, "'Having to Ask for Somewhere to Live, It's Difficult Indeed': Single, Female, Homeless. Australia's Shameful Crisis," *Sydney Morning Herald*, February 8, 2020,

https://www.smh.com.au/national/having-to-ask-for-somewhere-to-live-it-s-difficult-indeed -single-female-homeless-australia-s-shameful-crisis-20200127-p53uyg.html.

73. Matthew Palm, Katrina Raynor, and Carolyn Whitzman, "Project 30,000: Producing Social and Affordable Housing on Government Land," working paper, University of Melbourne School of Design, 2018, https://msd.unimelb.edu.au/__data/assets/pdf_file/0004/2876008 /Project-3000-Producing-Social-and-Affordable-Housing-on-Government-Land.pdf.

74. Ramon Oldenburg and Dennis Brissett, "The Third Place," *Qualitative Sociology* 5 (1982): 265–84; Paul Hickman, "'Third Places' and Social Interaction in Deprived Neighbourhoods in Great Britain," *Journal of Housing and the Built Environment* 28 (2013): 221–36.

75. "Australia's Changing Industry Structure," Australian Jobs Report, Australian Government, accessed June 2020, https://australianjobs.employment.gov.au/jobs-industry /australia%E2%80%99s-changing-industry-structure.

76. Timothy Moore, "Flat White Urbanism," *Conversation*, June 2, 2017, https:// theconversation.com/flat-white-urbanism-there-must-be-better-ways-to-foster-a-vibrant-street -life-78338.

77. Tony Dalton, "Another Suburban Transition? Responding to Climate Change in the Australian Suburbs," in *Urban Sustainability Transitions: Theory and Practice of Urban Sustainability Transitions*, ed. T. Moore, F. de Haan, R. Horne, and B. Gleeson (Singapore: Springer, 2018).

78. Timothy Neale, Jessica K. Weir, and Tara K. McGee, "Knowing Wildfire Risk: Scientific Interactions with Risk Mitigation Policy and Practice in Victoria, Australia," *Geoforum* 72 (2016): 16–25.

79. Jamie Tarabay, "Why These Fires Are Like Nothing We've Seen Before," *New York Times*, January 21, 2020, https://www.nytimes.com/2020/01/21/world/australia/fires-size-climate.html.

80. Margaret Cook, *A River with a City Problem: A History of Brisbane Floods* (Brisbane: University of Queensland Press, 2019).

81. "Regional Population Growth, Australia 2018–2019," Australian Bureau of Statistics, March 25, 2020, https://www.abs.gov.au/ausstats/abs@.nsf/PrimaryMainFeatures/3218.0 ?OpenDocument.

82. Brian Bennion, "Residents Angered after Disputed Unit Development Approved," *Courier Mail*, July 6, 2017, https://www.couriermail.com.au/questnews/southeast/residents-angered -after-disputed-unit-development-approved/news-story/66cddce6c4affc032dc1f07d43897f6a.

83. Residential Statistics, Queensland State Government Department of Housing and Public Works, https://statistics.qgso.qld.gov.au/profiles/hpw/housing/pdf/2JW2CBSCT3V330MWW2 TG835BEAZ7GQH3H4LCELQR4ATPU7IPV3YPJJOHTVASlAGB8HFILDN1CM62AO1ADXX 096KBZW5GW62CR98GK6R8Q5RT8QR7S7TBH0M8DKYIKQE4/hpw-housing-profiles#view =fit&pagemode=bookmarks.

84. Evgeny Morozov, *To Save Everything, Click Here: The Folly of Technological Solutionism* (New York: Public Affairs, 2013).

85. Richard A. Walker, *Pictures of a Gone City: Tech and the Dark Side of Prosperity in the San Francisco Bay Area* (Oakland, CA: PM Press, 2018).

Conclusion

1. Caitlin Oprysko, "In grievance-filled speech, St. Louis couple warn of chaos in the suburbs if Democrats elected," *Politico*, August 24, 2020, https://www.politico.com/news/2020/08/24 /mccloskey-convention-speech-guns-suburbs-401297.

2. Colin Gordon, *Mapping Decline: St. Louis and the Fate of the American City* (Philadelphia: University of Pennsylvania Press, 2009).

3. Joe Holleman, "Spotlight: Cocktails at Archbishop's House Builds Interest in Family History," *St. Louis Post-Dispatch*, June 25, 2017, https://www.stltoday.com/news/local/columns/joe

-holleman/spotlight-cocktails-at-archbishops-house-builds-interest-in-family-history/article
_48205209-b7f6-5232-b75f-67475d1eab0f.html.

4. Colin McFarlane, "Repopulating Density: COVID-19 and the Politics of Urban Value."
Urban Studies, June 2021, https://doi.org/10.1177/00420980211014810.

5. CNN/SSRS Poll, June 12, 2020, accessed September 2020, http://cdn.cnn.com/cnn/2020
/images/06/12/rel7a.-.reactions.pdf.

6. Stonnington City Council East Ward Candidate Statements, Victorian Electoral Commission Mailer, 2020.

7. Shima Hamidi, Sadegh Sabouri, and Reid Ewing, "Does Density Aggravate the COVID-19
Pandemic?" *Journal of the American Planning Association* 86, no. 4 (2020): 495–509.

8. William H. Frey, "Covid-19's Recent Spread Shifts to Suburban, Whiter, and More Republican-
leaning Areas," *Brookings*, April 22, 2020, https://www.brookings.edu/blog/the-avenue/2020/04
/22/as-covid-19-spreads-newly-affected-areas-look-much-different-than-previous-ones/.

9. Jessica Menton, "Get Me Out of Here! Americans Flee Crowded Cities amid COVID-19,
Consider Permanent Moves," *USA Today*, May 1, 2020, https://www.usatoday.com/story/money
/2020/05/01/coronavirus-americans-flee-cities-suburbs/3045025001/.

10. Ian Bogost, "Revenge of the Suburbs," *Atlantic*, June 19, 2020, https://www.theatlantic
.com/technology/archive/2020/06/pandemic-suburbs-are-best/613300/.

11. Brendan Churchill, "COVID-19 and the Immediate Impact on Young People and Employment in Australia: A Gendered Analysis," *Gender Work Organization* 28 (2021): 783–94.

12. This also involved a renewed emphasis on spatial control in a number of locations: see
Alison Young, "The Limits of the City: Atmospheres of Lockdown," *British Journal of Criminology*
61, no. 4 (2021): 985–1004.

13. Philip Oltermann, "Pop-up Bike Lanes Help with Coronavirus Physical Distancing in
Germany," *Guardian*, April 13, 2020, https://www.theguardian.com/world/2020/apr/13/pop
-up-bike-lanes-help-with-coronavirus-social-distancing-in-germany.

14. David Mark, "Australia Is Facing a 'Once-in-a-lifetime Opportunity' as Cycling Booms,
Advocates Say," *ABC News*, May 17, 2020, https://www.abc.net.au/news/2020-05-17/coronavirus
-brings-once-in-a-lifetime-opportunity-for-cycling/12247870.

15. Eric Klinenberg, *Palaces for the People: How Social Infrastructure Can Help Fight Inequality,
Polarization, and the Decline of Civic Life* (New York: Penguin, 2018).

16. Michael Manville, Paavo Monkkonen, Michael Lens, and Richard Green, "COVID-19 and
Renter Distress: Evidence from Los Angeles" (UCLA, Lewis Center for Regional Policy Studies,
2020), https://escholarship.org/uc/item/7sv4n7pr.

17. "The State of the Nation's Housing 2021," Joint Center for Housing Studies at Harvard
University, https://www.jchs.harvard.edu/sites/default/files/reports/files/Harvard_JCHS_State
_Nations_Housing_2021.pdf, p. 25.

18. Miriam Zuk and Karen Chapple, "Housing Production, Filtering and Displacement: Untan-
gling the Relationships" (Berkeley: University of California, Institute of Governmental Studies,
May 2016), https://www.urbandisplacement.org/sites/default/files/images/udp_research_brief
_052316.pdf.

19. Richard A. Walker, *Pictures of a Gone City: Tech and the Dark Side of Prosperity in the San
Francisco Bay Area* (Oakland, CA: PM Press, 2018).

20. Paul M. Ong, Chhandara Pech, and Megan Potter, "California Neighborhoods and COVID-
19 Vulnerabilities" (Los Angeles: UCLA Center for Neighborhood Knowledge, October 1, 2020),
https://knowledge.luskin.ucla.edu/wp-content/uploads/2020/12/CA_Covid_Vulnerabilities
_UCOP_v03.pdf.

21. Jung-eun Lee, "Insularity or Solidarity? The Impacts of Political Opportunity Structure
and Social Movement Sector on Alliance Formation," *Mobilization: An International Quarterly*
16, no. 3: 303–24.

22. Katharine Gammon, "How LA's Getty Center Built a Fire-proof Fortress for Priceless Art," *Guardian*, October 29, 2019, https://www.theguardian.com/us-news/2019/oct/28/california -wildfires-getty-fire-museum-art.

23. Rebecca Elliott, "'Scarier than Another Storm': Values at Risk in the Mapping and Insuring of U.S. Floodplains," *British Journal of Sociology* 70, no. 3 (2019): 1067–90.

24. Liz Koslov, "The Case for Retreat," *Public Culture* 28, no. 2 (2016): 359–87.

25. Abrahm Lustgarten, "How Climate Change Will Reshape America," *New York Times*, September 15, 2020, https://www.nytimes.com/interactive/2020/09/15/magazine/climate-crisis -migration-america.html.

26. Some, like journalist Matthew Yglesias, have argued that the US would be far better off with more residents. He makes the case in Matthew Yglesias, *One Billion Americans: The Case for Thinking Bigger* (New York: Penguin, 2020). A more tempered analysis of denser and more populous cities is made in by Billy Flemming et al., "The 2100 Project: An Atlas for the Green New Deal" (Philadelphia: University of Pennsylvania, McHarg Center, 2020), https://mcharg.upenn .edu/2100-project-atlas-green-new-deal.

27. John Stanley and Roz Hansen, "People Love the Idea of 20-minute Neighbourhoods; So Why Isn't It Top of the Agenda?" *Conversation*, February 20, 2020, https://theconversation.com /people-love-the-idea-of-20-minute-neighbourhoods-so-why-isnt-it-top-of-the-agenda-131193.

28. Imogen Tyler, *Stigma: The Machinery of Inequality* (London: Zed Books, 2020).

INDEX

Abundant Housing, 128
accessory dwelling unit, 13, 65, 96, 107
activism, 14, 16, 28, 34, 38–40, 132; anti-gentrification, 23; anti-growth, 57; astro-turfing, 48, 161
adaptive reuse, 62
Agnos, Art, 28
Airbnb, 14, 95
Arts and Crafts style, 80
Aspen, Colorado, 98
Association of Bay Area Governments, 25
astronaut families, 143
AURA, 106, 110–21
austerity, 137
Austin, Texas, 100–123
Austin Neighborhood Council, 102
Australia, 137–39
Auyero, Javier, 109

baby boomers, 56, 58–64, 71–72
Bacigalupi, Paolo, 164
backyard, 159
Bay Area Rapid Transit (BART), 20
Bay Area Renters Federation (BARF), 5–6, 31
Bellamy, Edward, 78
Berkeley, 2, 5, 39–42, 54
Better Boulder, 76
Boulder, Colorado, 74–99
Boyd, Robin, 140
Breed, London, 21, 53
Brisbane, 150–56
brownfield, 130

California Renters Legal Advocacy and Education Fund (CaRLA), 36
California YIMBY, 36
Casar, Greg, 102
Central Business District (CBD), 105, 125, 141, 143, 145, 150–53
Central Market Payroll Tax Exclusion, 29
Chiu, David, 50

class, 7, 14, 70–72, 140
climate change, 49, 53, 64, 116, 154, 156, 162–64, 172
Code-NEXT, 102
cohabitation, 101
college town, 77
community character, 3, 34–35, 57, 76, 109
community consultation, 130
community land trust, 113, 163
commuting, 61, 73, 92, 116; rail, 116–17
coronavirus, 3, 14, 18, 124, 138, 158–59, 160, 162
cosmopolitanism, 4, 141
counterculture 58; Austin, 102–3; San Francisco, 19
crime, 4, 8, 29, 77, 137–38, 144, 157

Davison, Graeme, 139
DeLeon, Richard, 28
Democratic Party, 52, 70, 120
densification, 7, 10–11, 15–16, 18, 71–72, 76, 95, 102–7, 109, 117, 131–36, 146, 151, 154–55, 163–64
developers, 6–7, 23–24, 32–33, 38, 43–49, 50–53, 81, 94, 97, 102–4, 111, 115, 121–22, 128, 130–32, 145–46, 151, 158, 161–62
domestic violence, 148
duplex, 54, 65, 96, 104, 107, 153

Easterling, Keller, 30
Ehrlich, Paul, 88
elitism, 57, 77, 96
eminent domain, 84, 87, 163
essential workers, 160
ethnography, 171

Fabians, 80
fair housing act: California (1964), 26; US (1968), 109
Ferlinghetti, Lawrence, 19

festivals, 104

financial crisis (2008), 7, 13, 20, 29, 31, 63, 65, 71, 124, 137, 160

flooding, 3, 87, 101, 140, 163

Florida, Richard, 103

food sovereignty, 151

Foote, Laura, 22, 67

Footscray, Victoria, 145

Fourier, Charles, 79

Garcetti, Eric, 53

Garden City, 78; association, 79

gemeinschaft, 100

generations, 61, 69–73, 102, 161

gentrification, 3, 6, 11–17, 23, 28–29, 34, 38, 43–46, 49–53, 58, 62–65, 101, 103, 107–9, 112–15, 121–25, 128, 141, 146, 160

Golden Gate Authority, 24

Graham, Steven, 31

Great Society, 19

greenbelt, 17, 75–93

Green New Deal, 14

growth boundary, 80–81

growth machine, 24, 28, 128

Haertling, Charles, 87

Hall, Peter, 130

Hanlon, Brian, 22

Hanson, Pauline, 143

height limits, 76, 89

Herman, Justin, 25

Hill, Octavia, 78

historic preservation, 62, 111

homelessness, 21, 150

homeownership, equity, 57

homes: row, 131; terrace, 139; tract, 125, 139

housing, 12–14; boarding, 147; build-to-rent, 145; competition, 109; council, 131; filtering, 12; financialization, 132; morphology, 62–63, 135; permitting process, 22; public, 13, 97, 155, 160; supply, 22, 161; supply skepticism philosophy, 12

Howard, Ebenezer, 78

hyper-prosperous cities, 21

Imagine Austin, 102

Immigration, Australia, 125, 137–38

In God's Backyard, 162

inequality, 16, 27, 60, 68, 78, 109, 123–24, 158

infrastructure, 21, 23–24, 29–31, 54, 63, 77, 93, 117, 120, 128, 138, 153, 156, 160

Isenberg, Alison, 25

Jacobs, Jane, 9, 25, 62, 111

jobs, 3, 5, 8, 21–22, 31, 37, 57–58, 81

Johnson, Lyndon, 19, 123

Keep Austin Weird, 105

Kim, Jane, 50

Knecht, Bob, 85

knowledge sector, 129

Lafayette, California, 43

Lamont, William, 91

lazy land, 149

League of Women Voters, 82

Le Corbusier, 79

Lee, Ed, 29

libertarianism, 10, 30

Linklater, Richard, 104

livability, 124

Livable Boulder, 96

London, 129–37

Lower East Side, 7

localism, 65, 68

MacGillis, Alec, 21

Malthusian, 88

Marvin, Simon, 31

mass transit, 63, 93, 160

media analysis, 167

Melbourne, 137–50

memes, 162, 172

middle-class, 5–7, 12, 16, 19, 23, 45, 58–60, 72, 129, 165, 167

millennials, 4, 7, 17, 24, 40, 56–58, 62–73, 119, 138

minimum lot size, 101

Mission District, 16, 22, 43, 46, 49, 113

missing middle, 117–18, 120, 132, 138

mixed-use urban development, 28, 62, 107, 115, 122, 141, 153

mobility, 8, 18, 30, 40, 58, 67, 71

neighborhood groups, 61, 169

newcomers, 67, 100

New Deal, 80–81, 108, 111

New Urbanism, 6, 10–11, 114

New Urbanist Memes for Transport-Oriented Teens (NUMTOT), 39

Newsom, Gavin, 53

NIMBY, 1–2, 17–18, 26–28, 33, 35, 39, 41, 54, 56–77, 167

Oakland, 5, 16, 22–23, 34–36, 38, 42, 45, 63

Oedipus, 1

old-timers, 75, 91, 100
oral history, 170
Orwell, George, 131
overcrowding, 4, 98
Owen, Robert, 79

parking, 3, 52, 101, 104, 106, 114–15
parks, 17, 84, 68, 84–86, 133, 159
peppercorn lease, 148
PLAN-Boulder, 82
population growth, 75
postindustrial, 105
precarity, 59
Pritchett, V. S., 129
Progressive Era, 7, 78
property rights, 135
Proposition M (San Francisco), 27
Proposition 13 (California), 27
proximity, 158
Public Housing in My Backyard
    (PHIMBY), 45
public land, 83, 149
public opinion, 128
psychedelic cowboys, 103

Queensland YIMBY, 151–52

racism, 26, 108, 123
real estate investment trust (REIT), 14
redlining, 2, 60, 103, 109
refugees, 138
regionalism, 92, 164
rent, 3–8; burdened, 95; control, 34; market
    rate, 35
resort communities, 75
resource hoarding, 60
restrictive covenants, 60, 108
retirement, 67
Reagan, Ronald, 26–27, 57, 68
Rocky Mountains, 75, 82
roommates, 98, 125
Rosewood Courts, 111
Roy, Ananya, 121

San Francisco, 19–55
San Francisco Tenants Union, 23
Santa Rita Courts, 108
Sassen, Saskia, 62
satellite communities, 75, 91, 119
Schumpeter, Joseph, 9
Schafran, Alex, 27
Senate Bill 35, 51
Senate Bill 50, 52
Senate Bill 827, 51

Silicon Valley, 20
Simmel, Georg, 9
single-family homes 19; zoning, 14,
    157
single-room occupancy (SRO), 21, 29
Skinner, Nancy, 50
smart cities, 30
smart growth, 33, 76, 78, 102
snowball sample, 168
social media, 37, 39, 126, 167, 169, 170
social movements, 64, 172; emotionally con-
    structed, 59, 66; participation, 65
South of Market (SoMa), 20
sprawl, 10, 17–18, 24, 26, 44, 57, 59, 75,
    81–85, 87, 89
Stand Your Ground Law, 61
suburbs: incorporation, 78; lifestyle, 61;
    retrofitting, 69
suburbanization, 24, 41, 59–60, 67–68, 100,
    122, 125–26, 138, 140, 151
successful cities; 58
Sue the Suburbs, 43, 69
Sunbelt, 164
super-commuters, 22, 160
Sweden, 127

Tale of Two Cities, 21
taxes, 2, 29, 45, 60, 86, 114, 117; mortgage
    interest deduction credit, 150; negative
    gearing, 142; revolt, 27
Taylor, Keeanga-Yamahtta, 109
Tedesco, Ted, 85
telecommuting, 159
Tenderloin, 21, 26, 29
Thatcher, Margaret, 57, 132, 135,
    155
third places, 150
Tory, 132
trails, 17, 75, 85, 89, 90
Transamerica Pyramid, 25
transit-oriented development, 53–54
Trauss, Sonja, 4, 5, 22, 31, 33–38, 42–46, 49,
    50, 52
Trump, Donald, 21, 36–37, 39, 68, 116, 143,
    157
Tugwell, Rexford, 81
Turner, Fred, 20

Unwin, Raymond, 80
upzoning, 28
urban planning, 10, 12, 15, 36, 40, 42; meet-
    ings, 65
urban sociology, 7, 100
utopianism, 80

Vancouver, 128
Varma, Deepa, 23
verticality, 4, 82
virtue signaling, 23

Weiner, Scott, 50–54
welfare state, 19, 21, 79
White Australia Policy, 141
white flight, 2, 126
Whitlam, Gough, 139
wildfires, 151, 163

Wirth, Louis, 4
Wright, Ruth, 85

Yes in My Back Yard (YIMBY), 3–7, 11–18;
    build more of everything philosophy, 23,
    42; groups, 36, 48–49, 127

Zero Population Growth, 88
zoning, 3, 4–5, 10–16, 28, 33, 36, 39, 44, 54;
    inclusionary, 94; meetings, 41, 58–60, 64–66
Zukin, Sharon, 103

A NOTE ON THE TYPE

This book has been composed in Adobe Text and Gotham.
Adobe Text, designed by Robert Slimbach for Adobe,
bridges the gap between fifteenth- and sixteenth-century
calligraphic and eighteenth-century Modern styles.
Gotham, inspired by New York street signs, was designed
by Tobias Frere-Jones for Hoefler & Co.